BU

BURN

A story of fire, woods and healing

Ben Short

SCEPTRE

First published in Great Britain in 2022 by Sceptre
An imprint of Hodder & Stoughton
An Hachette UK company

1

Copyright © Ben Short 2022

A CIP catalogue record for this title is available from the British Library

Hardback ISBN 9781529370348
eBook ISBN 9781529370355

Typeset in Monotype Sabon by Manipal Technologies Limited

Printed and bound in Great Britain by Clays Ltd, Elcograf S.p.A.

Hodder & Stoughton policy is to use papers that are natural, renewable
and recyclable products and made from wood grown in sustainable forests.
The logging and manufacturing processes are expected to conform
to the environmental regulations of the country of origin.

Hodder & Stoughton Ltd
Carmelite House
50 Victoria Embankment
London EC4Y 0DZ

www.sceptrebooks.co.uk

In loving memory of Pig
2008–2022
I think we did OK

'Keep a little fire burning, however small, however hidden.'
Cormac McCarthy, *The Road*

Prologue

Just as silver is a supreme conductor of heat, summer woods are the most excellent conductor of darkness. The moon is the shape of a severed ear, thrown down on a blue cloth, yet light does not fetch far inside the broadleaf border. Beneath the canopy, the bright pink petals of campion gutter; the luminous blue towers of bugle are extinguished, too. There are leucistic fallow deer in this wood, almost white, a herd which drew King John to hunt this ground in the thirteenth century. Yet such is the dark, they would be barely visible, even at twenty feet.

What am I doing here? I am a charcoal burner and the wood is my place of work. During the summer I spend most of my time inside its green walls, harvesting the timber I cut over winter, turning it into coal. I have two kilns. One, at the western end of the wood, sits under a broken crab apple. The Malus is disfigured, its leader ripped off by a summer storm. The kiln beneath has been cooling since early morning when I closed it down, killing its fire. Tomorrow I shall open it and shovel out the char, bagging it in brown sacks. My second kiln sits on the edge of a woodman's ride, which cuts east-west through the wood. I loaded it with batons of hazel this afternoon, and rammed a flaming, diesel-soaked rag down one of its vents, just after four. The fire in its centre quickly took: there has been no rain for several weeks and the material is bone dry.

A charcoal kiln may seem out of keeping in a wood. A large, steel, industrial barrel, it is bold, even rude, the nose-cone of a Steampunk space rocket fallen to earth. Yet despite this incongruity, the kiln is most certainly a thing of the woods. Loaded with coppiced hazel and set alight, it becomes almost alive.

In the settled dark, I put my ear to one of its vents. There is a pitter-patter, like soft rain falling on the earth. Crouching low and peering down the vent, I watch the wood tar smoking on the ground, a satanic, black ooze. As night deepens, the light from these vents project glowing beams across the woodland floor. It is as if the kiln has swallowed a small sun. The sight is both irresistible and terrifying, for inside the steel oven there is no mercy.

During hours of burning the wood inside is transformed, reworked. Water and hydrocarbons are expelled in what seems like slow torture, the process of pyrolysis. With only a small drip of oxygen entering the kiln, the hazel inside does not burn away, but is forced to keep its shape and take the pain. I sometimes think burning it to ash would be kinder. Yet this cruelty has history behind it. Charcoal was the smelting fuel of the Bronze and Iron Age. It propped up the Romans; forged their weapons; put fury in their armies. And although we mainly use it to brown sausages now, that darkness remains.

But beyond blood, charcoal burning has always been magical, a kind of dark trick. A piece of tree miraculously reduced to carbon, atomic number 6 on the periodic table, one of the building blocks of life. Open a cooled kiln and one's eyes fall on a dusty black ossuary, glittering bones of trees. A nugget flashes silver-grey like a jackdaw's mantle; another is painted with a cobalt flare, edging to purple, then gold. Pick up a piece and it weighs next to nothing, the wood from which it came released from the dead weight of its water and tars.

There is a bump inside the kiln. It is the wood stack dropping as the material in the bottom burns away. The sound draws me back to the present. For most people, being alone in a wood at night is not normal behaviour. The dark rattles us, dredges up primal fears, even if it is two-and-a-half centuries since anyone in these islands had to worry about wolves. Now all the old poachers are in their graves, who in their right mind lingers in woods after sunset? But, for me, these dim precincts offer a comfort, not a threat. The smell of woodsmoke and the kiln's gentle song, settle me. On such a night, every tree becomes sacred, a pillar of stillness. Standing under them, the dark bleeds in, then a quietness comes upon you.

I came to the woods over a decade ago. I came to the woods because there was a fire in my head.

1

My eyes rested on the hawk. It was like a feathered flame. Its head and body burned a reddish-brown and set the room's blue-green plasterwork aglow behind it. The bird bobbed its head, trying to get a sightline on the food I was holding. In a beat, it lifted off the glove of the man standing opposite me and dropped into the air between us. One wingbeat, maybe two, and I felt its weight land heavily on my own glove. The hawk immediately set about dismembering the dead chick I held between my finger and thumb. Its eyes blazed as it tore at the small body.

The distance the buzzard had flown in that brief second was about fifteen feet, the transverse length of my living room. Across from me, in the opposite corner, stood Dave. Looking at his face, it was clear the bird brought him joy. The pair had been together for sixteen years, ever since he had found her injured halfway up a mountainside in Wales. Dave had carried her down and brought her back to Hackney to fix her. Once she had recovered, he had returned to Wales to release her, but the imprint between man and bird had been too strong. Dave described how he had let her go, jumped in the van and bolted. The hawk had immediately turned in the air and followed the red Transit down the mountain track, worrying at the roof with her talons. There was no outgunning her. After two more unsuccessful attempts, he had brought her home to London, resigned she would spend the rest of her life in captivity. With homing, she would need a name, so Dave called her Manod, after the mountain on which he found her.

With the buzzard still gorging on the chick, my eyes slipped down onto the street. A row of pollarded plane trees shrunk to a vanishing point towards Queensbridge Road. The housing stock was early Victorian; handsome, semi-detached villas with tall sashes and doorway fanlights. Their grimy yellow fascias mellowed in the late afternoon sun, the lime mortar and old London brick more acquiescent than modern materials. As Manod continued to pull at the dead chick, I felt the street's passivity. The heat of the day seemed to have taken the edge off everything.

I had first moved to Hackney in the late nineties. Back then, every ground-floor window and nearly every front door had worn a barred grill. There had been a curious disconnect between the gentility of the architecture and such an overwhelming sense of barricade. Despite the fine housing stock, Hackney was one of the capital's poorest boroughs and the local estates were among the worst in London. As if proud of the area's roughneck quality, the local rag advertised itself each week with sandwich-board headlines that seemed a parody of inner-city violence: 'Schoolboy shot in gangland execution'; 'Man disfigured in blow-torch revenge'; 'Body parts found in London Fields suitcase'. Most of the trouble was gang-on-gang but there was always the risk of being caught in the crossfire. After a month or two living there you became inured to the violence and just got on with it. Yet in the half decade I had called it home, things were changing. While the area was still rough, the security grills were on the wane. The early colonisers – the artists and musicians – had made the place fashionable and big money was moving in. The newly arrived bankers and lawyers weren't going to blow a million pounds on a Victorian villa and then keep an iron grill on the front door.

Dave had seen it all. He had been in London Fields for thirty years, most of them squatting the building opposite. He told me nearly all the houses on the street had once been similarly occupied. It had been a period of great community. But not any more. As the grills and window bars came down, different barriers were being raised, 'The sort with a water-mark running through them' as Dave put it. These days he kept a low profile, apart from the occasional ride out with his old motorcycle gang, living a quiet life with his birds and partner.

I first met Dave shortly after moving in. I had just got back from the advertising agency where I worked, a white capsule of minimalism off Regents Street. The satisfaction from my job as a writer in the agency's creative department had long since waned and despite the buzz of riding home too fast through London's rush hour traffic on a Japanese sports bike, I would nearly always arrive home feeling deflated. It was a warm evening in late May and I was padlocking my motor-bike to the streetlamp opposite my flat, when suddenly I felt a presence standing over me. Looking up, I was met by two pale eyes. The stranger was tall and wiry, with a face like a mountain crag and DIY ink needling his arms and hands. He wore leather biker jeans and a white vest emblazoned with the words 'Outcasts Prison Fund' – if required, he looked like he could dish it out. I straightened up to meet him. The man had come over to explain that if I left the Kawasaki there it was likely to get stolen, that 'the kids on the estate rob sports bikes to order.' I told him it was alarmed and fitted with a tracker. He looked through me and said: 'On your head be it.' I let the moment pass. We started talking bikes and slowly the ice melted. The stranger told me he had been into them all his life and had started at eleven, on a Bantam. He explained he did airbrush graphics and was a bit of an artist, had two choppers out the back he was currently working on. I could envisage the style – lurid designs of breasts and skulls, the dark crossover of fantasy and porn beloved of old bikers. Not my cup of tea, but honesty was not what the moment needed.

After that Dave would often come outside and chat. If I was ever cleaning my bike, I could always rely on him to mooch over and chew the fat, keeping an eye on my sponge work.

At other times, I would get a knock at the door only to find him standing there, waiting to be invited in. Mostly I didn't mind – it was nice to be neighbourly and quite un-London like – and although he would stay for a couple of hours, I always found some pleasure in his company which blew away the cobwebs of my professional life. Sitting on the edge of the chair, rolling a liquorice paper fag, Dave would elaborate on his life.

From a boyhood in Ireland to a rambling young adulthood around East Anglia, he had mostly done itinerant agricultural work. He was good at fixing tractors, or coming to the rescue when a hay baler went wrong. But it was the working horses that had most enthralled him. On a few of the farms he had worked they had still used Suffolk Punches – willing, hard-working animals with a gentle nature. When he spoke of them you could see the best aspects of the man shine, the same love and tenderness you witnessed when you watched him handle his birds.

But there was a darker side to Dave. Much of his life had been violent. In his twenties and thirties he had got involved in motorcycle gangs and spent a couple of years inside. He had been glassed, stabbed and shot; lost friends in fights with the Hells Angels. The old biker told me he had been given his gang name – Dave Two Hammers – after his reputation of going into battle carrying a pair of lump hammers. I was glad he spared me the details.

On a few occasions Dave would knock extra early, usually on a Sunday. I would drag myself out of bed to be greeted at the front door with a freshly killed duck off Walthamstow Marshes. Dave liked to poach with his Saker falcon and

Sunday mornings were the quietest. He would usually bag two or three and always threw one my way – plucked and gutted – which I would cook for my dinner. But it wasn't all one-way traffic. Occasionally I would cross the road to his place on my own kind of poaching trip.

Dave's home was a detached four-storey house, the tallest on the street. It would have once been a handsome building, but long neglect by its owners, the borough council, had left it in a sorry state. Grass and weeds grew from the guttering and the slate roof was broken and pitted. Despite Dave's best efforts to patch it up with fibreglass, it had the structural integrity of a smashed poppadom. From my flat across the road, I would often see feral pigeons entering and exiting through the holes. Dave said he hadn't used the attic for years; the stench of ammonia from the pigeon shit made it uninhabitable.

The hallway was pure Dickensian, holes in the walls exposing ancient laths and plaster. The bannister spindles were wrecked, smashed by a biker mate of Dave's who had ridden his Norton Commando up and down the stairs while on speed. Most of the windows, especially at the back of the house, were only partially glazed. Dave explained when the wind found its way off the river, the old house would groan. Off the hallway to the right some old stairs fell away into the black hole that was the cellar. I always had a bad feeling standing there, the air from below smelled rank and evil. Dave confirmed my unease when he told me he used to play his drums 'down the hole', but had been so badly spooked on one occasion that he had not set foot below stairs for a decade.

Walking down the hallway and into the kitchen, the novelty of such old-fashioned privation turned to horror. The kitchen reminded me of the degradation in Don McCullin's photographs of Bradford in the late Seventies; black and white interiors which shamed us as a developed country. A compost heap of food waste grew mould beside the old sink and yellowing chip paper peeled from the walls like ulcerated tongues. I did accept tea when it was offered, but drank it with my fingers crossed.

Despite all this, I liked going there. The squat was the perfect antidote to the polish and zip I encountered every day in the office, a vast expanse of marble and steel which left me cold. Although Dave's may have been a health hazard, the advertising agency represented a clear and present danger to the soul. Beyond its sliding doors I often felt like a bird trapped inside a bell jar, being slowly deprived of oxygen.

When I had started out in that professional world, everything had seemed so exciting. My teachers were old school creative directors who still believed in the power of ideas and encouraged their young disciples to dream. We were the new generation, tasked not only to match, but to go beyond the brilliant legacy of our forebears, the men and women who had created ads that would get the nation talking. But in the last ten years the drive to produce great work was dying. Partly, it was that we no longer watched television in the way we used to; and partly that clients had become more risk-averse – always the enemy of anything brave and good. The occasional idea would glow and shine, but ninety percent of what I wrote ended up in the bin.

It was fair to say I was out of love with the business and that my days felt devoid of any real creativity. Plus, the office had never been my natural habitat. Most of my peers seemed unaffected but I had always been allergic. I felt only half-alive under strip lighting and uncomfortable with the warm electrical smell of computers en masse. The only time I ever forgot my surroundings was when I was immersed in a good idea, then the world lit up. Why did I stay so long? There were several reasons but the short answer was that like so many people stuck in a job that no longer suits them, I remained because I felt unqualified to do anything else. You kid yourself that the free agency bar and the parties – as well as the money – make up for the creative disappointments, but in the end you realise that such an arrangement is unsustainable and a shoddy trade-off for someone who needs to be more expansively creative. It was life and stories that really interested me – the same material which had once inspired all those great ads – and over the road at Dave's, it was there in spades.

You could say Dave had a way of talking. And despite the distraction of being perpetually engaged in rolling a fag, the old memories would tumble out with a casual, effervescent brilliance. While Dave perched cross-legged on an old machinist's stool, I would sit opposite on a worn sofa, and let his reminiscences flood over me. The squat was a natural storyteller's den. Sitting in firelight with wind in the chimney, Dave would regale me with tales of free festivals in the Welsh hills, or solitary forays on his motorbike around Stonehenge with just a sleeping roll bungeed to his bike. His stories were a lifeline. They took me away from the aridity of my present and back to somewhere greener, more fertile.

It was as if a river ran through Dave's house, a twisting, silver stream. It was the undercurrent of creativity and freedom which ran through his life. Those old hands that had once gripped a lump hammer in the service of very bad things could also fashion beauty. It was present in his paintings on the living room wall and in the leatherwork scattered across his desk; it was there in the engine block of a vintage Bonneville he was restoring which lay in bits on the kitchen table. Out the back, among numerous plants and medicinal herbs, it stood quiet and sober in the primitive wooden carvings he had fashioned with a chainsaw. And beyond that still, it sung in the aviary of broken birds he mended – the hawks, falcons and owls which were brought to him to fix – and would eventually be released back into the wild.

I looked at Dave's output. It inspired me, but also made me feel guilty. When was the last time I'd allowed myself to be so playful, to be even half as creative? As a child growing up on a small farm I had always been outside making things or, if the weather was bad, drawing in my bedroom. Yet I couldn't remember the last time I had picked up a pencil for the sheer joy of it. It all felt a bit tragic. A London adman living vicariously through his neighbour, an old biker and ex-con to boot. In my best moments as an advertising script writer, I couldn't have come up with that.

2

I sat in a corner of the ship's club lounge, loading peanuts into my mouth, watching a procession of geriatric humanity pass in front of me. A fair proportion could only move about with walking frames or with the help of a steward, while several more wheeled oxygen concentrators around with them, helping them breathe on the go. There was something unpalatable about the whole vision: exceedingly old and wealthy white people being serviced by younger foreigners, all with darker skin. I looked away and picked up my glass. The ice cubes jangled as I took a pull on the whisky, working it around my mouth as if trying to rinse away a nasty taste.

The meeting with the company's Marketing Director had been fixed for five o'clock. I was early. I wouldn't normally be drinking so soon, but the whole point of the trip was to get a handle on the cruise-ship experience and, before leaving, my boss had urged me to get stuck in, to act as I would on vacation. Behind this seemingly gracious offer was some hard business sense. The thinking was that such behaviour would help give the creative work that came from my experience more clout. We had not yet secured the business and were down to the last two agencies pitching for the account. It was worth a lot of money.

The Marketing Director was a young Italian woman in her late twenties. We had met the previous day on boarding and while she had appeared pleasant enough, she seemed a little square. Sitting in the bar, I could foresee the meeting ahead. The woman would deliver a long and turgid presentation of how she envisaged the company's new marketing campaign. It would be complicated and weighed down by cliché. My

job would be to unpick it and come up with something fresh
and elegant which could be translated in several languages.
Such a task takes a huge amount of energy, even for the most
ardent advertising creative, but after years at the coalface, I
was cynical and uninspired before I had even started.

The woman arrived chaperoned by the advertising agency's Account Manager. Although we were colleagues, I did
not entirely trust him. We executed the normal pleasantries
and settled down into the lounge's deep, leather chairs. I
made a stab at small talk while the agency suit ordered a
round of drinks. When everything was set, the Marketing
Director flipped open a laptop and dived into her presentation in faultless English. That, at least, was impressive. As she
spoke I played the good creative, feigning an interest in her
graphs and research group findings. All the while, the agency
Account Manager pinned me with his eyes, making sure I did
not shirk my obligations in the sycophancy department. He
wanted the business bad.

The briefing finally over, we fell into small talk and the
Marketing Director relaxed a little. I tried to prod her and
get some connection on a human level – it would help when
it came to presenting the creative work. I noticed a large dia-
mond ring and asked her how long she had been engaged.
'Six months,' she replied, adding her fiancé was also in marketing. I imagined their domestic life must be a riot. But the
Account Manager shot me a couple of dark looks, I was
going off-script. I reverted back to business and asked her a
few questions on the age and demographic of her customer
base. She explained the majority were over seventy and with
no irony confided that the ship did, in fact, have a morgue.
We had been sailing for less than two days and a couple of
the freezer spaces had already been filled. A tag line for the
new advertising campaign gifted itself to me – *Snuff it at Sea*
– and the devil in me wanted to share it. I resisted and in the

intervening pause the Account Manager suggested reconvening for dinner at eight, where I could present some initial creative thoughts. I could have strangled him. I had less than three hours to make sense of a seventeen-page brief and come up with something coherent. The suit grinned and ordered himself another gin. The Marketing Director excused herself and left us for a conference call with her team. I took this as my cue, gathered my stuff and went back to my cabin. There was work to do.

I sat on the bed with an A3 pad open on my lap, the pages of the marketing brief scattered about me on a sea of Egyptian cotton. I felt low. Like the bar, the cabin had pretensions of glamour but lacked any true style. It was the same feeling I had in every luxury hotel on every business trip, whether I was holed up in New York or Buenos Aries, Dubai or Sydney. In each one, the lack of imagination seemed like a small death to me; dead worlds made more bleak by the fact they seemed so highly valued.

Yet the brewing anxiety I now felt was not just down to my surroundings. I had been struggling with mental health problems for seven years and the stress of the situation – the pressure to crack the brief there and then – as well as the fact that I was cooped up in what felt like a prison cell with gold bars, was enough to bring it on.

If someone had been able to describe to me the very specific agony of a long-term anxiety disorder before I had started suffering from one, I would not have believed them, I would not have understood it. It is the most horrific strain of human torture, a savage condition, a wrecker of life. I would have periods of feeling better, but the illness would always return. I felt like a boxer who had been knocked down a million times yet staggered back to his feet only to be floored again in a bout lasting years. Inside I was pulp.

I had been diagnosed with something called Pure OCD. The root of it lay partly in my childhood, and could be traced back to certain events as well as wider environmental factors. As all the experts in the field of 'Pure O' will tell you, it is the fear and anxiety the thoughts engender which is the problem, not the thoughts themselves. What is more, in discussing details, you are actually encouraging a dialogue which is not just unhelpful, but potentially dangerous. So when writing about it, even now, this is a red line.

It is also important to separate Pure O from what most people think OCD to be – that idea of obsessive neatness, something which is thrown about quite freely today, almost as a joke. With Pure O we are not talking about the mental tick which requires all the coke cans in a fridge to face the same way, or cushions to be constantly plumped. No, Pure O is more vicious than that. For sufferers, you are trapped in a cycle of disturbing, intrusive thoughts which you try to neutralise with alternative, 'better' thoughts. Unlike obsessive hand washing, for example, the neutralising action is not manifested physically, but remains in the mind – 'pure' refers to this difference. The problem is that this internal dialogue only serves to strengthen the anxiety even more, and is a cruel quirk of cognitive wiring which traps people in a never-ending cycle of mental torment.

Sitting on the bed, the anxiety slid in fast and deadly. I could feel my body temperature rise, my breathing becoming shallower as the airways narrowed. At that moment I wished I could be anywhere but on that boat. If the anxiety was not toxic enough, the fact that I could not flee was like a short dagger rammed under my ribs. I was stuck, incarcerated on a coffin-ship somewhere in the Med, miles from land. The demon anxiety licked its lips, I was easy meat. I could feel the pressure of tears, but they would no longer come. After seven years I was barren, denied their sweet release which only made the illness crueller.

Burn

I picked up a pencil from the bedside table and tried to refocus on the brief. That was now impossible. Looking down, I noticed the lead point quivering – the fear had reached my extremities. Acute anxiety feels like this. Everything coalesces very quickly to a place which feels like you are on the edge of a sheer, dark cliff. To withstand the crush of panic and fear is something which takes years of practice. Even then you will suffer, but in a diluted form. The key is not to respond to the intrusive thoughts in any way, to let them come without attempting to neutralise them. This is not *impossible*, but probably the hardest thing you will ever have to do.

There are two problems. The first is that it is entirely natural to diffuse anxiety with positive neutralising thoughts – it is the mind's version of fight or flight. So, in *not* responding, the sufferer is actually trying to cheat nature, a hard-wiring in humans evolved over millennia. The second problem is that the long-term sufferer has already developed neural pathways which are instantly activated before one can consciously act, so that you have performed the unhelpful neutralising thought before you can stop yourself, keeping yourself in the evil loop. Over time you can build new, healthier pathways, but this takes a level of courage and willpower which normal life will never ask of a person.

I tried to stave off the fear, but the physical symptoms pushed on. My vision started to deteriorate, everything shook. Around me the bedsheets swam, silver runnels of cotton snaking down the bed. My mind flipped backwards, the cognitive gearbox was overheating. I was aware that the skin under my left eye had started to twitch. I looked down at the A3 pad. It was a white rectangle with a few hard, grey lines drawn and redrawn in one corner, so much so the paper was scorched through, eviscerated by the sharp point of the 2H pencil. From the marks you could see the hand was not well, the pencil clenched, the lines robotic and unyielding.

I could not remember making those marks. It was an imprint of illness.

It had been a day since I'd got back from Monaco where the cruise had ended, when I heard a knock at the front door from my roost in the upstairs kitchen. By the weight and manner of the knock I took it to be Dave. He never signalled his presence with anything other than several hard raps. No dum-de-dum-dum jollity, no hint of musicality. Dave never played the brass knocker, he just beat it.

I opened the door. Dave stood in the porch looking straight ahead, his pale eyes dulled, the man behind them missing. A traffic warden walked past, browsing the dashboard of a dark blue saloon parked opposite. It was the only animation in the scene. At last Dave's eyes registered mine. He slurred: 'She's gone.'

The man stepped over the threshold and drifted past me. It was late afternoon and I had only just risen, still exhausted from the work trip. I closed the front door and turned back to the stairs. 'Who?'

Dave remained ahead of me, slowly climbing the treads. 'Manod.'

I stood at the foot of the stairs, stunned.

'Just went out to see her but the cage door was open. Must've flipped the latch.'

It did not make sense. The two of them were imprinted, inseparable. 'Why?'

'Been actin' strange lately, real testy. Reckon she's after a mate.'

I didn't know what to say. I had no knowledge of bird behaviour and whether this was a credible explanation. I suggested he sit down and have a cup of tea. Dave stepped into the kitchen and excavated a pouch of rolling tobacco from his denim jacket.

'Got any whisky?'

I nodded and went to the cupboard. Dave sat down at the table, pushing the chair back against the wall and spreading his feet wide. He started to roll a fag. I put the Jameson's on the table and fetched a glass. The man shook his head.

'No – put it in the tea.'

While the kettle boiled we sat in silence. Dave pulled on his rollie, remote again, just staring out of the open window. I had never seen him like this – Two Hammers cowed – his eyes large pools filled with loss.

'She's gone home. Back to the mountains.' He pulled quickly on his fag as if to head off a spike of emotion. 'Just 'ope she makes it.'

The afternoon light was luminous and quite unreal. Across east London's terraced roofs, a seam of darkening clouds was moving closer. I felt my shoulder blades against the cool plasterwork of the kitchen wall and looked outside. The tips of the sycamore in the garden had started to dance. From the open window the May air mingled with the smell of Dave's tobacco, but beyond that intermingling, there was something stronger. It was the smell of a storm jacking up, of impending violence. All of a sudden the sky had gone very dark.

I poured the tea, then the whisky. And then the rain came down, in a deluge. It shook the chimney pots and rattled the slates. Below, in one of the gardens, a cat sprang for cover. I looked at Dave. His face had gone hard like stone. White trails curled from his rollie, the end of it a growing length of fragile ash. It seemed he had left the kitchen, I guessed in transit too. Clear of this weather front, cleaving the air west, as if pulled along some powerful, shining thread, towards home.

3

It was only a few hours after learning of Manod's escape that I resolved to leave my own life. The hawk had flown, obeying a desire for something she might not have understood but had acted on nonetheless. I pictured her noon-day breakout, saw her lifting the latch with her beak and in a blink, gone. Did the bird not feel the cruelty in the moment, the brutal finality of it all?

I was numb, sitting alone in the room where she had once been so present. The green-blue walls seemed drained of colour, the Georgian elm desk denuded of its shine. Manod had always glowed, set everything around her alight. With her gone, the moment felt stillborn. I closed my eyes and saw her high above the shires now, beating west. In that moment I could not imagine a creature more alone. Where was her comfort – was instinct itself a cushion?

But more than feelings of loss, it was the purity of her action which cut through me. Her flight put into the starkest relief my own sense of internment. For years I had been a prisoner to my illness – if only I could flip the latch and fly, too. I asked myself how the bird had done it. Through the boldness of instinct. There was a lesson there. For years I had been trapped by the never-ending loops in my own head; what some psychotherapists call brain-lock. This is Pure O: our cognitive sophistication as humans working perfectly against us, the apex curse of thinking. When you boil it down, we have literally become too clever for our own good.

Think less. If only it was that easy. The damaging neural pathways were deep ruts in my brain, like holloways scored from years of mental footfall. Analysing the reasons for it all was complicated, but on an immediate level I understood the pressure and stress of my working life certainly contributed. I was suffering from an anxiety disorder based on over-thinking. The kicker was that my professional life was entirely bound up in mental exercise. I had been trained for years to be razor sharp, to make lateral connections other people might not see. The problem was that these abilities mixed with a predisposition for anxiety meant I had the perfect skill set to become horribly ill. In the pay of OCD my brain was the most loyal and obedient servant.

I had considered leaving my job on numerous occasions, but that hot gut feeling to cut loose had been put on ice by fear and contrary professional advice. I had been seeing a therapist for several years. He was a good and intelligent man, a leader in his field. Yet whenever I expressed a desire to leave work, his response had always been the same: walk away and you will get worse. In the vacuum of unemployment, he said, the illness would completely take over. It seemed, to me, obscene. The man knew my pain but insisted I remain in a place where I could see no light. Yet I obeyed him, despite my better instincts to run. I had survived for seven years, I hadn't completely broken. But I was close. I had lost count of the number of days I had lain motionless on the sofa, the curtains drawn despite the daylight outside; whole weekends remaining as still as possible, any physical movement a precursor to mental agitation. Those were the really bad times.

But the hawk overruled the psychotherapist with shattering force.

Suddenly I felt the urgency in the moment. Manod had been in captivity for sixteen years, exactly the same time I had been in London. But if I was to run, where would I go – and to what? I hadn't always been a Londoner. My childhood and teenage years had been spent on a small farm in Hampshire. But I had been so long in the capital that the

17

country boy I had once been seemed terminally distant. After sixteen years here, who was I? Was there any wildness left?

My childhood home was a remote spot, the farm set in a landscape of undulating chalk hills and small woods which rose gently to a plateau of downland, almost the highest in the county. Come summer, the farm was pressed in on all sides by fields of barley and wheat. On balmy days these fields were our surrogate seas, the vast acres blown in eddies and waves. As a boy I would stand on the edge of this flaxen ocean yearning to dive in, to feel the soft caress of its currents. But by September, the golden water-body would disappear, all that was left a razed plain. Then the farmer would set it alight and my twin brother and I would dare each other to hack across the burning stubble, cinders scorching our face, neck and hands.

The mainstay of our childhood, however, were the woods and barns. In the height of summer, across fields of quivering heat, the wood's dark borders offered us sanctuary. Walking out of the field's harsh glare, our eyes fell upon a softer world: hazel coppice, dappled with pools of light, and within those pools, campion and ragged robin and goose grass as thick as river weed. We built treehouses there, set off the gamekeeper's vermin traps by poking them with sticks. When we tired of the woods it was the barns that drew our play; old buildings of brick and flint in which we'd hole up for hours making dens with bales of hay.

Yet the barns also offered more sober experience. Sometimes I would shake off my twin and visit them alone, in a sort of pilgrimage. To enter their cool shade was akin to stepping across the threshold of a church. Sitting quietly in the half-dark, I could feel the past, brush up against its ghosts, hear the echo of old country voices. They were everywhere – in the loose hay which lay about the chalk floor, in the cool stone walls and in the roof's beams and purlins. Alone but not alone, these were special times, imprinted moments.

I left the boy and came back to the man. Sitting squarely in the present, it was the country which called me, it was the country I needed to reach. It would not, however, be back to Hampshire, not to my childhood home. That place had long since vanished, smothered by money and the stale drip of gentrification. The lanes I had once beaten along were now the rat runs of shiny SUV's, their tinted windows and moulded bodies so incongruous and plastic. The agricultural ruins that had been my boyhood playground, transformed too. Once they had held the past so tenderly, but now they stood emptied of their ghosts, bland barn conversions surrounded by deserts of pea shingle; status homes sprinkled with Porsches and lead planters.

Even our local market town had been primped and poked to death, and was now suffering some kind of monied rigor mortis. Hampshire, cursed by its commutable position to London and its rural beauty, had become the new Surrey. In its furthest reaches, forty years ago, you could still have sought out colour, unearthed magic. But not now. Awash with money, but suffering an imagination deficit, it was dead to me.

There were other, more practical concerns. What sort of life would I build? How would I make ends meet? I was lucky enough to own my flat, but even with the rental income, after paying what was still a hefty mortgage, there would not be a huge lot left. To make matters worse, it wasn't as if I had a definite vocational calling, I just *felt* things. I was an artist but didn't know how to paint; I was a writer, but had never written anything other than advertising copy. I liked the idea of working with wood, but had no practical skill at all. To all intents and purposes, I was useless. Anxious thoughts circled darkly, my own inadequacy stung. My eyes fell on the velvet buttons of the living room's Victorian sofa. They stood out brightly, as if mocking me.

I made it out of London, but only as far as Cambridge. At a loss where to go, and what to do, I moved in with my girl-friend. While she went to work, I was reduced to filling time, floating around Mill Road Cemetery in the early morning, and at the close of daylight, feeling oddly removed from my own body.

My partner during those empty days was my girlfriend's dog, a venerable Jack Russell terrier. While the cemetery mirrored my mood, reflecting my own morbid introspection, the little dog shamed me. He was a rickety old thing, but still found some joy in life. Despite failing eyesight and legs he was no longer sure on, he had a dainty snout which quivered on the wind and brought him compensations. Seeing him chase a discarded fast-food container that skittered down the path in a breeze was memorable – a deranged pensioner seized, momentarily, with diabolical intentions.

But the reality of park life remained. Only the old or job-less spend much time in such places during working hours and yet, at thirty-eight and professionally in my prime, I had to count myself among them. While there was still some relief at having left my former life, it had already become a second-hand thrill, the empty days and an uncertain future smothering the novelty. Standing there, depression setting in my gut like a cold pudding, I knew I had to move on. But the answers would not come. Suddenly, I felt a yank on the lead. The dog had stopped to sniff around the base of a collapsing Victorian headstone. I couldn't tell who lay there. Over the decades the city's fumes had bored into the soft stone, eroding the name. An identity lost. I knew the feeling.

Bette, my girlfriend, was not a big drinker. Being petite, half a pint of bitter would usually suffice. I would meet her most days in our local pub, a backstreet boozer on her way home from the university where she worked. It tied in nicely with my own early evening dog walk, or at least that was the excuse. By the end of the day I often needed a drink.

The pub was comfortably shabby and I liked its ambience. It had no ambition other than to keep a good cellar and doctor to the steady drip of locals who frequented it. I generally got there before Bette, who would breeze in just after six. A quick peck and I'd ask her how her day had been. It always seemed fine, although I knew her job was quite stressful. When it came to my day, Bette never needed to ask; she had an excellent radar. If I was wobbly, I'd feel a squeeze on my hand and the same old mantra: 'One day at a time, sweet Jesus', and always a smile.

I had met Bette on an internet dating site a couple of years earlier. Our first date had been at the Fitzwilliam Museum, staring at glass cabinets full of armour. Perhaps that had been a sign – our relationship had never been straightforward and there were more than a few fights. It would be fair to say we had both brought baggage from previous relationships and arguments were not uncommon.

In hindsight, moving in together was probably not the best move. After years of living alone and being accustomed to having a girlfriend at a distance, it was a shock not only co-habiting with Bette, but also with her two teenage children. Yet they were good kids, and the adjustments they were forced to make for me were probably more challenging than my own. At times I felt guilty pressing myself on them, although I felt if anybody could cope, it was Bette. The woman was bright. As a child she had been a school refuser and as a young adult, a psychiatric nurse. But later on she had returned to education and ended up with a flurry

of degrees, including an MA from Goldsmiths, in some kind
of 'ology.

Bette had been the first person to suggest the illness was
Pure O. I had never heard of it before, and giving it a label
somehow helped. She had done her research and I think part
of her enjoyed the intellectual challenge, navigating the dark
maze that is psychiatry. She was also good at old-fashioned
caring – the ex-nurse would materialise effortlessly when I
was in a bad place. But despite this, our relationship was
always going to be a struggle. I was really not well enough
to sustain any sort of coupledom, as the battle with my own
head demanded too much. Looking back, there are things I
regret doing and saying, for which I am sorry.

There were good times. Not just the pubs, but walking
in Grantchester Meadows, and at weekends, out on Wicken
Fen. It was not just the irresistible sense of space the fen
imparted which raised my mood, but also that it seemed so
focused in its flatness, so wholly committed to its East Ang-
lian-ness. Any landscape that was pure and wore its heart on
its sleeve always cut beautifully deep.

One particular weekend, after getting back to the car after
a two-hour blast of Fenland air, I felt changed. All the introspection and mental fatigue had been blown away. In the car
park Bette looked at me with a worried face and asked if
I was alright. But I was feeling different; I felt wonderfully
well. In that moment I realised she didn't recognise me, didn't
know my face at all. I had always been ill, as long as we'd
been together. I think it made her feel insecure.

After that, I spent more time at Wicken Fen, while Bette
was working. Going out into the fen, I never felt entirely
alone. Often I was stopped by a presence around a bend in
the path, or a sense I had company just out of touching distance, among the sedge. While the ghosts of my childhood
were hale yeomen of Saxon stock, the fen held a darker, more

solemn spirit: insubstantial figures who would melt in and out of the sedge – shape-shifters, eel-catchers, webbed bogey-men.

And so I walked the land with a certain kind of reverence. My eyes, stilled by the muted beauty of the fen, settled on its dark pools and spires of saw-toothed sedge; the shaggy, ancient shapes of Konik ponies, quietly grazing there. I wanted to lie down on the damp earth and soak up this stillness; to transfuse the black water into my veins. The fen was a magical tonic, a world away from the push and aggression to which I had become so sensitive in modern life.

I even drew there. A crack willow split at almost ninety degrees and the bold geometry of the dykes cleaving the fen, silver ley lines reflecting the wan sunsets of this strange land. All of this seeped in and the effect was an animation in me, a reddening of the cheeks just as I had experienced as a boy. The office pallor was fading.

4

It had been three months since I'd flown the capital and I had begun to feel that Cambridge suited me. In London, the anxiety to which I'd been wired was almost like electrical pulses which would surge before blowing a mental fuse. Here, the voltage in my psychic circuitry seemed lowered. There was something in the city's light; something in the form and colour of its trees; something even in the atmosphere and conversation of the backstreet pubs that was mellower and different, as if the River Cam's slow drift had got into everything.

I had also acclimatised to the role of fen-idler. One evening over supper, Bette suggested I needed to make a change. She told me she had enquired about a voluntary group which worked in the gardens of a National Trust property, a few miles west of Cambridge. I dully nodded my head over the veggie curry. I was not sure I wanted to be a gardener and felt an unpleasant feeling in my gut which I knew to be the shadow-play of anxiety.

We visited the hall on a Friday and as we drove there, I remember feeling particularly nervous. Getting closer, I had the strongest urge to ask Bette to do a U-turn and point the car in the other direction, but knew it was useless. Pulling up the handbrake, she suggested we take a walk around the hall's formal gardens; the meeting with the head gardener wasn't for an hour. After a short green stroll and a weak cup of tea in the visitors' cafe, I made my way to his office, a small room at the end of a dingy corridor in a Victorian outbuilding. Bette waited outside.

The man was a remote and laconic Yorkshireman in his early sixties. He was not unfriendly, but there was a brusqueness in his manner which did not put me immediately at ease. In his defence, I was feeling unusually delicate and perhaps this skewed my take on his tone. Looking back, I do not remember too many details, except that he had the mien of a man who spent his days in dimly lit snooker halls, an unhealthy grey skin tone that seemed in direct contradiction to the fact that he worked out of doors every day. With a crackle-glaze of broken blood vessels over his nose, and a thinning scrape of dyed black hair, Monty Don he was not. Sitting across the desk on a plastic chair, the man asked me a few questions on my horticultural experience – none – and asked me to fill in a couple of forms. Taking the paperwork, and scanning it, he regarded me with his baggy eyes, concluding: 'Well, you might know bugger all son, but you look like you got some heft, so I fancy you'll be useful wi a fork.'

My first few days in the garden passed as a blur. The work was dull – mostly watering duty – and hour upon hour being attached to a hosepipe was not my idea of fun. But on balance, it was better to be occupied and I now at least had a group of people around me, a little more life than had been available in Mill Road cemetery. My fellow volunteers were, in the main, either retired or, like me, people of working age sidelined by mental illness. Several had disorders which went beyond anxiety and depression and, to an extent, helped me rebalance the relationship I had with my own problems. A symptom of being ill for so long is that one's world becomes quite narrow and you lose sight of the fact that there may be others in the world in a worse fix. Working alongside them three days a week cut me down to size. Despite my own version of hell which I had been living through, I was still privileged. I had some education, a family that was present, and an upbringing which had given me strong foundations. Some of my fellow volunteers seemed less well furnished in that regard and watching them turn up, week in, week out, filled me with something more than admiration. When you are mentally unwell, life is a grey world of falling ash, the only compass the faith one carries inside oneself, the belief that eventually things will get better. To remain on the path and not give up takes enormous grit. It is, to my mind, the purest distillation of human courage and around me in the gardens, it overflowed.

In particular I remember two brothers. Both looked like they had been through the mill, but working with me, they were never anything but kind and gentle. Gary was in his mid-forties. He was slight and pale and wore his white-blonde hair in a pony tail. He would struggle to meet your eye in conversation and the skin around his right eye would twitch. I had the strong impression he had suffered a serious mental breakdown sometime in the past. He seemed unusually brittle.

Mick was a couple of years older. You could tell they were related – the same blue eyes and shock of Viking hair – although the senior brother was thicker set and more effusive. Mick told me he was an army veteran and had been deployed in Basra during the Second Gulf War. During that tour, he had volunteered as a one-man infantry escort for a bomb disposal unit. The agreed term had been a month, but he had ended up doing four. The team had been involved in several incidents, and fired on numerous times, but towards the end of his deployment, their luck ran out. Attempting to clear a roadside bomb, two of the soldiers were blown up and a passing civilian car also destroyed, killing a young Iraqi couple and their new-born baby. Mick had since developed PTSD which he described as 'a horrible pressure in his head; a mash-up of guilt, confusion and grief'. He told me that being at war 'there are things that are not normal for a human being to see. Too many memories build up.'

Burn

Mick still suffered panic attacks and would sometimes find himself lying on the carpet at home, unable to get up, retching uncontrollably. One morning while we were out in the gardens, a dumper truck fired up in the yard beyond, the explosive crescendo of its diesel engine shattering the peace. The sound made Mick start and momentarily lose his balance. Gary, who was working nearby, dropped his spade and came running over, gently leading his brother to a nearby bench, where he just held him. I looked on for a moment, then turned away. I could not cry for them then – my own illness had robbed me of my tears – but thinking and writing about them now, my eyes stream.

One of the more common daily tasks in the garden was hoeing and cauterising the weeds which sprouted from the fine black tilth of the walled garden. While I was thankful for the work, there were days when it would drag and, over time, I began to find myself looking rather more up than down, my eyes drawn towards a line of woods fringing some higher ground, beyond the garden. I wasn't the only one who had noticed.

One morning over tea break, the head gardener informed me that the estate had a forester and that I should perhaps look him up. He baited the suggestion with the fact that the man was a bit of a character, lived in a converted fire engine, and that we might get along.

Believing it best to strike while the iron was hot, I sought him out that afternoon. I was told he was hedge-laying along the Avenue, a mile south of the hall. As I walked, my eyes fell on a hedge which ran parallel to the wide green strip. It had been cut and pulled over diagonally to create a kind of screen. Through the middle of the hedge, wooden stakes had been hammered into the ground at regular intervals to help add, what I could only guess was extra rigidity. These were bound at the top with a plait of hazel. It looked skilled work and almost sculptural.

After twenty-minutes, I reached a battered Land Rover with the oak leaf logo of the National Trust wearing thin on its side. The vehicle had been abandoned in the middle of the green runway, the driver's door open. The hedge work which had continued the entire length of my walk ended here, and beyond, the hedge stretched away, tall and ragged.

Suddenly, I heard a bark of pain from behind a tree, followed by a stream of Anglo-Saxon expletives. I cleared my throat and mustered a self-conscious hello. My opener was met by some muttering, before a man tumbled out, shirtless. He appeared to have been foraging for blackberries, but was now engaged in extracting a briar thorn from his upper arm. Plucking it out, he raised the barb to his face for closer inspection, twirling it around in his fingers, as if marvelling at its cruel genius.

For an instant I felt I was facing a wild man, an East Anglian wodewose. The hedger was a dark and muscular creature, with a weathered face strongly suggestive of a life out of doors. His head was covered in a thick mop of hair cut short at the back and sides, which made him appear somewhere between a shambolic schoolboy and Tarzan. I introduced myself and told him my reason for being there: that gardening was not grabbing me and was there a possibility of shadowing him in his work. He returned my opening salvo with silence. It suddenly occurred to me that I had not confirmed whether he was the forester at all; perhaps he was simply a trespassing madman with a weakness for hedgerow fruit. I quickly asked: 'Are you the forester?'

The man grinned. 'Some call me that.' I waited for something more. After several seconds I began to feel uncomfortable and, in desperation, motioned towards the hedge.

'Nice work.'

The forester gave a shrug and began to pick berries from a nearby briar, all the while keeping his eyes on me. The bastard's enjoying this, I thought, and decided to wind the conversation up. Just then, he cut in: 'Giz a hand.' With a jerk of his head, he gestured towards the hedge. Suddenly, I was aware of the singular remoteness of the spot and the absurdity in blindly following someone who might be a psychopath with a taste for murdering lone ramblers. The shirtless stranger stopped abruptly where the laid hedge reverted to wild nature. Slapping his hand on a tall, slim tree, he looked up its length. Still feeling vulnerable, I noted his strong chin and square jaw, thinking it would take a good punch to put him down. 'Field maple's a sod to lay. 'Elp me pull it over.'

The tree was all but bare, a few ochre leaves left in its crown. At its base, I could see a diagonal cut which travelled down the stem about seven inches. But the trunk had not been completely severed; a section of wood, perhaps an inch and a half thick, had been left uncut. I braced myself and together, we slowly hauled the maple down.

We briefly stood in silence. Then the forester asked if I was free the following week. It suddenly occurred to me that laying the maple might have been some kind of physical test. Despite not feeling entirely sure of what I was letting myself in for, I said yes. The man nodded, and I took this as confirmation I was now his helper. There was another uncomfortable pause. I noticed the hedge had begun to ink in. Apart from a dozen rooks in the neighbouring field, we were completely alone. Oblivious to the fading light, the forester had melted back into the hedge. I said goodbye but got no answer.

Over the following weeks, I began to learn the hedge-layer's craft and what had first appeared an impossible learning curve slowly levelled out to a simple joy. The relationship with my mentor had also developed and while I was primarily there to work, I found out he wasn't as fierce or feral as I'd first thought.

During those early days, my time was spent cutting out various shrubs and small coppice material from the hedge which the forester deemed surplus. I stacked the waste in a long drift running parallel to the hedge line, a springy froth of hazel, ash, maple and thorn. At first, I found removing so much growth counter-intuitive, my instinct being to leave as much in the hedge as possible. Yet, the forester insisted this was the only way and, over time, I began to understand that a thinned hedge just lays better.

But why lay a hedge in the first place? It's a fair enough question. Hedges are, first and foremost, living fences, their main purpose to prevent livestock from getting out of fields. Leaving a hedge unmanaged, will, over time, erode the efficacy of that barrier. The forester explained that as hazel grows taller, gaps eventually appear, while under the shade of larger hedgerow trees, more gaps develop where plant growth is compromised. To that end, it was sometimes necessary to fell the odd hedgerow tree.

Beyond slashing and stacking, I was also instructed on the finer skills of the craft. The forester showed me how to make the 'pleach cut', the all-important diagonal incision which severs part, but crucially not all, of the main stem. The reason for this is that the hinge of wood left uncut not only allows the plant to be laid down neatly, but also keeps it alive, a conduit for ground water and nutrients travelling up from the roots.

The forester used an old hedging axe for the job. It seemed a hefty tool for so surgical an operation, yet its simple physicality felt good in my hands. In my old life as an advertising creative, my weapon of choice had always been an N50 bullet tip marker – cheap, light and entirely disposable. Now I was holding something with a patina and a past.

A long line of Fenland hedgers would have used the tool and trusted it like a friend while working alone on the field edges. Looking at the axe closer, I noticed a faint mark on the head – the impression of a swan stamped into the iron. The forester explained this was the blacksmith's mark, his calling card. When tools were made by country smiths, these men often branded their creations with the name of their local pub. In this case, if you wanted an axe, or perhaps a new bill-hook, find The Swan and you would find the smithy.

Over that autumn and winter, I realised my body reacted well to manual work, but the glow I was feeling was not just down to endorphins. It was as if the forester's energy was catching. The man possessed a sort of unconscious wildness which leaked from every pore and working alongside him, I found it impossible not to be affected. Just being in his orbit made me feel more vital, as if the flat-pack modern person I had once been was put back in its box, and a new version of myself re-hewn from more elemental material. Just as Dave had inspired me with his creativity, the forester's primal energy shook me up. In him I saw a man as close to nature as one could get in our society, as close to an aboriginal Englishman as you could possibly expect. Blessed not only with extraordinary physical endurance and natural charisma, he was a well of knowledge and practical nous. He was not only a fine hedge layer, but also a shepherd, a blacksmith, a horse-logger, and an expert on funghi and soils. When he was not working, he liked to climb mountains.

Yet it was in his quieter moments that the force of his personality seemed most marked. In the forester I had a sense there was a deep and old knowing, as if he was tuned into a frequency most of us are denied, or at least cut off from. Often, while out in the fields, he would pause to listen to the birds. Watching him – the way he'd dip or cock his head – gave me the feeling it was less to do with ornithological curiosity and more like straight eavesdropping. The hedge-row birds would fire off at each other and slowly, a smile would appear on his face. Or, if we were out in the woods, he would sometimes turn quiet and still, and looking up through the trees, appear in silent communication with something *other*. I said nothing during these moments. Intuition told me it would be wrong to speak.

For all the forester's dynamism, it was these quiet moments in nature which stilled me most. I recognised them, in a small way, from my own childhood – those fleeting snatches of time when I remember feeling acutely connected. I saw that feeling reflected in the forester's face time and again. It was something I felt remote from yet wanted desperately to regain. At these times my modern uniform weighed heavily on me and I realised it would take time to shed, to slough that particular skin.

One late autumn day we were thinning a stand of juvenile ash on the outer rim of the estate. While the forester felled the small trees, I was the pack horse, dragging the cut poles onto the woodland track, or 'ride' as they are termed in forestry. During a tea break, the forester's terrier began making a commotion at the entrance to a rabbit hole in the hedge bank. Alerted by the din, the forester put down his tea and ambled over. The man ordered the dog away, which it did reluctantly, trembling a few feet from its master. Kneeling in front of the burrow, the forester brushed at the entrance, then picked up several droppings and rolled them between his fingertips. What information he was divining from this field craft I did not know, but it was fascinating nonetheless. Without looking up, the man asked me to fetch him a long length of briar. A strange request, I thought, but obliged him, wading into a cluster of brambles and returning with a ten-foot whip. I handed it to him and watched as he cut down its length a couple of inches with his knife, before splaying each end at ninety degrees. This done, he began to pass the cutting down the hole.

For a couple of minutes he prodded and poked, silent but for his breathing. Finally, he stopped and began to rotate the briar. I remained mute, mesmerised by the slow turning and the sheer oddness of the ritual. After five minutes, and the greater part of the briar out of the hole, the forester shifted back and paused. And then I heard it: a thumping sound, like a dry, fast, drumbeat. In a flash, the forester pulled hard on the briar and suddenly it was with us: a large rabbit, kicking violently, caught on the end. The forester grabbed the animal and, before you could say *knife,* dispatched the squirming creature.

I regarded the dead rabbit and felt instant pity. Seconds earlier it had been full of life, wedded to the clod, to the dew, to the smell of coming winter. Now it was just a slack rectangle of fur. I observed the delicate ears and subtle dun coat, every cell of which the fields and Fenland air had nurtured into being. I did not want the forester to see I was affected, so looked away.

He told me an old poacher had taught him the trick. He had splayed the briar's end so as not to skewer the rabbit, and as it turned the creature's fur had caught on the thorns. The forester asked me if I wanted it for my pot. I couldn't say no, despite having no idea how to skin and prepare an animal. The truth was that I was too embarrassed to admit this, so took the limp creature from him and put it in my bag. Later, walking back to the truck, I caught a glimmer of the Dog Star low in the sky. My mind instantly returned to the rabbit who was now far beyond even that cold twinkling, as far from his hedgerow home as could be imagined. I promised myself to do right by the animal that night and cook a stupendous stew; to honour the rabbit who, in his final bolt, had out run Sirius.

Fate called my time in the East. Bette and I were struggling and deep down I knew it was time to go. One evening after a particularly unpleasant argument, I retreated to the drawing room and sat for a long time in front of the fire. Sitting rigid in the old wing back chair, I watched the flames dance brightly in the grate. But the hearth felt cold, and the blazing beech logs colder still, like dressed stones on fire.

We were not getting on and the arguments were damaging us both. Beyond the unpleasantness of a relationship break-up, I had no life to go to, literally *nothing*. To have to go back to square one felt terrifying. I had been in Cambridge for nine months and adjusted to my life there. The fen had continued to work its magic, while several months out in the woods and fields with the forester had given me a purpose, a welcome green space I had been able to slip into each week. Now the ash storm had blown in, all that green had vanished. I considered staying put and getting my own flat, but Cambridge was Bette's city, not mine, and however much I had become attached to the Fen and the haunting beauty of the flatlands, it was not my home.

We did what we had to, Bette hurt and angry. And after it was done, and on the cusp of leaving, I went out to the estate for the last time. It was a Sunday, and unseasonably warm, and as I approached the shanty of farm buildings where the forester parked his fire engine, I felt oddly nostalgic, as if the chapter had already passed. Turning into the fold yard, I saw the man's red home blazing in the sun. Getting out of the car, it struck me as eerily quiet, normally any arrival would be greeted by his terrier sounding off. A note scribbled on the fire engine's cabin door explained it:

'Climbing in Scotland. Back in a week'. I had to smile, it was so in character.

I tried the door but it was locked, so I hung the parting gift I'd brought him in a plastic bag from the door handle. It was a small pen and ink drawing I had done of the laid hedge on the Avenue, the maple and thorn pleachers sketched in as sepia diagonals. Accompanying the sketch, a short note telling him I was off and that I'd enjoyed working with him. I scratched around for a few moments, not wanting to leave; took in the black weather-boarded barn and the horizon with its thin line of woods. But the forester was not there and the place felt maudlin without him. Suddenly I had the strongest urge to go, so jumped in the car and went, leaving nothing but dust and flatness and a pressing, East Anglian silence.

5

I headed south-west. My parents and brother were now living in the West Country and with no job or life to go to, it was family I needed most. Mum and dad had sold the farm several years earlier, and retired to Devon, while my twin brother had recently quit London and was now living in the back end of Dorset with his wife and two daughters.

That familial tug westward was something I too had felt as long as I could remember. Even as a boy growing up in Hampshire, I'd experienced a subconscious pull that way, a lure of the eyes west, as if drawn across a vast room towards a pretty girl. Yet in the moment that happy instinct felt debased, trounced by less useful feelings. A man in his late thirties, returning to live with his parents, his life in a few boxes. After years of independence, I felt like a loser.

In hindsight, I was lucky I had a family to scoop me up at all. Those at a crisis in their lives and without one, must feel particularly desperate. For the first few weeks, I reverted to the child again – cooked for, my washing done, no expectation to do anything at all. Most of the time I escaped in books – a hefty biography of Scott of the Antarctic and a few Boys' Own adventures – anything to take my mind off the fact that my life had come to a painful and shuddering halt. At the same time it was odd to realise the anxiety from which I'd been suffering had almost entirely vanished. Yet in the weeks that followed, a strange trade-off seemed to be happening inside me, like a psychological deal struck down a dark alley without my consent. While my anxiety had tailed off, there was now a duller weight moving in. It loomed over me like a zeppelin and as the shadow pressed forward, the voice of my therapist, lecturing me on depression and the danger of empty days, rattled morbidly in my head.

My defence was to out-walk it. I spent days on the road, the deep cut lanes that ran through the Blackdown Hills like mycelia. I walked over to see my brother and sister-in-law, too. They had rented a hillside cottage twelve miles away which straddled the county border with Dorset. Much like my feelings at Wicken Fen, there was a palpable sense of antiquity that leaked out of the land there, a low-grade electrical charge that prickled with the past and filled the air. The hill on which they lived was one of a number of greensand lumps that rose out of the Marshwood Vale in a horseshoe pattern. All had once been hill forts, refuge of the Iron Age Durotriges. A millennium later, the hilltop had hosted medieval fairs and later still, had become a notorious horse-racing venue for Gypsies. It was now owned by the National Trust and was a popular spot for dog walkers, all the old colour and rowdy bonhomie reduced to Gore-tex and labradors.

Yet walk the hill in the gloaming and you could still feel the older echoes; in the beech hangars and on the dusky hillside paths, imprints that do not go away. I lingered there and felt enlivened, this strange, thin place offering me a speck of light in my darkness, a whisper that there was still magic in the world worth holding out for.

It was time to get a job and I managed to find one on a building site. The work was uncomplicated – barrowing cement and a fair amount of digging – and while it was not exactly creative, there was a part of me which enjoyed its brute physicality. After a couple of weeks, I'd bedded in and made some friends. Sitting down over lunch, they asked me where I'd come from and what I'd done before. I was uneasy about mentioning my old life in London but decided honesty was the best course. When I told them I used to make television advertisements they could not believe it, could not get their heads around why an adman would swap life in the fast lane for digging all day, down a hole. I explained that the life had not made me happy, and that I had suffered mental health problems. Reference to a wonky head made them briefly awkward, but they quickly shrugged it off and for the simple reason I had worked in television, endowed me with a kind of celebrity which made me feel daft.

It was while I was labouring that I found a cottage to rent. One of the site carpenters put me onto it. He did a little work for the country estate that owned the place and had heard it was once again available to let, after being untenanted for years. The rent was cheap, and although the cottage was 'a bit on the rough side' as he put it, the views were glorious. I visited one evening after work. The property was perched on a hill, half a mile up a track, with only the ghost of a derelict farm behind it. It had been built as a gamekeeper's lodge a few years before the start of the Great War. Walking around it, I could see the carpenter's summation of its condition was accurate, although it was clear the house had once had pride and conscience in its raising. I wondered of all the men who had contributed to its build, how many had survived the war.

The second part of his assessment was also resoundingly true. Standing alone up the farm track, the cottage commanded the most intoxicating views, and if one fancied a sight of the sea, it would reveal itself from the track which rose gently behind the house. I stood there that first evening for several minutes, mesmerised by the beauty before me and the quality of the silence. Looking across a greenbelt of ash and oak, I could see the bay glittering in the distance, a tantalising, shimmering, far-off thing. My mind drifted back to boyhood days gazing at the eddies which rippled through the barley, the flux and flow of my surrogate seas. But here, salty air was in sniffing distance.

Eventually, I pulled myself away and came down from the track. Pushing open the garden gate I startled a jackdaw which sprang from a nest of twigs poking out of a chimney pot. I watched him dance above the house, a silver-black mote, before the breeze carried him away into a hedgerow ash. My eyes took in the cottage on a second sweep. While it could not be described as pretty, it was definitively honest. The back door was a portal of English oak, the lintel above it a hefty slab of yellow ham stone. Looking in through the front room windows, I spied a handsome brick fireplace with a dark Arts & Crafts surround. I could immediately see Dave sitting there, perched on his stool, proselytising. I missed him, missed his stories. But in that moment it occurred to me I no longer needed to experience one second-hand from a grotty sofa. Alone, on a far western hill, I was slap-bang inside my very own. I leant back against the wall and shook my head at the realisation. Dave would have sucked on his fag and told me to get on with it.

Once I moved to the cottage on the hill, the locals quickly made themselves known. Investigating the derelict farm which lay behind the house, I discovered a pair of barn owls nesting in a stone outhouse. The old building had a brick floor and over time this had moved and shifted so that it now resembled the gentle chop of a squally sea. Bricks rose in wavelets, then fell in long, shallow troughs. Sea-froth was provided by the owls' whitewash which was expelled from the rafters at intervals. This strange inland sea even had its own flotsam and jetsam – elytra, bones, scraps of fur – the indigestible parts of the owls' dinner which had been regurgitated onto the swell of fired clay below.

The pale hunters showed themselves at dusk, quartering the field which lay in front of the house. I had no television, so my widescreen was the large kitchen window which looked out over the woods and fields. I tuned in every evening, addicted to my own form of reality TV, glued to the owls' soft flight and silent efficiency, their orb bodies skimming the field, before dropping into the long grass to commit sound-less executions.

The owls were regularly joined in their killing by another animal, a solitary fox, who hugged the hedge line which ran up from the wood. Watching him, I always felt he was a fellow fixed on business, his gait never suggested leisure. Here was one of those characters who was constantly working, always out. Sure, the cubs rarely saw him, but to hell with work-life balance: there was country to sweep, chickens to slaughter.

I felt lucky to live on that hill. Coming home after a long day on site, I could feel the countryside gather me up. The building work was extremely physical but that was not the problem. Surrounded all day by sheets of insulation and concrete block, part of me withered. I ached for nature but instead got the dead smell of cement and the dulling aroma of new plasterboard. Labouring with the forester had been physical too, but that had been work in nature, and with nature. On the building site there was none of that transcendent magic. I watched the carpenters cut a roof, marvelled at their skill, but the planed Baltic pine with its straight edges was unrecognisable from the green-grey ash poles I had dragged out of the copse, or the maple and thorn I had laid in the Fenland hedges. On a construction site the breath of nature was entirely absent. I could feel the screws tightening in my head.

One Sunday afternoon I took a walk through the copse which fell away at the back of the farm. It was a mixed wood of Scots pine and Douglas fir, with broadleaf trees fringing the border. Inside, wind-throw was rife, many of the softwoods lying across one another on the ground like knitting needles thrown down in a fit of pique. Picking my way through the carnage, I was hijacked by a low mood. The copse was on a downer and its sadness was catching.

A buzzard caught my eye, flying low through the wood. I did not like it. A hawk somehow changes once it enters the trees. Long gone is that plaintive spirit of the high places, a distant speck beyond blood and earthly appetites. The woodland version is darker, hooded, more reptilian. Watching it, I could well believe it tore at flesh, ripped off faces. Death seemed invisibly to follow it.

I hurried through the copse and reached wood-end, which was marked by a small cliff that tumbled down onto a backwater lane. I looked over the edge: it was a good ten-foot drop and almost sheer, although this hadn't deterred a badger. A well-worn track advertised where he had gone over and as I shuffled nervously forward, I was reminded that if an over-sized weasel could do it, so could I. Gingerly I prepared myself for the descent. I wouldn't be going over snout-first like Brock, but concluded sliding down on my bottom was a more intelligent strategy. As I inched forward, I was yanked by gravity. Vainly grabbing at a mob of hart's-tongue ferns, I let out the kind of scream reserved for a man hurtling down a water slide into a pool of piranha. I can't remember any pain on hitting the ground, only the sudden sensation of all locomotion halted. Sitting in a heap on the lane, still clutching the ferns I'd torn from the bank, I was only too aware of how I might look to a passing stranger: somewhere between a Green Man and the local village idiot.

I got to my feet and started down the lane, quickly reaching a field gateway. Beyond it, the ground fell away steeply, before flattening out to a wide plain. In the distance stood a small stone barn – there, I had my aim. Vaulting the gate, I hurried down the slope, deliberately hugging the field edge so as not to be seen. I was now trespassing.

Looking on the hedgerow, I could clearly see it had been laid at some point, ancient pleachers of ash lurching sideways and walking beside it, I began to make a count of the number of plant species it held. This was a habit I'd acquired while working with the forester, who'd once explained a thing called 'Hooper's Rule', a simple equation used to date hedges. Named after its founder, the late biologist Dr. Max Hooper, this hypothesis puts forward the idea that there is a direct correlation between the number of woody species in a particular length of hedge and the age of that hedge. The equation works like this: age of hedge (in years) equals the number of woody plant species in a 30-yard section, multiplied by 100. Having counted half a dozen different plants over such a distance, I could be roughly sure the hedgerow was fifteenth century, around six hundred years old.

After a ten-minute hike, I reached the barn. The light had started to go and a heavy gloaming hung around it like damp sheets on a line. Tentatively, I circled the byre, noting its thick rubble walls and old tin roof. The door, an old ledge-and-brace type, hung at an angle, one of its boards missing. Just as it had been in my childhood, the old places held me in awe, even a humble cow shed. I slipped inside. Standing in the gloom, I had a strong sense nobody had been there in a very long time. I considered checking the wall plate, it was the only place you might find something – a horseshoe, an old gin trap, the sort of modest treasures I had hunted for as a boy.

I reached up and felt blindly around. Nothing. I moved down its length, patting the cold stone, hoping my hands wouldn't land on something living and curled, waiting for me to leave. Then magically, something flashed through the air, like a glittering silver lure. It landed softly on a seabed of cow shit beside me. I looked down into the murk: an old pocket knife.

Burn

I knelt and picked up the relic, wiping excrement off the handle. How long had it been there? I guessed decades, idly placed on the wall by a farmer and forgotten. Opening it, I saw the main cutting blade was well-worn, its edge wavy from uneven sharpening. The second function, a tin opener, was in better shape and snapped back pleasingly when folded shut. I looked more closely at the knife. Turning it towards what was left of the light, I could just about make out a manufacturer's name – Warris, Sheffield – and a date, 1952. It also carried a crow's foot mark assigning it a military provenance. Next to these details, a simple instruction: OIL THE JOINTS. I gazed on it a moment more, then put the find happily in my pocket.

Walking back home in the dark, I thought more on the knife. It seemed so random a discovery, so unlikely an event, as to be almost fate. Its instruction to 'oil the joints', felt less like a prosaic command at maintenance and more of a deeper, personal hint. My life hadn't exactly seized up, but there was a certain lack of movement. Working on a building site was paying the rent, but it wasn't a permanent solution. And while I had made good progress with my mental health and was at least functioning, labouring was a retrograde step. I needed to push on, to cleave a more creative path. I needed re-oiling myself.

6

It was a Thursday just after five, and I was on a slow mosey home after a day on site. I'd clocked the wood yard beside the road many times before; with its chestnut gates and bodger's shelter, a place that had always struck me as interesting. Yet on that particular day I noticed, as I slowed, something new, placed in the entrance. It was a sandwich board and on it, chalked in capitals, the words:

APPRENTICE WANTED

I was instantly jolted – a random but beautiful request. I felt a surge of adrenalin pass through me and knew I had to act. Checking the rear-view mirror, I threw the pick-up across the road and in through the yard's open gates.

Coming to a halt, I parked next to another truck – a tatty Japanese workhorse not unlike mine – the rear tub loaded with hazel rods. Beside it, on a curve, ran a length of chestnut fencing. The timbers were a weathered silver-grey and pleasingly uneven. I got out of the cab and took in the yard: the whole place smelt of wood. Above me, a spray of oak leaves moved gently in the breeze, while under a naked ash stood a wooden cleaving brake, an old billhook checked into the top of one of its posts. Beside the brake, arranged according to size, were hundreds of coppiced hazel poles – whoever owned the yard had been busy. Further back, towards the rear, an old canvas tarp hung over a ridge pole, a place to work under should the weather turn wet.

I was interrupted by a short man walking with purpose up the track which ran from the wood behind. I knew immediately this was his habitat – he couldn't have looked more like a woodsman. It was the sheer physicality of the man, swarthy from outdoor work, with forearms that reminded me of the mooring rope of trawlers down at Lyme. Sartorially, he fitted the bill, too: old-fashioned in a flat cap, jerkin and heavy boots he also sported a cotton neckerchief the sun-faded orange of an old Penguin paperback. The man could have arrived in a time capsule. The only thing which queered the pitch a little were his glasses, fashionable modern rectangles.

'Can I help?' The woodsman spoke with a kind of grimy London-suburbs elocution, and did not seem particularly friendly.

'Hello. I've, er, come about the job.'

The man did a stocktake of my face. I was aware that an apprentice didn't normally mean someone in their late thirties and I suddenly felt old. I filled him in on my experience, explaining a bit about my work with the East Anglian forester and that I would be keen to learn more. His only reply was that he couldn't pay much and that the days would be long. There was an awkward pause. Motioning over to the oak in the corner of the yard, I remarked how handsome it was. The woodsman just nodded. Feeling uncomfortable, I started to effuse about my favourite trees – English oak, black walnut, Scots pine – which was either going to endear me to him or blow the whole thing entirely. The man gave nothing away. He asked whether I had done much felling and if I had a chainsaw certificate. I gave him the honest answer – no – and hoped this would not count against me. Remaining the reticent countryman, he said he'd have a think and call me. Again, I felt him take a long look, perhaps too long. Could he smell the Londoner, get a whiff of the ex-professional burn-out? Before I left, I gave him my number and handing it to him, asked his name. With the same poverty of warmth he had displayed throughout the interview, he replied: 'Joby Cutler.'

Driving back to the farm, I turned the encounter over in my mind. The man was as closed as they come. His accent, too, had completely thrown me – a harsh costermonger English, with no trace of Dorset in it at all. Thinking of my chances, I wasn't sure if I had come across well or as a total imbecile. Slowly the idea took shape that I must have appeared a fey and inadequate middle-class fool. Favourite trees? He didn't want an effing poet, he wanted a grafter. I'd probably blown it.

Sitting at the kitchen table with an extra jumper on, I was doing my best to keep chipper. A sea-fret had rolled in off the bay and decided to squat on the land: it had been four days of near-zero visibility. Stuck inside, occasionally glancing out of the kitchen window, my eyes were met with a damp, grey curtain. It made me feel claustrophobic and low, a hostage to the weather. And still no word from Joby.

The only bright spot had been a visit by a peregrine that morning. He had appeared out of the mist, during breakfast, landing on a fence post less than three metres from my window. The tiercel took to preening himself, while minute pearls of rainwater sequinned his shoulder and wing. His field uniform of blue-grey appeared vaguely teutonic – the colour not unlike the Luftwaffe's *fliegerbluse*, and his head also brought immediate associations: the aristocratic curve of the bill and the black moustache, strikingly handsome, yet cruel – a fascist's face. I remained fixed on the bird, my porridge idly steaming, until he muted, and in a blink was gone.

I was still at the kitchen table an hour later when the phone rang. The voice down the line was not immediately recognisable. While not gushing, it was demonstrably matey and it took me a few seconds to twig. During our meeting the previous week, Joby had been abrupt, even terse – in five minutes he could not have said more than two dozen words.

Now, the easy familiarity in his voice seemed an utter contradiction. In tow with his estuarine twang, it sounded as if he was warming me up to help him do a bank job, or turn over a post office. But no, he wanted me to go up country with him and pick up some wood. Immediately I felt uneasy. Was this man a semi-criminal? Whether we would be paying for it seemed, at that moment, a moot point. I tried to prod him for more information, imagining some kind of woodland smash-and-grab, but he remained sketchy. It sounded as if he was driving.

I stuck to my guns. Was this a one-off job or the start of an apprenticeship? Joby slurred something about seeing how things go, a trial period. This didn't feel suitably fleshed out for my taste, but it was no use trying to get anything firmer from the man. He wound up the conversation, telling me to meet him at his yard at five the next morning. I asked if there was anything I should bring, but he'd already hung up.

I sat at the table stunned. Joby wanted me as his apprentice – but did I want him as my boss? I thought back to the peregrine: cold, ruthless, a creature entirely focused on self. Slowly, the raptor's profile transmogrified into that of the woodsman, and with the vision, a nagging thought: this could be a terrible, terrible mistake.

It was dark when I arrived at the yard, but the gates were already open. Parked inside, stood a white seven-and-a-half-tonne rental lorry – evidently we weren't just picking up a few sticks. I got out of my truck, locked up, and walked towards the rig. Joby was illuminated under the cab light, grazing on something in tin foil. A mug steamed on the dashboard, fogging part of the windscreen. I opened the passenger door and climbed in. The cab had that strong, unsettling smell of factory newness, the rubber foot mats pristine, the seats pert and unsoiled. Joby had done his best to deflower some of its virgin quality: feet up, radio on, A4 print-outs of our route scattered around like leaf litter. I noticed some CDs had been wedged forcibly into the cubby box, while several ratchet straps lay uncoiled in my foot well. I bid him good morning. He took his face out of the tin foil, like a dingo looking up from a carrion dinner.

'Awright.'

Grease and ketchup smeared his chin. He wiped the stubbly promontory with the back of his hand and pulled out a small parcel from a plastic bag beside him. He said his missus had made it for me, a fried egg bap. I thanked him and hungrily took the offering. While I ate, Joby slurped his coffee and explained it would be a two-and-a-half-hour trip at that time in the morning and there would be a couple of lads waiting for us. The way he said it, it just sounded dodgy. Joby drained his coffee cup and began screwing it back on the thermos. Half-concealing a belch, he started the lorry and as we crept through the gates, I was hit by a pillow and the words: 'You might wanna kip.'

We took a wide left out of the yard and onto the road. Five minutes later we were on the main drag, heading east. The earlier darkness was opening up to a luminous blue and details in the landscape – a hillside farm, a distant wind turbine – were forming, like the latent image bleeding through in a developing tray. Now we were on the road, it all felt rather exciting. Looking across at my driver, however, it was clear the novelty of the experience was lost on him. For Joby it was just another working day and his face reflected this: eyes fixed ahead, head set on business.

For twenty minutes we sat in silence, but as we passed Dorchester, I ventured a question. I really knew nothing about the man and wondered how long he had been working in the woods. To my surprise, he opened up. Joby told me he came from an old Traveller family but had grown up on a council estate in Essex. The area had been known as a stopping place for Gypsies long before the estate was built – the land previously just fields and a shanty of wagons and tents. In the fifties, the council had stepped in and raised houses, put in gravel roads. The Bohemia Estate was born. But while the Gypsies were forced to give up their nomadic ways, the estate remained unmistakably Traveller.

As a boy, Joby remembered ponies grazing in the front gardens and lads trotting sulky carts up and down the flashings. The estate's pub was even called The Woodcutter, a common occupation among Travelling men. At sixteen, Joby left and went on the road, journeying by bicycle with just a bender tent on his back. Following his nose west, he ended up fruit picking around Ledbury. After a season he returned to Essex and the estate, but soon realised he was no longer cut out for town. Shortly afterwards, he went back on the road, and found work cutting chestnut coppice in Kent.

He had dipped into the nascent festival circuit and met his wife while protesting at the site of the Newbury bypass. After travelling around the south-west for several years, they had settled in Dorset. The couple had been static for seven years now, living in a yurt which Joby had built on some rented land. They had a vegetable patch; kept goats, ducks and chickens. The news that he lived in a yurt and grew his own food came as a relief, and my fear that he may be a hardened criminal was all but batted away. Criminals don't live in yurts, don't nurture marrows.

Listening to him talk about his life in Dorset was fascinating, but I wanted to know more about the woods, and where and how he had learned his trade. Joby explained he had done itinerant woodland work all over the south: from Kent through Sussex and as far west as Hampshire. As a 'young 'un' he had done the bulk of his apprenticeship with a woodland gang in Sussex, a county with a long and proud tradition of coppice work. The men had been rough and uncompromising and didn't suffer fools. Some of the old timers he worked with had been in the woods since they were twelve. One old boy was so old he reckoned he had been born just after 'Victoria hopped the twig' and still did a full day on the saw. The gang had old-fashioned ways, held old-fashioned beliefs, and at times it sounded brutal. But all Joby would say was that it 'weren't always comfortable'. I liked his restraint, his lack of fuss. 'You'd be up at five in the summer, an hour later in winter, and work 'til you lost the light. And if you got something wrong – look out. Those old boys treated you just as they'd been treated and weren't slow to raise a stick.' But Joby insisted it had been the best way to learn and given him a work ethic most people today didn't understand. Like his teachers, the Gypsy was a man with lignin in his veins. Wood seeps in.

We arrived just before eight at the entrance to the copse. I got out, slightly comatose from three hours in a warm cab but the woodland air acted like smelling salts and quickly shook out the journey. Reawakened, I peered into the trees and an incalculable multitude of black stems, shiny from the night's rain. Their sheer multitude was baffling, utterly incomprehensible. Ranks of chestnut poles, perhaps twenty to every stump, thrust out in a 'V' formation. Regarding them, I sensed a certain hostility in their growth, their single-minded reach for the light.

Yet they hadn't considered the dank, phlegmatic, English air. No ardour can survive such conditions, for nothing is damper than an English wood after rain. A million twigs drip and sink the world slowly, agents of moisture lurk everywhere. Under such conditions, the black shafts of chestnut stuck up dumbly, their zeal dowsed.

It was also eerily still. A dense silence rippled through the wood, the trees working like a sonic baffle. No sound of traffic, no modern intrusion. Then I saw the willow form of a young roe hind nosing the ground some distance off – delicate, coy, beautiful. She hadn't detected our presence, there was no wind to carry our scent. In the absolute silence of the coppice we could have been in 1200. As she continued to browse, I saw her as the stalking woodward might have, breath held, yew bow under tension.

'Pricks,' said Joby, 'fuckin' clowns. Said they'd be 'ere.'

No, we were definitely in the twenty-first century – what's more, in a cold, wet wood near London on a Tuesday. Joby looked annoyed, his face leaking violence. 'I'll phone 'em.'

He dug into his trouser pocket and pulled out a mobile, stabbing in the number. Joby clamped the phone to his ear, and walked a few paces away from me, while I stood stupid in the drizzle, waiting. After a few seconds I heard him utter darkly, 'We're 'ere,' then a pause and the words, 'ten minutes'. Joby switched off the phone, shook his head and mouthed something inaudible. I was glad he had declined to swear out loud, it didn't feel right in the wood. Pushing his glasses up the bridge of his nose, he blinked. I thought of Mole from *The Wind in the Willows* but with anger management issues. The short man spat on the ground and suggested we wait in the cab. The hind had vanished.

Back inside, Joby had dried up. A frown had appeared across his brow and I suspected his mind was deep in business. I also noticed a billhook jammed in between his seat and the lorry's cubby box – was he expecting trouble? Suddenly I wished I wasn't there.

A few seconds later I heard them. It was the sound of a diesel engine in low ratio, but revving high, somewhere on the road behind us. Looking in the wing mirror, I saw them, a Land Rover Discovery tearing up the ride, pulling a plant trailer loaded with a mini-digger. The truck was modified with a bull bar, snorkel and a set of roof lights for lamping rabbits.

Joby stiffened, his gaze fixed forward. If I hadn't felt so intimidated, I might have laughed. The whole scene was like a rural English parody of a Scorsese movie, aping some sort of clandestine drugs meet. But we weren't in a multi-storey car park at night, armed to the gills, watching a blacked-out sedan approach. We were on a woodland ride in a rental lorry, waiting to pick up some wood. Despite Joby packing a billhook, it was hardly *Scarface*.

The Discovery's engine cut out and two doors opened. A couple of lads jumped out, one in his late twenties, the other a decade older. They didn't immediately look like killers, although the young one did strike me as a bit twitchy. He was tall and lean, with the floating head of a boxer. I noticed Joby was watching him too, fixed, in the same way a cat watches a mouse hole. As they walked towards us, the older one raised a hand.

Joby remained silent, his hands gripping the steering wheel. As the two men got closer, his stillness crystallised. At five metres from the lorry, he gave the command to go and exited the cab before I had even reached for my door handle. I swore and parachuted out of the lorry late, landing in a puddle – not the most auspicious start. We met on the ride and shook hands. All except Joby. He declined to shake but silently nodded. That was all he was going to give them. I didn't need to be told what this was all about. Joby was using everything at his disposal to gain the upper hand. This was business, Traveller style.

The older fellow knew the game. He let the affront of Joby refusing to shake wash over him, the subtext being 'It's no odds to me short arse.' Studying him, I realised he was actually the more dangerous of the two. He had slow eyes, a thick neck, and a weakness for gold betrayed on every finger. Instantly, I got a whiff of the man-nutter not far beneath the surface, easily unlocked by a few pints.

Dwarfed by the two men, Joby puffed himself up like a cornered animal showing itself to its full advantage. His arms were folded defensively, a barrier but also a tacit message advertising their muscularity. The older man apologised for being late, explaining they'd had trouble loading the digger. He asked if we'd had a good trip. Joby replied we had, there hadn't been much traffic, we'd even had time to stop for a coffee. It was regulation small talk. What was really being communicated was unspoken – two men sniffing around each other, working out who was top dog.

Slow Eyes spoke in the modern Sussex dialect: sprawling, lazy, town-stained. He seemed on good behaviour, although I sensed civility was not his default setting. There was something strained in his good manners, something which didn't ring true. Whether he was trying to lull us into a false sense of security, I couldn't tell, but it was obvious Joby would not be easy game.

We walked up a woodland ride to an area of open ground, fringed by an oak plantation. The verge of the ride had been cut back to create a depot for the harvested chestnut poles which lay all over the wet ground, arranged according to size. Joby scratched his chin, unhooked a tape measure from his belt and rolled one pole over with his boot. The thicker, straighter poles we would split in half and use as fencing posts. The rest would be cleaved into quarters to make the rails. Measuring up, Joby did not seem entirely happy: he said he'd specified at least eight inches for the diameter of the posts and these fell short.

I suddenly felt surplus to requirements and walked away to study a giant puffball growing on the other side of the track. But my mushroom spotting was checked by the sound of Joby's raised voice behind me. Looking back, I saw he had his hands on his hips and was shaking his head. I also heard him utter the word 'pal' which did not bode well. Clearly the men were talking money and Joby wanted a deal. Whether bartering for horses, dogs, wagons or even wood, prestige is attached to a Traveller's ability to make a good 'chop'.

After a five-minute rally of animated talk and possibly threats, Joby seemed in the ascendant. He had already finished off the younger fellow who was staring woodenly into the ground and had now turned the full force of his will onto the older man. The banter was less knock-about now, more serious. I watched as Joby bored into the remaining obstacle with cold focus and over two slow minutes witnessed the Sussex man fade.

I walked back across the track towards them, pretending all was well in the world. It was no odds to me how much we had paid for the chestnut and I took no pleasure in seeing a man so reduced. But Joby couldn't care less, he had got the price he wanted and stood there stripping fifties from a silver money clip, while the older man looked dazed.

It took us an hour to load the lorry. While we worked, a couple of chainsaws started up in the coppice behind – it seemed Slow Eyes and his partner had resumed coppicing. With the lorry heaving, Joby flung several tie-downs over the load and lashed it down hard. That done, we climbed into the cab and went on our way. As the lorry left the wood, Joby cracked a toadish grin and, as we hit tarmac, he sounded off triumphantly with a lairy toot of the horn.

The following morning I met Joby at the yard just before eight. I arrived to find him knee-deep in chestnut, material we had unloaded from the lorry the previous day. He was well into it already, busy cleaving the larger posts with a sledgehammer and wedges. It was a handsome sight, the stack of cleft wood multiplying, vivid strips of ochre against the backdrop of the yard. I stood for a moment and watched him work the sledge, knocking a steel wedge into the post-end, before using two others to work the split down the timber's length.

A few feet from all this activity, a small camp-fire crackled and popped, several off-cuts of sweet chestnut hurling sparks. With not a breath of wind, the woodsmoke rose languidly, the most unlikely progeny of the surly, spitting chestnut below. The beauty of it fascinated me. Making a fire is an act of love. It is always becoming, lending a space, humanity and comfort. Instantly, the wood yard was no longer just a place of work. Inside its gates, the dull modern maxim that divides life from work had melted away. The yard, the fire and everything in it simply said, 'All is life. Be.'

It was as if the fire had smelted a rough, hard mineral – that thing called work – and reduced it to liquid matter, something which could be cast more creatively. I studied the wood yard dressed with its gathered material and Joby's simple canvas shelter. This seemed a more beautiful alternative.

I asked the man what I should do. He asked me to run the side-axe down the edges of the cleft rails, giving them a rough chamfer. I picked up the tool, a beautifully weighted thing with an off-set hickory handle and took to my task. The work was not technically difficult, but very soon my forearms were cramping. Being the new boy, I was simply not used to this specific woodland exercise. When Joby suggested a break, I tried not to sound too eager.

We stopped for breakfast, Joby putting a pan on the trivet, and breaking in a couple of eggs. They were huge – at least twice as big as any chicken egg I had ever seen – and the yolks were a rich tawny brown. Joby explained they came from his own ducks and the yolks were so coloured because they would sometimes feed the birds ground acorns, rich in brown pigment.

The kettle began to sing over the fire, so I took it off the crane and poured the boiling water into a pair of enamelled tin mugs. Joby passed me a spoon, one he had whittled from alder, and told me he liked his tea milky and with two sugars, or 'three when graftin'. I shot a look at the pile of cleaved chestnut and quickly apportioned his mug the higher dose. Meanwhile Joby got out his knife and began to butter the end of a white farmhouse loaf. A novel way of doing it I thought, perhaps another Traveller's quirk. He asked me if I wanted a slice, but I replied I wasn't hungry. As we sat, words didn't come, but a breeze got up, stirring the branches of the oak above us. The cramping in my forearms had started to relent and life seemed good. I realised then that I must be getting used to him – we had sat in silence for several minutes and there had been no need to fill the gap.

Finishing breakfast, Joby asked if I would like to see the wood. I hadn't yet made it past a stand of hornbeam, just below the bodger's shelter, and was curious to see what lay beyond. We walked down past the ironwood, their trunks wrung in elegant barley twists, and followed the track as it careered right, then left, through a grove of young beech. Turning a corner, we surprised a jay on the track which took off and flew low in front of us, its brisk wing beat rattling the air. Joby put up an imaginary gun and blasted the woodland crow, before giving it a second imaginary barrel for good measure. At that moment the track opened up to reveal an escarpment which dropped away, quite dramatically, at our feet. Joby stepped forward, looking towards the sea and a stagger of distant sea cliffs, then turned to me with a rhapsodic grin. 'Beats a council estate, don't it?'

Below us, the wood folded around itself in a vast semicircle like an amphitheatre; a fine place for viewing the tumbling drama below. Joby explained that the rock beneath was largely greensand, and this was the reason the beeches here had grown so big. Apart from their muscular monopoly, one could also make out some oak and the darker outlines of holly further down. At the very bottom, two hundred feet below, a burgundy blush of alder, heavy with catkins.

My eyes followed the woodland track as it dropped over the edge. It appeared Joby, on making the track, had not mitigated against the wood's steep gradient by putting in switchbacks, but rather trusted his pick-up, as well as his own nerve, to get up from the bottom when required. I noticed clouds moving among the alder beneath us, reflections on the water, the land down there pockmarked with ponds. Joby explained that the ground in the lowest part of the wood was saturated by springs and too waterlogged for planting, so he had drained it by digging ponds. They not only captured the water and dried up the land in between, but also encouraged biodiversity. It was a good habitat for grass snakes, and also a perfect place to rear ducks, he explained.

Joby motioned me forward and started to clamber down. I followed him and we traversed the sunny slope, picking our way across ground that he had recently thinned of trees. Bramble tore at my trousers and at intervals we passed stacks of felled beech which Joby had buttressed with heavier butt ends, to stop the stacks from rolling. In the gaps, new plant-ings of sweet chestnut stood sentinel in their guards of spiral mesh, while every few yards a stump rose out of the ground, memorial to a felled tree.

We pushed on across the hill and back into the trees. We had entered the kingdom of beech. Here, a dense silence reigned, for it is a feature of beech woodland that very little grows there. They are bullies, land-grabbers, winner-takes-all trees, their dense canopy casting a deadly shade. In the stillness, my eye caught an apparition, a drift of white. Sketches of fret were moving between the trees, ghosting silently through the deeper wood. I asked Joby what it was. Casually, he told me he had the kettle on, and suggested we take a look. Confused as to what he meant, I paused, but Joby had already gone and was walking in the direction of the haunting, like a doomed priest.

I hurried forward. I had lost him. Scanning the wood, I caught him turning down a narrow ride which cut through a patch of laurel. He disappeared down the dark tributary, like flotsam floating out of sight down a green drain. I pushed into the dark, eager not to lose my guide. Once clear of the laurel, the track widened and the light returned, and with it the tang of woodsmoke.

Rounding a bend, my eyes fell on a large circular object, the colour of a port wine stain, its metal surface livid with heat. Joby was standing beside it, watching the chimneys, slim panatelas of steel which were energetically pumping thick, white smoke into the air. The man looked up briefly. So this was his 'kettle', a charcoal kiln and, in its way, a kind of ghost.

Thrown untidily about the pitstead were his tools – a shovel, a rake, some old tarps. A pair of red welding mitts stuck upright on two hazel posts, stiff with wood tar, oddly grotesque. To one side sat a dumpy bag, distended with small black chips. I picked a piece out and turned it in my fingers. The flat surface shone an iridescent blue, edged with an after-burn of bronze. It felt weightless and tinkled in my hand like glass.

On the far side of the kiln was a heap of larger, partly carbonised sticks. They were ebonised seaside rock, satanic candy. Putting one to my nose it smelled faintly aromatic. I threw the black stick down and turned back towards the kiln. It was a cheerful thing full of industry, and if one could imagine it sentient, something that loved its job. I asked Joby when he had lit it. He scratched his head. 'About six this mornin'. She'll be done 'round nine tonight.'

It had only been going a few hours and was still in its most elemental phase, belching hydrocarbons into the atmosphere.

Burn

I watched the smoke, transfixed by its shapes, its helicoid mass. From the chimneys grew giant florets of vapour, nightmarish excrescences like a super-crop of gruesome cauliflower. The florets expanded, then multiplied, their silent blooms the colour of winter slush. Twelve feet above the kiln, the smoke started to disperse, then higher still, it appeared diluted to almost nothing, broken up in a tide of sea air which drew back through the branches of the wood.

The kiln jogged something powerful in me. I had come across charcoal burners once before, but that had been long ago, close on thirty years. My memories had since been without sound, just faded impressions, like charcoal drawings which had not been fixed. But the sight of the kiln and the smell of its industry had sharpened their ghostly forms.

Autumn term, 1979. A school trip to a local wood, the air thick with cold, the dying sun paper thin. A church bell rings out four times across the fields, its bright timbre unimpeded in the grainy air. Kids stand around: some are bored, others are spooked, I am transfixed. The men we watch work silently, bagging up the day, sweeping up the wood. One of them comes forward. He has a dark beard and a battered hat. He is falling into silhouette but his features can still be read. A kind face, the eyes bright and clear. He asks me if I like the wood – I am without words, I am shy and only eight. I nod. The man smiles and turns away. Across the glade three kilns smoke idly. I walk over and stand close to one, bathing in its glow, its ambient heat. From inside there is a sound of popping. It is the wood slowly baking, the hazel turning to coal. I feel at peace. I want to stay.

7

After two months working in Joby's wood, I began to think about moving there. The house on the hill was too big for me and while I loved its location and had become fond of my wild neighbours, I couldn't justify the rent. Yet, money aside, there was something else chipping away at me. Since working in the woods I had discovered a lightness which was like music in my blood. The trees held an energy which seemed healing, a glow I carried long after leaving them. And as I felt myself treading lighter through life and the old illness receding, I realised I would be happier with less, much less. I would still need a roof over my head, but the wood and its lucent green canopy had prompted me to ask, why such a heavy one?

So it was ideal timing when the phone rang one night after supper. It was Adam, an old family friend. We hadn't spoken for over a year – he was a busy headmaster and I'd been distracted myself of late – but when you are old friends such fallow periods do not matter.

We talked. Caught up on news. Fell into old, familiar patterns. One predictably reliable focus of conversation had always centred on what could loosely be described as 'wagons', a vague genera of wheeled, vintage homes, which could encompass anything from a tin-clad shepherd's hut to a gaudily painted Gypsy caravan. Adam had a sizeable collection and could talk on the subject for hours. But I was never bored. They too had been on my radar from an early age.

August 1985. I am fourteen and have a summer job pulling weeds from the arable fields which dominate the landscape around my home. 'Roguing' was the agricultural term for this seasonal work. A few of the local boys did it. You'd see gangs of them walking in lines through the barley and wheat every summer, stripped to the waist, trailing sacks in which to deposit the rogue weeds. It was monotonous, dry work and by the end of the day even the bounciest among us would feel deflated by boredom, punctured by the heat.

I walked home every night along an old drove road, a two-mile hike over the Downs. Half way back, I would pass a collection of barns, a satellite to the bigger farm several miles away. The place was always deserted, I never saw another soul there. In an open-sided hangar, stacked to the roof, giant bags of nitrate fertiliser. You could climb them, or stick your penknife into them and watch the tiny white balls of fertiliser trickle out.

Sometimes I'd shoot rats there. I would often leave my air rifle in the hedge on my morning commute and reclaim it on the return journey, stopping to enjoy half an hour's sniping before supper. Country kids can be bloodthirsty and I enjoyed killing with my gun. But behind the barns there was a different lure. One powerful enough to make me occasionally put down my rifle.

It was an old hut on wheels, what had once been a temporary home for the most revered of all farm employees, the shepherd. These huts were pulled out onto the Downs to provide him with shelter while he folded his sheep, or during the long weeks of lambing. Once a common sight in the chalk country, they were now obselete. A good proportion had been destroyed by the farms which had owned them, the carcass burnt and the ironwork sold for scrap. A few survived.

Looking at the hut, I could see redundancy and neglect had taken its toll. Now a decaying box clad in rippled tin sheet, the original black paint had worn away to a patchy veneer. Above the door, a cast iron-maker's plate with the faded name TASKER embossed in relief. The letters of the once proud name had been rounded and worn by weather, as if the hut sought some anonymity, its reduced circumstances bringing shame. The large iron wheels remained magnificent – wide rimmed and finely spoked, with a removable plug in each hub for greasing. A holly tree had grown between the spokes of one. Its scratchy leaves played a skiffle tune against the hut's tin side in the breeze.

All children are drawn to dens – and this was a ready-made one. Yet I did not feel inclined to play there. Perhaps it was that I was getting older, but the hut somehow demanded respect. I had the country deep in me, the flint and the chalk, and as a son of that soil I recognised an elder, even an inanimate one.

Standing before it, the blood-lust of idle murder shrank away. A stillness stole in. It was the idea of the man who had filled this space – his quiet shiftings in lamp light, nursing orphan lambs; or kneeling beside the stove, thorn wood crackling in the grate. I had not known the shepherd, but it was enough to look inside the hut to feel you had. Along the end wall, the remains of his wooden bed, the mattress decayed and mouse-eaten and below a small sliding window, an old medicine chest.

In 1985, *Country Living* had not yet cottoned on to these humble agricultural marvels, but as a fourteen-year-old boy, I had. As Adam talked, I detected some excitement in his voice. He was calling to tell me that an old fella up the road – something of a recluse and an eccentric – had a collection of huts and living vans he was planning to sell. Adam had persuaded him to give us first dibs. I left for Shropshire the next day.

Owen lived on the top of a hill in a tumble-down, half-timbered house, the sort which dot the landscape in that part of the world. The oak frame had weathered a silver-grey and the daub infill, a pale ochre. When we knocked, the old man answered shyly, peering around the doorway like a dusty ascetic. A dim hallway stretched behind him, on the walls faded wallpaper and a brown bakelite switch. The place could not have been decorated or rewired for over sixty years.

We waited on the doorstep while Owen gathered his coat and wellies. At the end of the hallway stood a silent, long case clock. It was either broken or unwound; the only sound was Owen's mutterings as he struggled with his boots. Eventually, Owen appeared from the house with an old spaniel in tow, its eyes woebegone and timid. The pair led us through an ancient cider orchard, the dog stopping occasionally to sniff at the base of the veteran trees. According to Adam, who'd done a recce the previous day, the wagon with my name on stood in the next paddock.

It was definitely not a shepherd's hut, its charms were less obvious. A drab green cube clad in tin sheet, it declared itself more 1950 than 1850 and my vision of Gabriel Oak instantly died. No self-respecting shepherd would have leant inside its doorframe, no sheep would have hunkered beneath it. But in the wake of my initial disappointment, something flickered. While not antique, the hut had some history. Moving closer, I made out traces of signage beneath the olive green paint: Shropshire County Contracting Van – Telford. My wagon snobbery faltered. I gleaned from Owen the hut would once have been a mobile shelter for a road gang, a refuge from the weather while repairing the county's highways and byways, its drains and culverts.

I stepped inside. The living van shared similar dimensions to a shepherd's hut, but with two large windows it felt far brighter. Its floorboards were thick and solid, and the walls were good. There were watermarks on the ceiling – probably leaks through joints in the tin sheet – but that could be fixed. After my initial dismay I was feeling more positive. Certainly not a chocolate box hut, but something more real. I bought the county works van off Owen for one hundred and forty pounds. I didn't think this a bad price and felt it ungallant to haggle. On shaking the old man looked at me shyly.

'You don't want a dog to go with that hut?'

'A dog?'

'Yes. A working man needs a dog.' I looked down at the old, tumour-riddled spaniel beside him.

'No, I'm sure she's happier here.' Owen scratched his stubble chin.

'Not her – got another – yours for a pound.' Before I could reply, the old boy had started back towards the house – talking dogs seemed to have given him some zest. We followed him at a short distance, and was beckoned into a fold yard. Stopping at a stable door, Owen grinned at me, advertising a row of rotten teeth, and pulled back the door bolt. The stable had a frowsy air, tired straw poking across the threshold like a Mary Quant fringe. Suddenly, the double blink of a fluorescent tube light killed the murk. Owen stepped inside.

'Come on you. Time to go.'

That sounded ominous. A second later the old man reappeared, dragging a short length of baler twine and, attached to the end, a small and skinny pup.

'Found 'im stray up toward Broadstone, day before last. Chewed through his leash. By the look of 'im, a Traveller's dog. There's a site up there – rough lot. Didn't fancy takin' 'im back.'

The pup looked out of sorts and certainly undernourished. If there was ever an animal that needed some luck, here it was. He had a dull coat – probably worms – and the legginess of youth. I put him at a year, tops.

'Mangy looking mutt, Owen.'

The old man felt the dog's withers.

'He'll pack out, don't you worry.' Owen took a small treat out of his pocket and offered it to the creature. Its eyes bulged as it sniffed at the rough hand, then took the morsel sharply. I looked some more on the dog. His body was white, the only markings a dusting of brown spots on the back of his ears. The head was interesting too, the skull ovoid, the nose long and tapering. He looked to have some English Bull terrier in him, but was softer, not the full package.

'Looks like there's some Bully in there.' Owen nodded.

'Aye. Don't know what with. Parsons terrier if I 'ad to guess.' The pup lay down on the concrete yard and made himself small. Owen scratched his chin. 'Typical tinker's dog – they like their fightin' crosses. 'E's a bit sensitive 'round 'is back end, mind. Reckon e's been kicked there a few times.'

I whistled to the pup. Instantly, his face was alive. All of a sudden I had every compunction to take him on, to go with the gift. I had pined for a dog during my London years, but had always demurred, feeling my lifestyle was not conducive. But free of those shackles, there really was no reason. I thought of Joby – perhaps he wouldn't be keen – it would be a gamble. I turned to Owen.

'Why don't you keep him?'

'Not fair on my old girl – been just the two of us this fifteen year. Rather see our time out as is.' I looked over at Adam who had remained silent the whole time. A grin had appeared on his face.

'Got Dorset written all over him, cuz.'

I bent down and offered the pup my hand. He sniffed at it tentatively. Shy now I thought, but he would grow into a right bruiser. As I studied the dog, Owen said something which I didn't take in – it was just sound. Then I knew. The dog was coming home with me. Joby would have to lump it.

The Gypsy stood with his hands in his pockets and his gut hanging over his belt, regarding the new arrival. In the field opposite, a flock of Poll Dorsets – mothers with their lambs – were out in force.

'Wass 'is name?' asked Joby.

'Haven't thought of one yet.' I replied. The man pushed the glassy rectangles up the bridge of his nose and blinked.

'Better do. If he gets in wiv those sheep, farmer'll shoot 'im. Least wiv a name you got summink to put on 'is headstone.'

I looked down at the pup. Being a terrier there would be some mischief there. Despite the insensitivity of his conclusion, Joby had a point.

We'd got back to Dorset the previous day, after a five-hour trek down the west of England. I'd left the van at home, but in getting to the woods that morning had told Joby all about it. He'd seemed interested which had given me the impetus to float the idea of moving it to the woods and living there permanently. To my surprise, the Gypsy agreed – no point throwing away good money on rent when you had alternative means, had been the gist of his answer. I explained I wouldn't be moving immediately. I would have to see out my notice on the cottage and had some work to do on the van. Joby shrugged, adding it was no odds to him, and I could move when I liked. He added that he wouldn't ask for any ground rent, the agreement being I'd be his nightwatchman while he lived off-site, in the yurt. The pup was only a scrappy half-pint now, but he'd soon be something more formidable, a proper 'yard dog' as Joby put it, just the kind of animal to deter the wrong sort from having a snoop around. As we stood there, a breeze got up and I noticed the pup sticking his nose into the wind, floating on it the scent of baby sheep. I suddenly felt pressed to give him a name.

'You reckon you'll take to it?' Joby was done with dog-talk and had moved onto the van.

'Take to what?'

'The life.'

'Reckon so. Van, dog, kettle over the fire – what more could a man want?' Joby looked at me with a sneer of amusement.

'Hot water, TV, central heating?'

I knew Joby was sceptical. And to be fair, I was an easy target. I think what most grated with him was that he could clearly see the middle-class romantic in me and doubted my staying power. After a month or two of wagon living, I'd fold. But what he didn't know was that beyond certain poetic sensibilities, I had some steel. What I'd suffered in the past had given me a strong tiller.

As far as creature comforts go, there was a pinch of hypocrisy in Joby's own position. A few years before settling in Dorset, he'd done a stint in an off-grid woodland community near Yeovil. It had been a viciously principled set up, no modern technology allowed on site. But after a few months, he had been turfed out when one of the community elders found a battery-powered, portable TV in his yurt. So while he had Romany blood, Joby seemed to me more of a woody, New Age chancer.

Even with the good fortune of stumbling on the living van and Joby's generous offer to live in his wood, I was not naive enough to think that I was now cured, riding a zip wire to a perfect life. I could not afford to think for one minute that the battle with my own illness was won. Keeping things simple was the only way forward. Getting caught in the spring traps modern life sets would only make the fight harder. In my slow recovery from years of poor mental health, what I needed most was the free air created from living life on my own terms. I knew I could never go back into the System and be at the mercy of all its rules, red lines and judgements. Operating in that environment while struggling with acute anxiety had been torture. The System does not have time for anyone who is not a reliable servant. And when you wake up in the morning with anxiety that is frying your soul, how can you brush that off because you have a 9.00am meeting about an ad campaign for a new brand of toothpaste?

Over the following weeks, I worked on the van, reno-vating it between woodland shifts. I'd fitted a small stove and chimney, knocked together a folding table, made a bed and put up some shelves. While I worked, the pup mooched about, flitting between short periods of playful animation and committed idleness. As the van interior took shape, so did my thoughts on a name. The pup was clearly a cross, but the bullish physicality of one half of his lineage shone through. He had filled out a little too, probably more down to regular meals and the worming tablets, but I'd also noticed the pink edging the black snout, the porcine gut, and the back legs which seemed distinctly hammish. If he stayed in the sun too long he would glow rose pink through his short, white coat. Sitting on the wagon steps, nursing a brew, it came to me. The pup was part-pork, a quasi-hog. I'd call him Pig.

With the van habitable and my notice on the tenancy seen out, we left the house on the hill. As I drove down the track for the final time, Pig sat on the passenger seat, occasionally throwing a look at me over his shoulder, as if for reassurance. Looking at him, I felt some responsibility. I wanted a good life for the dog as much as for me. He deserved some luck.

Arriving in Joby's wood, we parked the van against a cliff of sloping greensand, just off a woodland ride which ran up towards the kiln. During the first night it rained heavily and I awoke to a considerable amount of standing water all about the place. Springs proliferated in the wood and had conspired with the greensand and clay to create the sort of light brown slop found in a baby's nappy. My outdoor kitchen, too, looked pitiful. With no awning raised, everything was soaked – at least I'd be spared the washing up. Joby looked at my set-up and shook his head. It wasn't up to scratch. The first tenet of wagon-living is that if you are not properly organised, and the weather fixes on being awkward, things unravel very quickly. Pulling a face as though Pig had curled a turd on his boots, Joby called me a 'mumper', the Romany word for a tramp.

But it was the look on the pup's face which cut deeper. Pig stood on the threshold of the van looking towards me, grave and sore. He was a born Traveller's dog – he knew too.

Was this all too much? Had I bitten off more than I could chew? My old colleagues, those admen commanding legions from their glass offices or sitting in the comfortable chairs of their private clubs, would have thought so. And I wouldn't have blamed them. My situation was so far from their own, so remote from any acceptable form of existence they could understand, they would only have reached one conclusion: he's cracked.

When once I'd had waiters bring me bottled spring water in some of London's finest restaurants, I would now be fetching my own, hauled from a well every morning and boiled on a cast iron stove. And instead of boozy evenings spent in fashionable East End pubs, I'd now be seeing out the light in a space no bigger than a stationary cupboard.

Yet without doubt, I was better off among the trees with Pig beside me than I had been in my West End office, surrounded yet utterly alone, clinging to the last vestiges of sanity a man can call on. While my new life in the woods was extreme, it was a necessary redrafting. A mental and spiritual reboot which nature had ordered.

My eyes were now on the small things. Fetching my water in a pair of stainless steel milk churns, the shape of rhubarb forcers. Standing beside the well, scooping leaves off the water, rescuing a drowning beetle. Carrying the heavy, clanking churns back up the hill, each footstep lightened by birdsong. Getting back to the wagon, I'd light the stove. The water heated soon enough, steam curling from the bowl. Then I'd dip my hands in and feel the heat prickle my skin, a good thing.

It may sound trite, but when life is reduced to the basics, they themselves become rewarding. A hot wash in a tin bowl and the soft pressing of a warm flannel on one's face. Hanging the towel on a string line above the stove to dry. The smell of freshly brewed coffee colliding with the smack of early morning, forest air. Watching the sun move west over the wood, scanning the horizon, sniffing the forecast.

But wagon living isn't all roses. Our fantasies of such a life are so limited, so dumbed down by cliché. Of course there are certain freedoms which go with this lifestyle and a great deal of happiness to be had, but our mental shorthand does not include the long, dark nights in small spaces and the heavy reek of paraffin lamps. Neither is there room in our imagination for the fires that smoulder and the chimneys which refuse to draw. We don't for a second consider the freezing mornings or unwanted visitors in the middle of the night. Forget the easy clichés, it is the practical hardships one has to wrestle with and the new rhythms one must master which give the most satisfaction; it is those moments of quiet purpose, done slowly and freely given, which truly speak.

Another challenge which my new life presented was returning to the woods after dark, a situation I had always found disconcerting. Perhaps I have seen too many films, but car lights in a wood are always spooky. Halogen beams penetrating layers of trees, lights sweeping the underwood, throwing up faces and body parts of startled animals – the burning eyes of a dog fox, a badger's thick rear end oscillating into darkness, the mosh-pit spasm of a spooked herd of deer.

As I drove down the track past stands of hornbeam, the trees made it no easier, going to work on my imagination. They crowded in, bending down, as if cursing a noisy trespasser. A car has no place in a wood, especially after dark. It is in many ways an act of aggression, disturbing the natural rhythms and fracking the night. If you walk in you are accepted. But to drive in, it warps the energy there.

8

5.00am. A blackbird lets rip outside my window and I curse
its dark heart. A warm dream curtailed, I find myself hurled
from sleep into the pre-dawn gloom of a cold wagon. Pig
stirs. He needs a pee. He throws his head aslant, imploring
me, his skull the shape of a lead bossing mallet. I pretend I
haven't noticed, but all too quickly feel a phantom throb in
my bladder. I shake myself free of the bed. Bare feet greet
boards. I duck under lines of washing I have drying across the
middle of the van, but am caught by a pair of underpants that
hang shrivelled, like an old man's testicle, under the window.
They catch me below the chin and as I step forward pull back
over my face. I am momentarily blinded in a confusing world
of grey-white. Tearing them off, I catch Pig eyeing me from
his bed. He regards me with indifference. Physical comedy is
not his bag – at least not before breakfast.

7.30am. Fuelled by strong coffee, I make my way up to the
yard. In over a year of working with Joby, there was never
a day when he was not there before me. I had no reason to
feel guilty about this as my working day formally began at
eight, but something in Joby's manner always gave me the
impression I was disappointing him. He would often point
out he'd been there since six, which only made me feel worse.
It seemed to me that part of the man liked to keep me down,
to remind me in small and regular ways that he was the boss.
This struck me as totally unnecessary. I was more than aware
of my own lack in so many areas and would never have
pushed my status as anything but the grateful apprentice.

Despite this, I enjoyed my days. It was a vest and shorts April
and I was simply happy to be outside. Joby's agro-forestry

71

project was still in its infancy and there was plenty to do. He'd already done a huge amount of work himself, having taken a steep and neglected Forestry Commission patch and turned it into something which had started to resemble a working wood. With ponds dug, a well sunk, scores of the beech felled and a network of rides excavated, I had to take my hat off to him. Joby was a human dynamo, a real dog. From my advertising days I knew what hard work looked like, but that had all been mental graft. Working with the Gypsy represented something new and I relished the challenge.

Fencing had been the first job to tick off. Joby had suffered problems with cattle getting into the wood from an adjacent field, browsing the young trees and trampling the ground. To stymie these bovine raids, we spent two weeks making a chestnut post-and-rail fence which ran the entire length of the wood's eastern edge. Most of my time was spent digging post holes, perhaps forty all told. It was murder, the ground mean and flinty, and my wrists took a hammering. But Joby had mixed up the ground-work with more creative tasks. Some days I was engaged in shaping fencing posts with a side-axe and one morning he handed me a froe and told me to get busy splitting more chestnut.

The froe is an interesting tool, the shape of an L. Think of the upright as the handle, the horizontal bottom as its metal edge. It is used to split or 'cleave' wood down the grain and is an integral part of every green woodworker's tool kit.

To cleave a length of wood, you first hammer the blade of the froe across the pole end which creates a small split. You then place the pole in something called a 'cleaving brake' which locks the wood in position. By working the froe's handle like a lever, the split is quickly opened into a running crack. Eventually the crack travels down the entire length of the timber until it shivers in two with a pleasing pop. Cleaving wood is a basic greenwood skill and means you can split long poles with ease, creating two perfectly symmetrical halves. Joby had made his own froe, the blade fabricated from an old lorry leaf suspension spring. He'd shaped it, sharpened it and fitted it with a turned ash handle. It seemed the man had craft as well as grunt.

Working with the froe I'd be serenaded by birds, and occasionally look up to watch a family of long-tailed tits scuffing the hedgerow. A wren would often appear too, flitting in and out of the woodpile next to me, his throat rippling as he poured out his song. It never ceased to amaze me how such a tiny thing could project so loudly. In the field beyond, the Jersey cattle gorged merrily on spring grass while swallows sliced the air in between the herd, picking off insects which rose from the ground, disturbed by the grazing. Like the creatures of air, field and wood, Joby seemed to be enjoying the fine weather, parading around shirtless. What most amused me was that while he had no scruples about revealing his gut, he never exposed his legs. The pot belly was tight as a timpani drum and browned quickly to a deep mocha, but his lower limbs never saw daylight. Whether it is a rule that Travelling men do not show their legs in public, or that Joby was just embarrassed by their lack of inches, I do not know, but the Gypsy remained in corduroy all summer.

While I laboured, dragging fencing posts and rails, Joby dedicated himself to higher matters. His role was directing the assembly of the fence and in this he was very particular. The fence had to flow, to glide over the land – a poorly chosen rail could throw the whole thing out entirely. Chestnut, by its nature, is a wonky wood, and when utilised as a fencing timber this is part of its charm. But it takes somebody with an eye to get it right. Joby knew exactly how to work the wood, how to construct a barrier which courted with and danced over the ground. As time went on, I began to regard the fence as a kind of sculpture: natural, cleaved wood locked together by simple mortice and tenon that would turn silver-grey over time and mellow against the backdrop of the wood. It was more than fencing. It was land art.

The clenched fist of a summer storm swung off the bay and delivered a haymaker to the wood. Joby stood in the yard, arms dangling, as if punch drunk. We'd been working through the deluge for two hours, cross-cutting a stack of beech trunks and were both sodden. I was praying for him to call it a day, but knew he wouldn't. Giving into a bit of weather was, for men like Joby, an affront to their masculinity. The Gypsy grinned through it, sticking his jaw into the gale, as if to say: 'That the best you got?'

The wind hissed through the trees. A gust rocked him on his heels. I cut in: 'This is daft, Joby, let's get out of the rain. We can work under the tarp.'

The man shot me a look of pure disdain. He didn't like it, didn't appreciate being told. But in such biblical conditions, he knew it made sense.

'Come on, I'll get a brew on.'

Bloodied by the south-westerly, his head dropped. Joby cursed and dragged his body over to the shelter at the back of the yard. I started to make a fire while he dumped himself silently on a round of oak. As the fire crackled and found some heart, his trousers began to steam. I passed him a mug of milky tea.

'Here you go – three sugars.'

We sat in silence for a few minutes, listening to the rain's tattoo on the tarpaulin, the Gypsy slowly coming down from the adrenalin of the fight. Finally, he spoke.

'S'pose we could crack on wiv some hurdles – got an order for three dozen that needs finishin'.' While Joby could just about accept submitting to the weather, he couldn't completely demean himself by finishing early.

For an experienced hurdle-maker, his hands are his tools. They are used to thump, bend and twist the wood into place.

Watching Joby work, the hazel looked so pliable, so biddable a wood; there was even a sense the job might be pleasurable. Yet he had the knack, I was not so blessed. My hands, unconditioned to the particular punishment hurdle-making doles out, were soon a bruised and swollen mess. As I looked down at them, a mental inventory of pain began to run away with itself and I started to consider going back out into the rain. Water cannon seemed preferable to woody GBH.

Yet it wasn't just experience that had hardened Joby's hands to the physical beatings. They were also built for it. His palms were shovels, plates of meat with thick, fleshy digits and broad hammer thumbs. In wincing discomfort, I pointed this out. Joby grinned and held up a paw, his fingers dangling downwards. 'Like pig's tits,' he offered, laughing. Shadowing him, I did the same. But my hands were different, 'piano player's fingers,' I remarked. This was a gift to the Gypsy, a naive tit-bit thrown his way. I watched as his eyes glittered and the old sneer broke out: 'Yeah Beethoven, but 'ow often do yer need a Joanna in the woods?'

Throughout these ups and downs, one thing remained constant: my love of charcoal burning. I'd done over twenty burns with Joby that summer and part of the satisfaction in it was the feeling that we were doing right by the wood. Nothing was ever wasted. When a tree was felled, the larger bits would be milled for timber or cross-cut for firewood. But the smaller material also had an intrinsic value which Joby would not ignore. It was the perfect size for charcoal, another revenue stream for the wood.

A hot, filthy job perhaps. But compared to the way in which charcoal used to be made, we were in clover. Prior to the invention of metal kilns in the last century, charcoal burners produced their coal in woodland clamps, vast conical stacks of wood built around a central flue and covered with straw and riddled earth, making them airtight. This was rough work, the whole process taking a couple of weeks, and during the burn the clamp had to be monitored both day and night. If part of it collapsed – which often happened – things had to be remedied fast. Too much oxygen getting in could mean the loss of several days' work, the charcoal crop reduced to ash. For this reason, those on night shift would sit on something which could only have been invented for a watching charcoal burner, a piece of furniture with more than a hint of sadism in its design. The stool only had one central leg, meaning the man sitting astride it was forced to balance it himself. This required being awake. Drop off and the ground would quickly deliver a hard slap.

By now, I knew my way around a kiln and the basic method of using one. A poorly laid hearth will hinder the even spread of the burn which will lower the final charcoal yield – either ashen hot spots where the wood has burned too long, or cold areas where the wood has not charred sufficiently. The desired state was always an even burn, the wood carbonising at the same rate. You could say Joby was hot on this.

The term 'charcoal burning' is itself a misnomer. Charcoal burning is rather the baking of wood under controlled conditions, the amount of oxygen inside the kiln restricted, so complete combustion of the material inside is avoided. During the early stages, it is important that air from the outside can flow unobstructed into the kiln's centre. For this reason the charcoal burner creates channels with pieces of wood from the outer vents towards a central charge. These air channels are then overlaid with batons to stop the material loaded on top from blocking them and choking air flow. The charge itself is most often the part-charred pieces from a previous burn. Being kiln-dried they are already more combustible than ordinary wood and excellent fire starters. Burners of old called these 'bones' or 'brown ends'. Of course, all of this lower wood is sacrificial, and will eventually burn away to nothing, but that is not a concern. The heat it generates will bake the wood above, creating charcoal.

There were no short cuts in the laying of the kiln's hearth, although I discovered methodology does differ in later parts of the process. Some burners light the kiln through one of the vents, pushing a flaming rag into the centre with a long stick. Others drop burning embers down a central chimney, a vertical shoot which is built as the kiln is loaded. Joby preferred doing it this way, it was how he'd been taught in the Sussex woods. In this he would not deviate.

Yet however conscientious one is in preparing a burn, the wind will often have its say. Wind means more oxygen getting into the kiln which will make an even burn harder to achieve. Working in woods by the sea, we often had this problem and tried to gag its influence by using wind-breaks of cheap shuttering board placed in front of the vents, most often on the south-westerly side of the kiln, the direction of the prevailing weather. Once lit, Joby or myself would return to the kiln every three hours to rotate the chimneys, which would help maintain an even temperature inside the kiln. Most often the burn would be done in around sixteen hours – the smoky cotton wool vapour of the early stages thinning to a dry, blue-tinged fret. With that as a sign, we would remove the smokestacks and fill every vent with sand to stop further oxygen entering the kiln, thus extinguishing the fire.

A day later, opening the kiln to see what the burn had brought us was always a moment of great anticipation, and played to the child in everyone. We'd often walk up to it with a flask of sloe gin and a fried egg sandwich, woodsmen's perks that would add to the sense of occasion. Even Joby, so long in the charcoaling game, would seem a little dizzy before the big moment. The lid was a six-foot steel round and between us we'd slide it off, the air silvering with charcoal particles drawn up from inside. This was the stuff that demanded we wore dust masks when grading and bagging, nasty particles that can hook into the lung walls and kill you later down the line.

Joby would put on a pair of swimming goggles against the dust, swing a stumpy leg up over the side and dive in. He would start shovelling immediately. We had a grading table pushed up against the kiln topped with wire mesh. Joby would deposit shovelfuls of charcoal onto it and I would pull it down towards me, bagging the larger lumps for barbecue charcoal while the dust and smaller particles – the 'fines' – fell through the wire and were saved in a dumpy bag positioned underneath.

Mostly we'd work in silence but at some point Joby would lose his composure. It would start as a staccato titter, contained within the rubber housing of his mask. After a while he would have to remove the muffle and let me have it. Joby never tired of the joke, it never failed to tickle him. It was the charcoal dust plastered around my eyes, the fine black residue which stuck to my lashes and rims. Faced with such a vision, some might reference an Eighties' goth, or more imaginatively, a silent film villain, but Joby was more basic than that. Through the prism of his macho brain, I was simply 'a fella who liked dressin' up as a bird' and with that he'd change my name to Shirley. I never thought it that funny, but Joby did. He had a unique laugh, a contagious donkey-like bray, but with darker hints towards the back end, a kind of auto-erotic wheeze. I'd try to remain immune, but it would always get me, this sexed-up guffaw. Looking at him standing in the kiln, dusty black and shaking with giggles, he resembled a dark woodland imp. And then the laughter would empty out of me: simple, stupid laughter. Laughing at Joby Cutler; laughing at myself; laughing at the daftness of it all. And with it, tears, good tears. That hadn't happened for a very long time.

9

With summer gone, we went to the Chase to cut hazel. It had been an early start, Joby instructing me to be up at the yard by six. I'd woken an hour earlier to Pig's snoring and lay there for several minutes, listening. There was a strange comfort to the sound, the regular porky wheeze followed by a contented porky rumble. It was the sound of an animal at peace, snug in the dark of his wagon.

I got out of bed and checked the fire. A few embers were clinging on. Placing a small faggot of sticks over them, I opened the damper and the fire instantly took. I peered out of the window to check the weather. There was a glow in the east and studying the tree tops, barely any wind – instinct told me it would be a fine day.

By now, Pig was up. He stood at the van door waiting to be let out. I opened it and watched as he paused on the threshold, his nose wrinkling in the air. I fancied I could read his mind. 'A light sea breeze with a hint of badger.' He took one more hit, then dropped down the steps to do his business. While the dog was out, I bolted some porridge and sorted my chainsaw and kit. With the coming light, the edge of my bill-hook gleamed silver. I took an old rag and wrapped it around the mottled blade, fixed a flask, and was out.

Ten minutes later we were hurtling along one of Dorset's main arteries, towards the Chase. Joby was silent, local radio filling the void. After a forty-minute drive Joby found a pull-in and parked. There was a nip in the air, but it was bright, just a sketch of cirrus cloud above. Carrying our chainsaws and kit, we started across a swathe of newly cut coppice towards the area of hazel we were designated to cut, when Joby ended his verbal fast.

'Let's crack into it for a coupla hours, then 'ave a break.' He tapped my petrol can with his boot. 'Might 'ave t'borrow some of yer fuel – bit short today.' I nodded. It was always understood we helped each other out in the wood.

My eyes took in the coppice. Beautiful hazel coppice. It had probably been worked and managed like this for centuries. I could make out the separate blocks, the hazel at different stages of regrowth advertising the wonder of the coppice cycle. The area was given over entirely to the hazel – long, straight rods unencumbered by light-stealing, larger trees. Such woodland husbandry did not exist further west. This was the coppice country of Hardy's Woodlanders, a culture of nurture and cyclical harvest. Push further east and you'd find more of it in Hampshire, Sussex and Kent. An old crop of England's South Country.

The word 'coppice' comes from the French *couper* – to cut. Coppicing exploits the capacity of many tree species to put out more shoots from their stump once they are felled. The stump of a coppiced tree is commonly called a stool, although in Dorset it is referred to as a 'mock'. There is evidence of coppiced timber having been used in the construction of a causeway called The Sweet Track, built in Neolithic times. The trackway was discovered in 1970 during peat excavations on the Somerset Levels, the original timbers preserved in the anaerobic conditions of the bog. Sent to a lab and analysed, the track was confirmed to have been built in 3807 BC.

Traditional coppice is cut in what is termed 'rotation', a wood divided up into separate areas, known variously as 'coupes', 'fells', 'cants' or 'panels', depending on where you're from. To cut a copse is to 'peel it'. The classic rotation of a hazel copse is seven years, that time period allowing the hazel to grow to exactly the right size for working. Common sense thus asserts a hazel copse be divided up into multiples of seven – each block cut one after the other, over successive winters – so that by the time you return to the first block, it is ready to cut again.

There is oak and ash coppice, hornbeam, alder and sweet chestnut too, but the most common species is hazel. Hazel was particularly useful for making things like wattle hurdles which shepherds would use for folding sheep while out on the Downs; or in the manufacture of woven crates for transporting fragile goods like pottery. The reason for this is that hazel's wood fibres are particularly flexible and in weaving the wood to make these items, the hazel often has to be twisted and turned back on itself. Most species would break; hazel can take this rough handling.

The coppicing industry shrank to virtually nothing during the last century, when new materials such as plastic and steel became available, replacing the woodland products which once made it tick. Denied their livelihood and with no economic future, the coppice workers walked out of the copse, almost for good.

The trees, left uncut, eventually became 'over-stood', the material no longer useful for anything except charcoal or firewood. A copse which has fallen out of a cutting rotation is termed 'derelict'. Sadly, most of our small woods and copses remain this way. Joby was determined to remedy this, at least in his own fashion. A large part of his income came from the wattle hurdles which he made and sold as garden screens or fencing. Cut the wood, create a product, make a sale. Joby liked a sale.

'Get a fire on. I need to sort my saw.'

'Get a fire on!'

I hadn't heard Joby the first time, I was still in copse world.

'Sorry – miles away.'

Joby shook his head. He was kneeling on the ground, bent over a disassembled chainsaw. I watched as his thick, grubby fingers pulled off its star-shaped sprocket. The metal was badly worn and he was replacing it with a new one. I moved off and started picking around for kindling. Once the fire was going, I hung the kettle. After five minutes, Joby had done the repair. He looked up, wiping his forehead, leaving a smear of oil and sawdust across it, joining his eyebrows into a greasy mono-brow. It made him look primitive.

'We'll move down the copse, 'bout ten metres apart. Cut everything in front of you in a five-metre spread. And make sure you cut it low, don't want no snots pokin' up.' I nodded. I'd heard the phrase before. A snot was any stem sticking up too far, a trip hazard.

We started our chainsaws, two 50cc engines tearing up the peace. Angling the nose of mine down, I began to sever the hazel rods, cutting them as close to the ground as possible. But after twenty minutes I was conscious Joby had moved ahead. I felt an itch of anxiety, but there was no gain in rushing. The Gypsy woodsman had years of experience on me, I could not expect to work at his speed. To try and keep up, to push it, would be the classic tyro's mistake.

This is where modern technology is unhelpful. The chainsaw empowers us to do more, in shorter time, but also brings with it an infection. Working a mechanical saw, you quickly become tuned with the machine, its rage and power are irresistible. The saw screams, curses, dares you to work faster. Experienced woodsmen are wise to it, the beginner always falls.

I wonder what yesterday's woodmen would have thought. I imagine a group of them standing around a modern forester. They would be in their old clothes, mostly wool and corduroy, although one might wear a leather army jerkin brought back from the First World War. The modern forester is dressed in lurid, branded armour, and fires up his chain-saw, sinking a felling cut into a tree. The men would flinch at the sound. They witness the saw scatter the tree's innards across the ground – the thing is insatiable. One of the older woodmen pulls on his pipe, agog at its speed and efficiency, but disturbed by the lack of feeling. The tree falls and crashes to the ground. The men gather round, laugh and joke, but are rattled.

I rev my saw. It spews pale flecks of arboreal offal over my clothes. I tell myself to slow down, not to get over-excited. But hopelessly addicted, my trigger finger depresses the throttle again, and the whirring teeth bring carnage. As the hazel is severed, I watch their tops nod, see the sticks fall. Beyond, the coppice is a dense thicket, a tangle of wood. Peering into the deeper copse there is a softening of edges, a dimming. These are holy places. The departed men and women who once worked these woods are within touching distance. Working the coppice, I always feel them. The chainsaw is loud and unseemly, but the ghosts do not scatter. They remain, watching. Their eyes fall on the drifts of hazel and the cut coppice drawing out behind, like the train on a bridal dress.

We kept busy the whole winter, wood cutting. Light was an issue not just in the copse, however. Living in the wagon that winter was a hard slog, driven largely by the lack of illumination. It is a simple truth that when it is dark by half past four, and your home is no bigger than a garden shed, it is a long evening to kill in a small space before you can realistically turn in. I had no electricity, and while the hurricane lamps I used did give some light, it was the sort of low-grade illumination that can, over time, get you down. That said, I did not sink to my old level, the nature of my work and the wood giving me extra buoyancy. And feeling low in November certainly was nothing new. Even in London, I always felt my mood on the slide at that time of year, the period when the dark and the shorter days would really close in and bite.

During those long wagon nights, my mind would wander. I often thought of Dave, hunched over the fire in his Hackney burrow, shutters closed, London banished. And then there was Manod. She would come to me occasionally, as if in a dream. The hawk roosts on a North Walian crag, a granite throne. It is colder in her world, everything is sharper. I picture the tail, the fine head, and the hook beak standing proud against Orion. Her eyes pierce the darkness and winkle out the stars.

Such visions would stir bouts of loneliness, so I grounded myself in books. I had a small library in the wagon, including a slim volume on charcoal burning which Joby had leant me. As I read about the old burners, they appeared to me wildly vivid. The original name for a person who practised the craft was a 'wood collier', but it was the names of the men themselves which proved most irresistible. There was Humphrey Crow, Francis Grimes, John Rooke, and best of all, Jim Shady, a Wyre Forest charcoal burner who worked alone and lived entirely on tea. Was it coincidence that all these names seemed a nod to their blackened faces, the result of ingrained charcoal dust?

Like the Gypsy, these itinerant workers lived on the edge of society, respectability's outskirts. The charcoaling season lasted from April to November and so for eight months of the year they disappeared, melting into the deep woods, before re-emerging on the cusp of winter to go back to their homes. Ephemeral, mercurial, unfixed; was it this shifting quality which society found so intimidating? Studying the accounts of their lives, it seemed to me that this fluid existence directly paralleled the processes they presided over. The alchemy of turning wood to coal. Lords of flux. Masters of existing nowhere.

The news I received that late spring morning hit me with the force of a splitting maul slammed into end-grain oak. Joby delivered it as if it was of no consequence.

'Gonna have to lay you off.'

I stood beside the charcoal store, stunned. 'What?'

'Money's tight – sorry.'

I couldn't believe what I was hearing. One moment we had been unloading fencing stakes, a second later nothing made sense. The consequences were only just percolating through.

'Why now? Bit sudden, Joby.'

'Had a letter from the Revenue. They're after me for a few quid.'

'How much?'

Joby sniffed. 'Enough to 'ave to let yer go.'

It didn't wash. Joby flew under the radar, was of No Fixed Abode. For all intents and purposes, didn't exist at all.

'Right. So how'd they find you?' The short man looked down and toed the ground.

'Fuck knows. Reckon some cunt grassed me up.'

Probably a lie, but something I couldn't disprove.

'Does this mean I've got to leave the wood?'

Joby nodded. The hurt piled in.

'How long have I got?'

The Gypsy pulled a queer, pained expression as if to project a kind of mental juggling. 'End of the week.'

It was already Thursday. I muttered something I now forget, shook my head. After a year of working together he was dropping me just like that. Joby adjusted his necker.

'Had a chat with the old fella over the road – the one wiv the farm. Said you could pull in there if you were short of a place to go.'

So other people had been told before me. I now felt stupid.

'Right. Should I go over and have a word with him?'

The Gypsy nodded and for a second time I felt sick. Asking the question, I had half-hoped he might have had a change of heart – or told me the whole thing was a wind-up. But it was as if a wall had gone up.

'So out by Sunday then?'

The Gypsy wouldn't look at me.

'Yeah, sorry pal.'

Joby got in his truck and drove out of the wood while I leant against a plank door, empty. The place had been my home for over a year. We'd done an enormous amount of work there together and had, I'd thought, developed a kind of mutual affection. I looked out at my small green world. The stillness in it was broken. Perhaps the Gypsy had never really wanted a woodland apprentice. What I'd been to Joby Cutler was cheap labour. Looking at the drainage dug, the charcoal store built and the fencing done, it all became clear: I was no longer needed. I was down the road.

10

The broken white line in the middle of the tarmac straight signalled where Dorset ended and Devon began. Beyond, over a tall conifer hedge, was George Marden's land. Peering through it, my eyes fell on a farm whose only crop seemed neglect. The yard itself was a litter of tired outbuildings slowly sinking in squalor. The farmhouse did nothing to improve matters, a two-storey eyesore rendered in a concrete screed. Farmers are mostly practical men and the homes they build are often a reflection of this. But George's house seemed almost deliberately ugly.

I walked along the hedge line to the yard entrance. A metal gate barred the way. Farmers of old hung hag stones on their entrances to ward off witches and protect their livestock from the evil eye. George was more modern than this and had cable-tied a couple of plastic signs to the steel rails. One read 'Visitors by Appointment only' and the second 'No scrap', each one a coded 'fuck-off' to anyone bent on trespassing. A third sign made of ply had the name of the grim plot slopped across it in white paint: Hilltop Farm.

From the evidence of the sign I took it George was no artist. And looking at the frontage of the house, no gardener either. Along the path, a herbaceous border of black plastic bags vomited rubbish, while in front of the house a rockery of tarmac planings disgraced what would have been a lawn. Gingerly, I opened the gate. I was aware I had no appointment and hoped George wasn't the kind of old-fashioned farmer who let off a shotgun first, asked questions later. Stepping forward, I checked for movement in the farmhouse windows, but the curtains were drawn and all that was returned was a blankness. Under the near gable, jerky movements of small life forms – George's chickens. The fowl were kept in grass-less pens divided by thin, nylon netting. In one, a large, surly cockerel bristled with congenital aggression.

I gave the cock a wide berth and went round to the back door. Knocking on it, nothing. Looking in through the scullery window, newspapers piled high on a broad sill, years of tabloid sediment. And between the paper and glass, an insect ossuary, their remains drilled by the hard light. I pulled back and began to retrace my steps. But clearing the gable my heart jumped, as I caught sight of a figure coming down the track towards me. I raised my hand in greeting, but the gesture was ignored. I started up the track towards him.

George's gait was a low-slung waddle. He was a thick-set man with a long, heavy torso and short bowed legs – the sort of physique I recognised from my rugby days as one that befits a good tight-head prop. All the physical indicators pointed to a man that could call on phenomenal natural strength.

'Hope you don't mind me bothering you, I'm from over the road, been helping Joby in his wood.' George dropped the sack of chicken feed he'd been hauling.

'Wass yer name?'

'Ben.' I offered my hand. The farmer's eyes played over me, before he reached across.

'George Marden.' We shook. His grip was crushing.

'Fair bit of land you got here,' I ventured, my hand still smarting. The farmer nodded, looking over to the nearest field, part obscured by a heap of spoil dancing with weeds.

'Been 'ere all me life. Jus' before mother died, promised 'er I'd look after the place, keep things goin'.' I politely smiled, aware his caretaking had perhaps slipped.

'Joby mentioned I might be looking for somewhere to park my van...'

'Yes, think 'e did... Well, that's alright, you can dangle 'ere a while.'

'That's kind, thanks. How much can I pay you for rent?' The farmer shook his head in a dense, violent manner, as if worried by a wasp.

'Don't worry 'bout that – be nice to 'ave some company.' I instantly felt uncomfortable. While I appreciated the offer of a stopping place, I didn't want to feel obliged to be his new best friend.

'No, really, I'd prefer to contribute, it's only right.' George looked away momentarily and scratched his neck.

'S'pose you could 'elp me hay cartin'. Always easier with two.'

We talked a little longer – about the farm, about the weather. George was a powerful man, but when he spoke all his physical potency was dashed. Words exited his mouth fast and in a high register. There was also a slight speech impediment, consonants and vowels mangled through his oddly small teeth.

The farmer explained that over the years he'd had a few people stay on the land, but in the end most took advantage of his good nature. It was an odd offering, a case of over-sharing, and left me struggling for something to say. I could see how the wrong types might try and take advantage of him, but suspected he wasn't as daft as he appeared.

I told George I had a dog. He liked dogs and asked what sort. Worried the Bull terrier part might not scan well I fudged it, describing Pig as a 'rough terrier cross'. But the farmer was too tickled by the name to take in anything about his breeding – calling a dog after a hoofed farmyard animal seemed, to him, hilarious. When the giggles dried up he asked if the terrier was trustworthy around sheep. I told him not to worry, I'd keep Pig on a short leash. That had him on the ropes again, folded over, sucking in the air. Then his face darkened as he looked down towards his chickens. Said if the dog got in among the hens, the cock would turn nasty.

'Vicious bird,' he squawked, pulling up his shirt sleeve to reveal several deep scars chiselling his forearm. 'One night I fell in the pen, belly full o' cider. Well, that cock took agin me. Went at it with some purpose.'

George looked over at the cockerel, the pain of the encounter still etched. We stood for a moment in silence, just the velvet knock of the breeze in the nettles. I changed the subject and asked if I could look where I might put my van, but the farmer hadn't heard me and seemed locked in the memory of the chicken-mauling. I repeated the question and George finally jerked out of the reliving and pointed up the track, adding there was plenty of room at the back of the farm. I thanked him and offered him my hand – another wincing handshake. Then he picked up the feed sack and went slowly down to his hens and the nemesis cock.

I turned up the track. In the margins, hanging on spears of dried grass, a sloughed snake skin. And here and there in the ruts and divots, black road planings puddling the ground. Further up, a huddle of derelict pig units claimed the right side of the track and behind them, an old Dutch barn. It reminded me of a similar one we'd had on our farm as a boy, yet in salty country so close to the sea, the iron looked less hearty. At the back of the yard the track dissolved into an area of rough ground and a pressed figure of eight where George turned his tractor. Loaded against the hedge, more agricultural wrack: a bent and rusted cattle-crusher; a dozen oil drums; and in the deeper thicket, a hillock of greening tractor tyres.

I looked across the turf. Despite the poor nature of the ground I was not unhappy to be there. The littering was hard on the eyes but there was a simple compensation in the openness of the fields, a relief after dark months locked in the wood. As I stood there, taking it all in, a fox snuck out of the hedge and trotted across the hay meadow, full of noonday pomp. I watched him as his rust form was lost in the tall grass. So this was to be home. In crossing the road, I had not just crossed a county boundary, but a cultural one too. The farm was pure hillbilly. The only thing missing was the banjo.

We moved the van on a Sunday. It would be my last time in the wood. Although it had only been a few days since I'd received my marching orders, the place already felt remote. Walking into the yard, I'd always felt the trees' green welcome, but now the ash and oak appeared indifferent, as if they'd never known me. Joby, too, had drawn back and would not show his face. But I knew he would be watching. Hidden behind hazel, he would have to witness my departure.

Travellers demand firm endings. When you are out you are out. This can seem a harsh law to outsiders, but when you consider the history of their race, it is not difficult to see why. The Gypsy has been persecuted for centuries and has had to build walls. They are part of a survival mechanism which has become innate and hard-wired. I had done nothing wrong, but this ability to cut off came easily to Joby. While I had been useful to him for a short time, when the moment came to sever our relationship he had not had to think. He had acted like a guillotine.

I could do with some of that hardness. I was still raw from my axing and needed my own inner map to help me move on. The road helped in that respect. The tarmac was a clear line and hard border, past and present tangibly separated. Although I'd see the drifts of kiln-smoke from Joby's wood come summer and my heart would tug, the road was a half-mile straight of black macadam that would not bend.

Besides, I had stuff to do, a new camp to sort for starters. George had helped me haul the van into place with his tractor, siting it on a piece of level ground I'd cleared the previous day. I angled the hut so the back door faced the hay meadow – handy for fox-gazing. Scattered close by were piles of old hay and bits of tin sheet. George told me to keep an eye out for adders. I was not keen on our only venomous snake as a close neighbour, mainly for the pup's sake. But it would be good to see them as their numbers were in sharp decline. To have snakes on the farm would be a sign that the ecology of the place was still working.

Over the next few days I organised my camp. The van needed some repairs, and following my early oversight in Joby's wood, I also thought it a good idea to construct a rough awning and decking. The ground was hard clay now but that was only with the blessing of dry days. Come the rain things would be different. A toilet was my only other consideration. George had offered his, but I thought better of it and sought my own location. Walking down the hedge line, I found a private spot, behind a decaying horse box. I dug a deep pit and fashioned a bench seat with a hole, raised on two rounds of ash.

Between jobs, I had a chance to poke about the farm. It was immediately obvious George's front yard had been no anomaly: neglect ran clean through his land and in every corner, the bachelor's hoarding instinct ran amok. In the Dutch barn, among hay bales, stood a derelict Aga and a covey of ripped-out kitchen units. In the old dairy, a mountain of newspapers and discarded magazines. Sifting through them, *Fiesta* and *Farmer's Weekly* seemed the mainstay of George's literary diet. The hoarding and general chaos was so in your face, I wondered what prompted it. Putting on my shrink's hat, I considered it may be the consequence of a need to fill some void, of satisfying some unmet emotional need. But the way George talked about his parents certainly shelved any notion that he had been unloved. He still visited them every week in the graveyard, telling me he liked to keep them informed on what was happening.

Burn

My simple hunch was that his hoarding was a consequence of general anxiety built up over years. He'd probably been born with a propensity for it but environmental factors had contributed to its development. On the surface George appeared breezy, but I was conscious of something suppressed, a weight which hung about his corners. Perhaps because of the way he talked and walked, he had always been ridiculed – by teachers, school peers, locals in the village – labelled as daft, no good, a bit useless; the sort of negative in-drumming that can damage a person. After all, it was not hard to imagine the climate he grew up in, a Devon backwater of the nineteen-fifties not the most forgiving of places.

If truth be told, George wasn't really a farmer. Running twenty sheep doesn't count. But it had been different with his father. George told me the land had been won in a card game sometime after the war. At first it hadn't been a good prospect, the fields a plateau of rock and scrub. But between them, George's parents had cleared the ground, pulling up the gorse and removing every field stone by hand. It was back-breaking work and in the end it told. One night, George's old man was late coming in for his tea. The boy was told to go out and fetch him. Rounding the back of the barn, he found him slumped stone dead in a wheelbarrow.

As the weeks passed I got to know George better. Most mornings he would knock on the van door and come in for coffee. I didn't mind, I liked the company. While I fixed a brew, he would prop himself in an old armchair. It was an elegant junk shop find, but too narrow for a man of his girth, so he'd sit wedged between the dusty pink arms, bolt upright. I'd ask him what he had on that day and he'd regale me with a long list of not much at all. Soon enough the coffee pot would gurgle and save George the trouble of sounding busy. He'd never drunk espresso before and said it made him feel sophisticated. I told him it was Italian. He hadn't been abroad and asked what other countries were like. Sometimes he sounded like a child. But I played it down for the most part; I didn't think going into too much detail about the places I'd been or my old life in general would help us find a level.

One of George's most endearing qualities was the way in which he interacted with Pig. They were chums. As soon as he sat down, the pup would be up on his lap. The farmer would talk to him softly, grabbing his scruff and massaging the whole dog as if he were pizza dough. It was a physical approach but such muscular affection did not seem to bother the terrier. He was even at ease when George took a noseful, sinking his face into the back of his spotty ears. With most people, Pig would have drawn a line at such intimacy, but with George he submitted wholeheartedly. Animals, in my experience, are a good barometer of people.

With no rent to speak of, and only the pick-up to run, I didn't need to earn much money. I still pulled in a little from my London flat, so we were never going to starve, but cash flow was often tight. Fortunately, George insisted on paying me for my help hay-carting. The work already had happy associations, childhood memories of working with my great uncle on his small Hampshire farm. George would come and knock at the van when the day was cooling. The cut hayfield looked so spruce then, the pale stubble like a vast sisal rug. The old farmer would start enthusiastically, chucking bales onto the trailer for me to load. There was a sense of him both enjoying his brute strength and a bit of transparent showing off. But he'd soon fade and then I'd be the bale-boy, throwing the hard-packed rectangles up as the load grew higher. The work came easily and we both enjoyed it. I'd drive the David Brown tractor around the field with George standing aboard the trailer, pointing and hollering at the next stack to load. He really was king of the hill in those moments.

With the light going and no rain forecast, we left the loaded hay cart outside for the night. As I stood in the gathering dark, I watched George walk home. He was a strange fish, a bundle of neuroses which all seemed neatly played out in his odd farmyard shuffle. As he rounded the chicken pens and disappeared out of sight, I couldn't help feel some affection for him.

The next morning, George knocked at seven. He seemed distressingly cheerful, as if our working partnership had given him new impetus to start farming properly. George chucked me the tractor key, told me to reverse the trailer into the barn. The David Brown started on the button, a little black smoke from the silencer and our working day began. As I let out the clutch, George guided me back: 'Yeah, keep goin'... Left hand down... Bit more... Bit more... Whoaaa!' The tractor lurched to a stop, several tonnes of sun-dried grass wobbled. I turned the key and pulled out the engine stop. Jumping down, I could see George leaning on a pitchfork, surveying the dumped kitchen units in the back of the barn – we'd have to move them first. Picking up a magnolia-painted cupboard, I began to walk it back when George shrieked, pointing at a movement in the hay. It was an adder.

The snake decided on a swift tack towards George. I was surprised how quickly the flushed reptile glided across the ground. It was beautiful and quite mesmerising, yet at the same time awful – some ancient wiring in my brain interpreting the sinuous advance as bad news. George remained rooted to the spot. Rather than run, his heavy body opted for a comedy jig. I began to laugh but the farmer was in no place to see the funny side. With a whoop and a squawk, he raised his pitchfork. I shouted at him not to kill the snake and he froze as the adder shot between his legs and out into open ground.

George twitched and jumped a couple of times in the air. I was suddenly watching bad ballet, Nureyev gone to seed.

It was clear the man was not a fan of snakes, especially poisonous ones. I tried to calm him down, but he was horribly distressed, the relief of seeing the snake gone colliding with the adrenalin still coursing through him. We sat down on a bale of hay. Slowly, very slowly, George calmed.

'Pesky adder. Never liked 'em. Used to be more of 'em round 'ere, specially when ma and pa first moved. Rocks, gorse, ideal ground.'

The man looked down, idly scuffing a divot in the barn's chalky floor.

'Kids once put one in me satchel as a joke.'

It suddenly all made sense. George rummaged in his pocket and pulled out a handkerchief to dab his eyes. On it, embroidered in a burgundy cross-stitch, were his initials. I asked him if he'd done the needlework. He looked up, red-eyed, and told me it was the work of his mum – he'd had the handkerchief since he was ten. There was a pause before the dam broke and the bale rocked with the shuddering of his heavy shoulders.

As summer advanced, I made the most of the long light, spending most of my time out of doors. There were odd jobs for George – making some hen houses and hauling firewood from the copse at the northern perimeter of his land. The corrugated iron barn also required re-painting, which he deemed should be a paying job. The task seemed endless, but such chores offer compensations. Slopping on red oxide does not require much thought and gave my mind a ticket to wander. Perhaps it was the heat of those late summer days and the still, windless air, but charcoal burning filled my every thought.

On more than one instance, while lost in a vision of smoking kilns, my nose caught the taint of woodsmoke and I'd look up to see a thin trail rising from the trees on the other side of the road. It was at once beautiful and painful and watching the smoke lift out of the canopy, my brushwork would die. I missed the wood and the rituals it had given me. I missed the banter too, even Joby's mordant quips. I had always been most happy with a purpose and odd-jobbing wasn't the same. In the evenings I'd go through my tools, cleaning, oiling and sharpening. The billhooks were primed, the axe's edge keen and glinting. But secretly I knew it was all pointless. The tools were redundant, nothing more than museum pieces. It cut into me, this woodless life, and over the coming weeks I could feel my mood slide.

One Sunday evening, while sitting on my field loo, I hit a low. George's place was a dump and I felt the life I'd tried to create was a sham. In that moment my old life with all its money, parties and false kudos glowed brighter. I reached for it, but only felt the vast distance I'd strayed. I'd been insane to leave it, to chuck it all in.

For the first time in a long while, my illness got a grip. Over the next few weeks I could feel myself turning inward, all the joy and wellness of my recent past trickling away. I holed up in my van, saw less of George. But it was different from before. The old anxiety had mutated into a broader, deeper low. Compared to the spikes of panic I'd suffered in the past, this was less viscerally painful, more like a slow bleeding out. The low had a double terror in it. Not just the pooling blackness, but a fear that I was back in my cage and this time the latch was nailed down for good.

Depression changes your world because there is no light. How does it feel? At the time I wanted to die. A blade would do it. I had an old German trench knife on the shelf above my bed. Stab, stab, stab in the stomach. No, *stab, stab, stab* – at least do it right. But no blood would flow, only ashes. I thought about the boy I had once been, so unfettered in spirit, so open to wonder. I could not betray him.

So you sit with your agony, snookered by pain. Not wanting to move an inch, not even a millimetre. Moving is to be
back in the world, fully conscious in a nightmare which feels
murderous and bleak and real. I have sat like that more times
than I care to remember. A world of grey motes blowing
inside you. A depression that has no answer.

One evening in the wagon I could feel the edges of the
trapdoor under my feet. A voice kicked inside me: 'Get up.' I
couldn't. The voice repeated the order: 'Get up – walk or die.'
I roused myself, forcing every particle of will to pull myself
out of the chair. Pig eyed me shiftily from his bed, he didn't
recognise his master anymore. Putting on my boots, I wanted
to cry. 'Walk,' the voice commanded, 'just like you did as a
boy – into the fields, into the woods – healing is there.'

So I walked. Through the ten-acre field with the spreading oak; through George's flock of ragged sheep; through
a small, dark copse towards the boundary lands. Standing
on the edge of the known world, the little boy would have
whooped with excitement, hollered with glee. I could not
share his joy.

On the edge of the field stood an old hedge bank knotted
with the root-work of vast beech trees. Behind them, the sun
was in a slow red dive west. It would soon be dark. I shuffled
over to one of the trees and placing my hand on a low bough,
tried to feel some sign I was still me.

The bark was cold and smooth and slightly rippled. I
leaned in further, resting my forehead on it. And then, in the
thickening hush, a shiver of vibration, a minute tremor down
the branch, as if the tree was communicating some message
to me. Looking up, I noticed the twigs dancing lightly in the
breeze. And in that movement, that gentle rocking, the old
giant seemed to speak: 'I live. You live. This breeze lives. We
are all connected, it's okay.'

The dip in my mental health had scared me. I'd slipped by getting too comfortable at George's and the illness had done what mental illness always does – takes over by degrees. But slowly, over weeks, I started to feel myself again. I can't say how it happened, it was just a steady correction as if all my atoms, cells, those cosmic materials which make up a person came back into balance. With this gradual reconfiguring, I began to see things more clearly. Energy started to flow back. Most pressing was the understanding that I needed to find a wood to work, it was no good drifting.

My better mood lasted a few days. Then walking down to the standpipe to get water one morning, the spring in my step faltered. As I rounded the old pig units, a desecration. The old king of the yard, George's nemesis cockerel, lay dead. His end had been excessively violent, blood pooled everywhere. One beautiful, glossy wing lay amputated, glistening with saliva. The head looked like it had been put through a mangle, before being swung against a concrete wall. I stood fixed on the horror. A fox could certainly kill without conscience, but this seemed beyond his work, more darkly creative – it had hate in it. As I stared, George appeared around the corner.

'What did this?' The farmer looked sheepish.

'I, er, got meself a hound.'

There was a moment's silence. An emerald tail feather blew across the ground and over his factory shoes. George swallowed and attempted a smile that instantly died. He motioned for me to follow him down to the house.

We turned the corner and beside the front door, shackled on a chain, stood a dog. It was huge, what appeared to be some unholy cross between a ridgeback and a jackal. The body was brindle, but through the neck and into the head its coat changed to a lustrous black. Instantly I thought of Anubis, Egyptian God of mummification and the afterlife.

The creature looked into me and growled, a deep, guttural warning. I stepped back, the hairs on my neck raised. A demon dog, with spikes for ears and eyes that were dark, red pits. I felt as if I was looking on something against nature. I turned to George. He started to gabble.

'Girl in the chip shop had it. Couldn't control it, she said. Asked if I'd take it on. Thought Pig could do with a friend.' I looked at George. I had a fondness for the man, and was familiar with all his quirks, but until that moment had never actually considered him insane.

'George. That dog will kill Pig, no question. We can't stay here now. We have to leave.' The farmer looked at me like a scolded child and fingered his sleeve.

'He's alright I reckon. Just out of sorts with the move.'

I could feel my anger rising – such delusion – there really was nothing more to say. I picked up the water jack and walked back to the van, the vision of the black head still haunting me. Getting inside, I shook off my boots and made up the fire. I sat there for a long time. The anger slowly passed. Disappointment moved in.

11

There was a house going near Lyme, or more accurately a hovel. It was the home of a painter who was off to overwinter in India and had advertised it on a short-term let. The deal was we could have it until March. While the place was a tip, the timing suited us. We'd take it on for the dark months and find a new stopping place for the van come spring.

I told George we were leaving. He said he was sad to see us go. Bending down to say goodbye to Pig, I could see he was choked, he was soft on the little dog. I let them have their moment then opened the truck door and called the animal in. I thanked George for everything, shook his hand and we rolled out of Hilltop for the last time, the farmer a large blot of loneliness in my mirror.

A few miles south of the farm, we reached our new home. Sunken and shabby and hiding down a green lane, the bungalow certainly had layers. And from a distance, the white weatherboarding made un-new by sun, wind and rain was undeniably attractive. But living in it, the spell quickly died. Behind the sofa, black mould colonised the wall and in the kitchen, even the tea cosy felt damp. The windows of the shack were particularly gruesome, the glazing bars rotted to nothing, just anorexic slivers of wood. To counter this, our landlady had lined their insides with cling film as a form of budget double glazing. The decay I could accept, but to view the world through an artificial polymer seemed so depressing.

I actually felt guilty bringing Pig there. We had already known a level of domesticity which would have been a challenge to most, but you cannot compare wagon-living with a life in bricks. When choosing to overwinter in a wagon, you are fully complicit in the choices you are making: space and light will always be compromised; simple household chores like drying clothes take on a new dimension; and unless you have a good stove, you will always wake up cold. But choosing to live in a house one expects to be served better. Part of the problem was the bungalow sucked up damp like a bloated willow pollard. To compound matters, the stove was a parsimonious little thug and failed miserably at its primary task, to give heat. As I poked around, trying to light it, Pig would appear beside me. The dog always appreciated a good fire but knew it was pointless. Looking at the animal and sensing his disappointment, I felt like a bad parent.

Damp and a constant chill were not the only challenges we faced. The bungalow's roof space was occupied by an army of rats who seemed to time their manoeuvres just as Pig and I were retiring to bed. Wrapped in a damp flannel of darkness, my ears would prickle and skin crawl, for there is something uniquely unpleasant about the sound of a rodent army on the move. Come dawn, their operations would cease, but some ignored the curfew of daylight.

One morning, while I was making a cup of tea, the head of a rat appeared through a hole in the kitchen ceiling. The shock of it made me curse. I picked up a grapefruit and threw it at its head, missing. Rats and damp were certainly not ideal, but we'd sit it out, knowing we'd be back in the wagon come spring. What was getting me down more was a feeling of drifting. Without work or company the days felt empty. I remembered the warnings of my therapist and the sting of fear I'd felt back in my Hackney flat. Those dark mental cycles had thinned over the last two years, but as my experience at George's had proven, given certain conditions, the old patterns could worm back in.

My days needed filling. My wallet, too, was near-empty. It was clear which way my heart was being pulled. I wanted to go back to the woods and fields; to put in a hard day's work again. I yearned for the curious sense of wellbeing that tired muscles deliver the mind and the simple satisfaction one feels at the end of a long day, whether that be a section of hedge laid or a block of hazel cut. The woods and fields had always been in me, even in my darkest moments. I needed them again now.

My deliverance came quickly and quite unexpectedly. Browsing through the local paper one evening I came across an advertisement in the classifieds. Its brevity verged on rude.

HEDGE LAYER REQUIRES LABOURER.
MUST BE RELIABLE.
CALL MR. WATTS AFTER 6PM.

The ad seemed as much a dare as a job vacancy, so I picked up the phone and dialled.

I'd arranged to meet Ralph Watts early the following Monday. When I arrived at our rendezvous, I found a ratty red pick-up idling beside the churchyard wall, exhaust fumes insulting the morning air. Ralph was sitting in the driver's seat, smoking a pipe. I tapped on the window and waited several seconds before he decided to unwind it. As the thin blue haze lifted I was met by eyes that were pale and cold like flint. The face was lined and creased, with a lank moustache and a thinning mullet of dry, blond hair. The man looked like a cross between a surfer and a plains drifter who had at least sixty summers under his belt.

'Morning Ralph.' The man took me in.

'Morning Winkle.' The flat tone hovered between friendly and not.

'I'll, er, get my stuff.' Not a flicker from the man. I turned away, before checking myself. 'I've got a dog with me – do you mind if he comes?' Ralph's eyes narrowed.

'What make?' I didn't understand and paused to answer. Ralph seemed impatient.

'What breed?' I coloured and gave him a half-truth.

'He's a terrier.'

The man sucked on his pipe and nodded. As I dropped my kit into the rear tub of the pick-up, I noticed a young collie lying under the aluminium hood. His eyes gleamed and his tail thumped the rags which made up his bed. Certainly friendlier than his owner, I thought. I looked around for my own dog and caught him lifting his leg against the church-yard wall. 'Come on Pig, get in.'

The white terrier trotted over and sprang into the back. Immediately, the two dogs eyed each other. Between them lay Ralph's hedging tools, a sea of agricultural flotsam. I noticed a long-handled slasher, what countrymen-of-old would have called 'a thing of purpose'. It was a vintage tool but the han-dle had been remade, a long-grained piece of ash cut from a hedge and tapered with a drawknife. It was secured in place by a roofing nail which had been hammered through and bent over to serve as a lynch-pin. The object had finesse as well as brute force in its making. I thought of Joby.

I walked back to the cab and tried the passenger door. Locked. Ralph leant casually across and opened it. Again, I noticed the eyes: an empathy-free zone. I slid into the passen-ger seat among a fug of pipe smoke and engine-warmed air. As I put on my seatbelt I glimpsed Ralph checking out the white dog in his rear-view mirror.

'What's its name?' he asked.

'Pig,' I replied. There was no hint of a reaction, or play of a smile. After a moment's silence I returned the question, asking him the name of his collie. Ralph bit down on his pipe stem:

'Bryn.'

'Ah, a good name' was all I could summon. Ralph put the truck in first and we pulled away. I asked if Bryn was a working dog. Ralph distractedly replied, 'No chance. Thick as a brick.' We hit second, then third. The man continued. 'Wanted to shoot 'im, but 'er in doors wouldn't 'ave it.'

I suddenly lost all appetite for conversation and looked away. We left the village and the lane opened out onto a long straight but the pick-up's speed remained at twenty-five. It seemed that while the man was breezy about killing, he was less comfortable behind a steering wheel. You could see it in his bearing, the shoulders hunched and the long neck craned forward like a turkey offering itself for execution. It felt rude to stare, so I transferred my attentions to the truck's cab. It was the usual genera of working man's cockpit, a dumping ground of accumulated rubbish. Among stray pellets of animal feed and a litter of work receipts, several tins of pipe tobacco. One had migrated into my footwell. The label on the tin read 'Presbyterian Mixture', which sounded both dark and wilfully austere. Ralph had found his brand.

We travelled inland. The fields glistened a hard white, still petrified from the overnight freeze. We passed standing cattle throwing long shadows, steam rising off their flanks in the windless air. Even the inland oaks seemed solemn. The conversation in the car remained stilted, but I persevered and eventually Ralph started to defrost. He asked me where I came from. I replied Cambridge, but carefully avoided the "L" word. I had been in the country long enough to know that if you mention London in certain circles you are setting yourself up for a harder road. I figured I'd have plenty to prove to Mr. Watts and didn't need the deeper examination that would come with that tag.

The lanes deepened and were fringed by high hedges. Passing a length of hedge which had been recently laid, the character of the lane was instantly changed. Early morning sunlight blasted the road, giving everything a golden glow.

My eyes fell on the hedge work. It was a beautiful job, the hedgerow's frosty top glinting like quartz. Beyond lay drifts of brash and further down a converted ambulance parked on the verge. The back doors were open, exposing a gurney laid out with tools. As we passed I noticed a man in a donkey jacket lifting a kettle beside a fire. Another with long mutton chops and a tam o'shanter stood sharpening his billhook. Ralph pipped his horn and the two old hedgers waved.

We continued driving for ten more minutes, finally coming to a stop in a field gateway. Ralph turned the key and silence. Opposite, under a hedgerow ash, stood a lay-by filled with black road planings. Ralph eyed the heap.

'Stops they Travellers pullin' in.'

I did not offer an opinion, only a weak smile. Ralph turned to me and in that moment I felt like I was being regarded by an animal. It was not aggressive, but his gaze was intense and made me uneasy. I reached for the door handle and bundled out. Ralph followed. As we began to unload our gear from the back of the truck, I saw Ralph was eyeing Pig – he'd noticed the Bull terrier part.

'So you got one of they.'

It was not a compliment. After a protracted pause which seemed designed to maximise my discomfort, Ralph pointed over to a wood a quarter of a mile distant. 'We're headed that way. Council wood, 'bout fifty acres. Got a few soft rides to cut there. Bit o' crash, bang, wallop.' I nodded. So it was felling, not hedge laying, which was the order of the day.

We smashed it up that morning, cutting a wide corridor through the wood. Birch, young ash and hazel took the brunt of it as Ralph crackled with energy, the joy of physical work rising off him like steam. While Ralph sizzled, my job was to clear the fallen poles to one side, laying them in the woodland gutter like tall drunks. Just like Joby and the forester before him, Ralph was an old-world grafter. He was lean and sinewy and carried no fat. Hours of heavy work wouldn't touch him. In that moment it struck me he was the extraordinary double of Tollund Man, the Mesolithic hunter-gatherer dug up some years before in a Danish peat bog.

A physical likeness was not the only parallel. The Meso-lithics were not big on health and safety and, in this, Ralph followed suit. For a man so acutely cautious behind the wheel of a car, he transformed once his finger found the throttle of a chainsaw. It was as if he had a personal gripe against the vertical and in his fever to fell, the trees came down so fast, I was nearly hit three times. Nothing was spared, not even the holly. This seemed counter to my understanding. I had once read that woodmen never touch an old one; they are regarded as magical trees, fairy trees, superstitions hang around them as vivid as their berries, as prickly as their leaves. Watching Ralph preparing to level a particularly beautiful specimen, I had to step in.

'Why don't you leave it?' He looked at me like I was a fool. 'It's in the way.'

'But aren't they sacred?' Ralph's lip curled and he straight-ened up. 'Sacred? You some sorta hippy?'

'It just seems a shame. Such a beautiful old tree.'

Ralph hawked and spat and shook his head. My senti-ment, it seemed, did not dignify a response. I cringed as he bent down and drove the chainsaw into the trunk. The leaves shivered as creamy white heartwood spurted out. Ralph stepped back and gave the holly a shunt with his boot. It hit the ground with a metallic rustle of leaves, its death rattle. The woodman switched off the saw and looked about. Twi-light was sinking in.

'Time to pack up.'

We ambled back to the pick-up in silence. Rooks were returning from their feeding grounds and bickering loudly in the treetops. After a terminally slow commute back to the village, Ralph paid me for the day in fifty one-pound coins. Getting out of the truck, I turned away almost lopsided with the change. I said goodbye but all that was returned was a half nod. The pick-up continued to idle. I looked down to see Ralph was still watching me, his face drawn, the eyes more vulpine than hollow.

'I'll see yer tomorra if I get through the night.'

The next morning started wrong. Ralph had picked me up at the church and we'd set off for the woods as before. A few miles out of the village we approached a lonely cross-roads where Ralph had slowed and stopped. Looking left, one could make out a small red dot travelling along the road, gaining at a moderate speed. It was still two hundred metres off, but Ralph, unbelievably, concluded it too risky to cross.

Clutch control was lost on the man. The nose of the pick-up parried with the junction's white line while we waited for the oncoming car. As the pick-up dithered, the cab filled with smoke, Ralph's anxiety making him suck harder on his pipe. Through a blue tobacco fog, I faintly made out a passing post office van and a bemused postie, staring.

Scanning right to make sure the road was clear, my heart sank: at one hundred yards, a tractor. But I couldn't bear it any longer and suggested, perhaps too forcibly, that Ralph should go. The pick-up lurched forward and glanced into the opposite hedge. A gang of sparrows exploded from within, unleashing birdy profanities, as Ralph righted the vehicle back on the lane. After a few seconds he stopped, his eyes flashing anger.

'Next time Winkle, keep it shut!'

I bit my lip. The Winkle moniker was getting hard to take, but having a strip torn off you in your late thirties was worse. We spent the rest of the commute in silence, tension bubbling like a thick stew.

Parking in the field entrance, Ralph broke the deadlock, explaining the day's task, a stretch of hedge which needed laying at the far end of the wood. It was, in all, four hundred metres and would take us a couple of weeks. Ralph told me the locals called the place 'Big Wood', which at fifty acres it undoubtedly was, yet this name did not seem sufficiently trollish. Whether I was simply spooked from the previous day's show of bad felling, or rattled by the morning's drama, I couldn't be sure, but a sixth sense moved inside me urging caution.

We got to work, Ralph thinning the large hazel mocks which dominated the boundary. Much of it would simply be cut out, rather than laid in the hedge, the derelict hazel too big and unwieldy. I was tasked with cutting out the rubbish; the nettles, bramble and elder which Ralph deemed should go. While I worked I noticed there had been men in the far end of the wood before us. Across the wood bank, a large area had been coppiced to leave a crop of oak trees, several emblazoned with a fluorescent red dot. This was the mark of the executioner, applied by forester's aerosol. The red ones were coming down. The council were cashing in on their timber trees.

My eyes fell on the brash piles scattered across the wood, the bark curling and studded with pox. Mooning out of the brash, the round ends of larger poles, perhaps six or seven inches in diameter. These were the classic product of derelict coppice, hazel which hadn't been managed for decades. The piles themselves were now a teeming habitat for birds, beetles and other invertebrates, and in that they had a value. But the sheer extent of the material left to decompose was shocking. I thought of the old woodmen. They would not have countenanced this. In their world, everything was used, right down to the twiggy brash ends which would have been collected and bound into kindling faggots. But the world no longer had time for the old-fashioned woodman. It simply did not pay for the large, modern contractor to process hazel in that way. I stared at the waste and a thought flickered. Perhaps a small, one-man operation could still find some use for it. It would, after all, make decent charcoal.

At lunch, beside the fire, I mentioned my idea to Ralph. He listened without comment, making me feel my suggestions about charcoal burning were naive. As my enthusiasm for sharing petered out, he drained his cup, concluding, 'Might work. Ask the land agent – 'e's 'ere tomorra.'

A rare gleam of positivity from the man. I felt a flush of warmth. But as I got up and prepared to go back to the hedge, Ralph ordered me to sit. 'Hold yer 'orses Winkle. Hit a flint before lunch. Gotta give this chain a tickle.' I did what I was told, sat back down and watched as he went about sharpening the dull teeth. The saw doctored, we got to our feet and walked stiffly back to the hedge. In the meantime, Pig and Bryn had begun a game of chase. As the dogs came through on a second pass, the collie sprinted low between us, knocking the underside of Ralph's saw with his head. In seconds the piebald skull had turned crimson, blood geysering from a deep incision left by the freshly-honed cutting teeth. Ralph spat out a torrent of abuse and called the dog in. Bryn obeyed and curled around his master, his eyes bulging with fear.

'Useless bloody cur. Nothin' but trouble!' The blood was by now all over Ralph's hands, which Bryn began to feverishly lick. 'Quick, fetch my grip – got some duct tape in there.' I stood on the threshold of going, aware of the urgency, but paralysed by the rank meanness of Ralph's suggestion.

'Duct tape? Shouldn't we go direct to a vet?'

Ralph scowled and snarled back: 'Bugger that. 'E's not costin' me vet's fees as well as an afternoon's wages. Duct tape and fast!'

I ran back to the fire and unrolled the bag. A round of scrim-backed tape lay inside. I'd used the same stuff myself on a variety of things but couldn't recall emergency wound-dressing as one of them. Returning to the scene, I could see man and dog had not moved. Ralph was wiping blood off the dog's head with his handkerchief while pinching the wound shut with finger and thumb. He looked up at me and growled: 'Just wind it round 'is swede. And don't be too careful 'bout it, we're not wrappin' mother's Christmas present.'

I wound the grey adhesive around Bryn's head. With each turn, the dog looked more depressed. When Ralph felt it sufficient, he tore off the tape with his teeth and plastered the end down, hard.

'Now git!'

The dog knew the routine. Humiliated, he wandered back to his bed by the fire and slumped down – he'd displeased his master once again. Getting back to work, Ralph said we'd have to work late. There were a few small hedgerow trees that he wanted out of the hedge, and we were behind schedule. Seeing that we were losing the light at six I wondered how that would work. Darkness and tree felling don't mix.

We'd got through a stand of field maple before the light had started to go, but by this point Ralph was at twenty yards near invisible. I had heard him restart the saw for one last push when suddenly and violently, the moon was occluded by the crashing silhouette of a falling tree. In those last seconds my life did not flash before me, but instead, a more depressing vision. It was the gurning mooncalf that was Ralph Watts, a cretinous, murderous hedge-waif, a simple man killer.

I came to in a cage of thorn, face down on the hedge bank. The tree – a large blackthorn – had hammered me into the ground like a hedging crook. Vision was reduced to a blotchy indigo-black, animated with moving auras of green and

111

purple. There was a taste of blood and soil in my mouth. I cannot exactly remember what I said but the fifty one-pound coins I'd earned the previous day would have been instantly relinquished had there been a swear box around. Ralph's reaction? That it was my fault.

'You bloody idiot Winkle, can't you move quicker than that?' I could not believe my ears, the man was clearly ill.

'You are joking. You nearly killed me!'

'Yer should be watchin' more carefully.'

'What, in this light! Do you see feathers on me Ralph – I'm not a fucking owl.'

Silence. And then, as he walked away, the cruellest whisper thrown to the dark: 'Bloody townie.'

At that moment I had the sudden impulse to be excessively violent. But I knew I had to suck it up, no good would ever come from a stand-off with Mr. Watts. Slowly extricating myself from the thorn's clutches, Pig appeared next to me, ears down, anxious. My face was scratched and bleeding, but I'd dodged any serious injury. I made my way back to Ralph's truck, imagining revenge scenarios of the most violent and satisfying kind. The bastard was already inside, having a smoke.

I pulled the door open and got in. After a couple of seconds' silence he turned to me with a stilted grin and rattled a tin under my nose.

'Humbug?'

I took the sweet as the peace offering it was intended to be. It was the closest thing I ever got to an apology from the old goat.

It was mid-afternoon when the land agent appeared. Ralph saw him first, sidling down the edge of the wood towards us. The old hedger turned to me shiftily and spoke like a hunted animal.

'Crafty bugger. Thought 'e'd creep up on us down wind. Could smell 'is aftershave a mile off.'

I ignored the remark and continued working, crooking down a long length of ash. From a distance the land agent hailed a greeting. It was stock upper class.

'Ah Ralph... Good to see you.'

I looked up and saw a man in his early sixties. He was polished and urbane, his moleskin trousers tucked into designer wellington boots. Ralph suddenly appeared deferential and meek. He introduced me and we shook hands.

'Bill Cope – pleased to meet you.' As he regarded me, he noticed the facial injury. 'Been in the wars?'

Ralph broke in. 'Cut 'e self shaving.'

I let the lie go, there was no point contradicting him. The pair drifted off down the hedge line, Ralph pointing out this and that. After ten minutes they returned.

'Well, all seems in order, Ralph. I'll be off.' As he turned to go, I made my move.

'Could I walk up to the gate with you, Mr. Cope? I have a couple of questions regarding the wood.' The land agent smiled.

'Of course.'

We crossed into the wood via a stile and followed a rough path to a ride. I'd started to explain my thinking regarding charcoal burning while Cope listened. As we pushed up the ride, I again felt the wood's particular energy, of something ill at ease between the trees. Cope looked at the piles of brash under the oaks.

'We had a charcoal burner here in the Seventies, an itinerant. He was here for a couple of summers as I remember. Old chap. Probably dead now.' I studied Cope. He was looking deep into the trees as if something was troubling him. The cloud passed and he turned to me. 'Yes, don't see why you shouldn't give it a go.'

A small flame of joy danced inside me. I would finally have my own wood to work. We made it to a steel five-bar gate at the main entrance. Cope's car was parked on the other side, a shabby saloon which seemed at odds with the gentleman beside me. Cope spoke, 'I'll sort you out a licence, so it's all above board.' The flame inside me was not just dancing, this was now disco. 'All I need is a pound to make the licence binding.' I drove my hand into my trouser pocket and pulled out some change. Fifty, sixty, seventy. I was thirty pence short. Cope held out his hand. 'That'll do. I'm sure the council can make up the difference.' I slid the change into his palm. He rummaged in his pocket, pulling out a key on a plastic fob. 'This is yours, the key to the wood.' It was quite a moment. As he handed it to me all I could say was thank you, which didn't seem nearly enough. Cope opened his car door, smiling. 'I'll pop over with the licence as soon as it's done. Keep up the good work on the hedge.'

As he drove away I looked down at the object in my hand. Not only the key to a fifty-acre oak wood, but one to a whole new chapter. And on the fob, scribbled in biro, the title of the plot I'd been granted. Not the dull but factually correct 'Big Wood' of the locals, but a far older name and one which seemed closer to its dark essence: 'Gribble'.

12

I now needed a kiln, a ring of pressed steel to unlock my future. I racked my brains for the name of the company which had fabricated Joby's. I had a vague recollection they were based in Yorkshire so went online and found an engineering firm in East Riding. The company specialised in custom-built portable loos and, to my delight, also manufactured charcoal kilns. I picked up the phone. A dour Northern voice answered, as flat as the Humber shore. The man confirmed he could make me one but warned it would take a couple of months as they were in the middle of a large order 'makin' portable shitters bound for India'. While the delay was not ideal, I decided to commit and paid the deposit.

While I waited for the kiln, I continued running the gauntlet with Ralph. But somehow we made it through and spring came back around. Pig and I had moved out of the shack by then, and waved goodbye to the rats. To finance the remainder of the kiln purchase I'd also had to sell the roadman's van. Without it, we were forced to down-shift and sleep in the back of the pick-up: Gribble was now our home. Then one late afternoon in April, the phone rang. The kiln was ready for collection.

We left Dorset late on a Wednesday evening in a rented Luton van. I preferred to travel at night, the roads would be empty. By 2am we were on the southern approaches to York. I was flagging and needed to get my head down. We pulled off the main drag and rattled along B-roads looking for a stopping place. I found a green lane and drove down it, pulling up against a high hedge. Getting out of the cab I immediately felt a change. It was colder here, the sky clear

115

and shot with stars. I opened the van's tailgate to expose a grim bedchamber. A thin mattress and duvet lay crumpled against the bulkhead. I called Pig over and lifted him inside. I crawled in and shut the back which closed with an ominous clunk. I walked across to the bed and lay down in my clothes. Pulling the duvet around me, I felt the dog settle. Could I see stars through the fibreglass roof? I was asleep before the answer came.

I woke up late, of my own accord. Coming round, I had no idea of the time but the strength of the light coming through the roof suggested the sun was already high in the sky. I stood up and put on my shoes with that particular thick head that comes with a driving hangover. Pig yawned and performed a perfect downward dog. He'd want his breakfast. We moved towards the back of the van. There was a moment of anxiety when I feared we were locked in, but the tailgate eventually lifted to reveal a quiet Yorkshire lane. Pig stuck his nose into the breeze.

'Different air here, Pig. Drier than home.'

I jumped down and walked to the cab to fetch our rations. With Pig head down in his bowl, I put a coffee pot over the flame of a small camping stove. While I waited for the coffee, I scanned the lane. Its mossy centre suggested it was little used. Opposite, a fingerpost sign advertised two villages that meant nothing to me. Physically the sign was not unlike the way-markers of home, a simple wooden board painted white with black letters. But while the Dorset fingerpost ended in a gentle curve, here they were pointed. The difference seemed apt, echoing regional stereotypes: the West Countryman slow and sanguine, the Yorkshireman more to the point.

By my reckoning we were somewhere south-east of York. I had to find a main road and get my bearings. I finished my coffee and set off. It was flat country with large arable fields dominating, broken up by small woods. We passed tinker cobs tethered on grazing chains and farmsteads hidden behind dark windbreaks of trees. A mechanical digger stood stranded out on the wash. Everything seemed locked down, closed.

The industrial estate was located on a joyless tract of land that had once been an airfield. Under a vast, grey sky Nissen huts and old hangers mingled with modern portakabins and cars. I found the fabricators down a cul-de-sac on the far perimeter of the estate. The parking area was littered with hulking pieces of machinery, some swathed in cellophane wrap.

As I opened the van door, my nostrils caught the tight, acrid smell of hot metal. A middle-aged man approached in a boiler suit. He was tall and lean, with cropped hair and a blunt face. He opened his mouth and a gold front tooth flashed.

'You 'ere ferkil-un?'

I had no idea what he meant.

'Sorry?'

He repeated: 'Ferkil-un?'

He motioned over to a group of newly fabricated charcoal kilns beyond the hangar.

'Oh, for the kiln – yes. Sorry I'm late.'

'I'll get forklift.'

I nodded and he turned away. Waiting, I surveyed the industrial shanty around me, the fantastical pipework, the odd ducts and vents. The man returned slouched on the forklift, one hand on the steering wheel. In a beat, he had the forks under a kiln and had raised it off the ground, several feet. A quick two-point turn later and he was trundling towards me. He hollered: 'Open back.'

Of course, the tailgate. The man waited while I opened it, then loaded the kiln with professional ease. In seconds, half a tonne of pressed steel sat in the Luton's back.

'I'll get re-seet.' I nodded as the man jumped down and sloped back to the site office, his long neck creased like vintage leather. Returning, he handed me the docket, on thin white paper.

'Well thanks,' I replied, 'Guess that's it.'

The man attempted a half smile. Climbing into the van, I shoved the receipt into a door tray. I sat for a moment feeling oddly charged, knowing my future lay stowed behind me. I turned the ignition key and from the hangar, the blue strobe of a welding rig crackled. Electricity was in the air.

Finding my way off the industrial estate proved more awkward. Reversing too hastily down a third wrong-turn, I hit a wall. I got out to survey the damage. Both rear lights were smashed and I'd put an ugly dent in the bumper. Fortunately, I'd taken extra insurance out on the van, so wouldn't be liable for the repair bill, but the rental guy would correctly label me an idiot.

We crossed the Humber in light mizzle and once in Lincolnshire set a diagonal course for home. I was lost in charcoal dreaming and Pig was fast asleep when, in my mirror, the blinking neon blue of an emergency vehicle curtailed our peace. I hoped for an ambulance. No such luck, police.

I pulled over and waited. A female traffic officer appeared at the window. She was a tough-looking, high-cheeked blonde with eyes heavily loaded with mascara. I wound down the window and smiled. In a less than musical accent she bade me good day.

'Good afternoon constable,' I replied. The cop looked at me closer, took in the sleep-deprived face, the swarthy beard, the battered trilby hat. She'd also clocked Pig, made a note of breed and probable temperament. It didn't take a genius to see the conclusions she was working towards. The Bull terrier, meanwhile, glared at the policewoman. He was in a foul mood, it was always the same when he had his kip disturbed. A low bass warning rumbled from his throat. The officer pinned the animal with her eyes. Her tone was colder.

'Any idea why I've stopped you?' I had no time to answer. Pig tore across the cab towards the uniform, fuelled by resentment and an instinctive dislike. I grabbed him and threw him back in the passenger seat. Instantly, the cop ordered me out of the van. As I shut the door, Pig savaged the door panel, his cortisol levels blown through the roof. Visibly ruffled, the traffic officer marched me around to the back of the van and told me it was a disgrace. Looking at the mangled electrics, I tried to appear contrite, explaining I had no idea they were damaged. But I am a lousy liar.

Thinking things couldn't get any worse, she then asked me what I had inside the back of the van. I cringed as the tailgate lifted. I knew the kiln, a large metal lump, would not look good given the assumptions she was making about my ethnic group. On seeing it, she simply shook her head. I argued that I had a receipt for it in the cab, but the cop wasn't listening. She wanted to run a check on me and ordered me to her vehicle.

At this point I decided to enjoy the experience. I'd never been inside a police car and thought I might stretch it out. The inside was meticulously clean, an air freshener dangling from the mirror with the name 'Black Ice'. The traffic officer bent forward and began typing something onto a small, touch-sensitive screen buried in the dashboard. She asked me my name, address and date of birth. When I said a I was of No Fixed Abode and living in a wood, I could tell she thought she was on to a good thing. She asked me my occupation, to which I replied, 'wood collier'. The policewoman looked up, her confidence momentarily stalled.

'Wood what?'

'Wood collier. I make charcoal in the woods, officer.'

Reluctantly taking my word for it, she turned back to the touch screen and typed 'wood colier' into the required box. It was a gift I couldn't pass up.

'That's a double 'l', officer.'

Her jaw tensed, a nostril quivered. She made the correction and the small computer returned a flat beep. The traffic officer shot back.

'No, can't find that here.'

'OK, try charcoal burner.' Again, the same outcome, a negative, electronic fart. I could feel the balance of power had shifted. Confidence was now in her court. 'What about woodsman?' I tried, but still no joy. The policewoman looked at me and with clear emphasis proclaimed:

'You're *not* on the list.'

The tone irked me, but it was the statement which really got under my skin. 'Not on the list' – what bloody list? Whatever grim inventory of respectable occupations the list actually amounted to I had no idea, but it was clearly obvious not being on it was a very bad thing. With relish, the officer explained she would have to put 'No Category' in the box. As she typed it in I could almost hear her tut. After several seconds the check came back: no criminal record, no traffic violations, clean as a whistle. Disappointment oozed from her face. Smiling, I pushed the front brim of my trilby up an inch.

'Take it I'm free to go?'

The policewoman looked at me drily and dredged what little satisfaction she could from the situation by ordering me to stop at the next garage and get the lights fixed. As I got out of the car and walked away, she took one final swipe, 'And get that animal tethered in the vehicle – *It's the law!*'

We made it back to Gribble just after eight. As we drove through the gates, the sun was behind us, still an hour of daylight left. I was too tired to deal with unloading the kiln, so parked up and got a brew on. We'd spend another night in the fibreglass crate and sort things out in the morning.

I sat and waited for the kettle to boil. The evening was still, not a breath of wind. The drowsy call of a wood pigeon floated over from somewhere deep in the trees. Not to be outdone, the kettle began to whistle. I poured the boiling water into my mug and dropped a teabag in.

My mind returned to the encounter with the traffic cop. The whole thing did not sit well. I'd taken umbrage at having to answer to anyone, perhaps too much. At the time, the whole name, rank, number charade had made me feel reduced, as if those small details amounted to the sum of all I was. In the end it had turned into something no more evolved than a playground squabble.

I looked out into the wood, the green depths closing in with the dimsey. In the stillness, the trees themselves seemed to breathe, one long, synchronised out-breath. I had a sudden and profound sense of a deep power, one which passed right through me. I looked up as if with a new pair of eyes, took in the patrician oaks and the hundreds of species which called them home. In all of this there were no boxes, no divisions, just a symphony of vibrations echoing back without end.

13

I sited the kiln inside a ring of seven oaks and began with a ritual. As flames swarmed through the small fire I'd made, I closed my eyes and meditated on the moment. A new beginning, a new life, burning in an ancient oak wood.

The place, however, was scarred. Beside my new camp ran a woodland ride. The track was part of a grid system which had been put in a year before by the council to aid the extraction of timber. The hardcore which had been used to make up the tracks had come from a demolished hospital. Spring and summer growth had softened their aspect, but if you looked down, there were still signs, things that had no place in an English wood. Staring up through the broken brick, a doll's face, and a little further down the ride, the gruesome remains of an Action Man. The rubble in this part of the wood had come from the hospital's paediatric unit.

Sitting by the fire, my mind naturally bent to the children. Just as with animals, the idea of innocents suffering was always hard to bear. But the present demanded action, dwelling was no good. I got up and walked over to the kiln, it needed filling. Up until that moment, all I'd seen was the volume of free material available to me, the tons of hazel gifted by the wood. Now, with sharpened focus I saw the whole truth. In front of me lay two years' hard labour: dragging, hauling, cutting and burning. No Joby Cutler with his grimy banter, no Ralph Watts to keep me on my toes. Looking across the wood and its endless piles of brash, I felt like someone left to clean up after a vast and raucous party. Pulling the larger hazel from the rotting heaps, it soon became clear those responsible for dumping it this way could not have made things more difficult. The poles were overgrown with matted grasses and did not give up their booty without a fight. The air turned blue as I cursed the idiots who'd buried good wood under bad. By the time I had a truck load, I was exhausted. I fell into the cab, my legs ringing with nettle stings. Pig sat in the passenger seat, impassive, a hairy white buddha. He seemed oblivious to my suffering, and in a moment of churlishness I felt moved to enlighten him.

'I'm doing this for you Pig, *for us.*'

This was a lie. I was doing it for me. Perhaps the dog already understood this. He turned towards me, before dropping his gaze and licking the end of his penis. I shook my head, clutching for words and stuck the pick-up in reverse.

We reached the kiln and I started to unload. The poles had been cut to eight-foot lengths, but would need to be cut down further to be kiln friendly. I started to stack them neatly on the ground. I'd learnt with Joby that it always paid to build an orderly woodpile. A tidy stack can be cut through with long dives of the chainsaw, severing multiple poles in one go. The timber locks together in a neat woodpile and generally remains more stable. Not only is this more time efficient, but also means you don't risk finishing your working day with one foot less than when you started. People will often stick their hoof on a single round of wood to stabilise it while they cut. The wood spins, kicks back, and they end up sinking the chainsaw through their foot. This can be messy when you consider a cutting chain at full throttle travels at twenty metres per second.

The saw made quick work of the hazel, the new chain cutting like a dream. Everything was now set for loading. It took me an hour and a half to fill the kiln, a satisfying process witnessing what had been waste wood being used for something which would bring in a profit. What was less encouraging was the amount of hazel left in the original pile. I'd estimated that I must have hauled at least a tonne and a half of wood that morning, enough I'd thought, for two burns. But the kiln seemed to swallow the hazel with ease and all that was left were a couple of wheelbarrow loads. I couldn't remember Joby's being quite so greedy.

Despite the reality check, I felt a little giddy. I stood on the threshold of my first solo burn. The names of the old charcoal burners I'd read in Joby's book were suddenly rekindled. Was Jim Shady alongside me waiting for the gush of the lit flame? Did Humphrey Crow linger among the trees, eager to catch the tang of woodsmoke? Winding a pair of old boxer shorts around a hazel stick, I doused them in diesel. If the old charcoal burners really were present they'd be holding their ghost breath right now, hanging on every move. I rolled the lighter's wheel and a long flame streaked. As I watched the silent immolation of cotton I felt the sacred intensity of the moment. The small flame which is passed on from charcoal burner to charcoal burner flickered and glowed.

I knelt down and pushed the conflagration through one of the air vents towards the charge. I could hear the dry nest of sticks catch – a sharp, urgent crackle. A drift of smoke appeared almost immediately from the top of the kiln like a wood spirit vacating. The noise must have roused Pig, who sidled forward and lifted his nose for a hit of woodsmoke. His tail gave a lazy wag. He then cocked a leg and peed against the kiln wall.

After ten minutes the smoke which had been rising stalled and eventually petered out. I bent over the kiln's edge and put my ear to the wood: the vital signs had died. Anxious, I lit another pair of underpants and shoved them down a second vent. Almost immediately, the kiln returned a crackle. I looked across at Pig and grinned. We watched as the smoke drifted up, but after several minutes the thing guttered once again and the fire died. I began to fret. I didn't care if I'd have to strip off and set fire to the boxers I was actually wearing – that would be a minor inconvenience – but having to unload all the wood and re-stock the charge would be soul-destroying.

On the third attempt at firing, the charge took. Over twenty minutes the reedy white trail grew into a giant barley twist of smoke. In contrast to the still, placid oaks, the helix was all snarl, a posturing aggressor. I stepped back and retreated into the trees, in awe of what I'd created. In charcoal burning parlance this early phase is called the 'free burn'. Charcoal burners will explain this happens when the kiln and vents are left entirely open, giving the fire as much oxygen as possible and time to take hold. But at that precise moment, this seemed far too dry an explanation for it. What I was watching had all the joy of a wild creature freed from long internment. The smoke punched into the air, pulling faces at me. 'Free! Free!' it rejoiced, as it raced clear of its steel bounds.

With the kiln emptied and fifty bags of charcoal filled, I now needed to sell them. Approaching the village shop, my first on a long list of possible local outlets, I wasn't full of confidence; despite my adman past, I was no natural salesman. To mitigate against this, I'd prepared and rehearsed an introduction, cleaned myself up by taking a strip wash in the woods. The black eyeliner, however, had refused to budge and made me feel self-conscious.

Entering the shop did nothing to ease my anxiety. The formica shelves were big on surface area but lacked product. Were the owners selling up? Was this the last of their stock? A single strip light cast a jaundice yellow over a clutch of over-ripe bananas. Beside them, a pork pie sweated in clingfilm.

I approached the counter where a tall, thin man stood reading the *Racing Post*. He seemed closed and tired, his mouth set in a sour hook. As he looked up, I caught a tug at the side of his face. I ignored it and held up the large brown sack I was carrying, bearing the legend: British Barbecue Charcoal.

'Good morning. I make charcoal in the woods a couple of miles from here and wondered if...'

The man cut me short. 'No thank you.'

I was stunned by his brevity. He hadn't even had the good grace to hear me out. I stood speechless for several moments, processing. It must have been the eyeliner. I understood the sooty make-up was a bit of a curve ball, especially as I appeared in every other way your normal middle-aged bloke, but still, there's manners. The man suddenly piped up.

'You might try The Green Dragon. They sometimes do barbecues.'

I smiled gratefully but he had already returned to his paper. I picked up the sack and left.

I found the pub, a modest building of brick and flint, two hundred yards up the hill. Over the door hung a shabby, fibreglass dragon. The lizard reeked of inadequacy, a tubby runt with wings woefully under-engineered to keep him airborne and with looks only a mother-dragon could love. As I stood regarding him, a young woman appeared from around the corner carrying a vegetable box. She wore clogs and a pair of black and white checked strides which declared her a chef. The girl smiled and said something about the dragon needing a makeover. I didn't have the heart to tell her it needed more than that. She looked down at the bag of charcoal I was carrying and asked the price. 'Seven pounds,' I answered. The girl didn't bat an eyelid and said she'd take twenty. I nodded, slightly dizzy with the ease of the sale. While the chef disappeared to get some cash, I went back to the truck and started unloading. Stacking the bags beside the front door, I was aware of being watched. The googly-eyed dragon was staring down on me from above. Looking up, I thought he needed to find a new career. He wasn't frightening anyone, bar the most lily-livered knight.

Getting back to the woods with a wedge of cash in my pocket, I felt like I'd won the lottery. It was the first sale I'd earned from the kiln and wasn't much – coppers compared to what I used to earn – but that was not the point. In London I'd burned money: eating out, drinking, taking cabs; the four figures under 'Net Pay' on my monthly payslip, almost meaningless.

Working in Gribble, converting waste wood into cash, seemed infinitely more rewarding. I would never be rich, but this path offered a different kind of prosperity. With the sun on my back and the charcoal money safely stowed in an old cake tin, I went back to refill the kiln, re-energised and hungry for more.

Over the summer, I averaged two burns every seven days, yielding around eighty bags of charcoal a week. The weather was warm and with the sun out people were buying it. At moments in my day, I'd stop for a cup of tea and would find myself chuckling at the odd, crazy, miracle unfolding, as if I'd stumbled on a life so beautiful and simple it shouldn't be allowed. I knew I would never be going back to my old life. The corporate world and all its trappings had been carbonised.

One late afternoon, I decided on a ramble through the woods. It was especially still, the smoke from the kiln's chimneys pumping neat verticals through the canopy. Leaving the camp, I called Pig, but he wouldn't come. I tried to coax him out from under the pick-up but nothing would convince him.

Alone, I walked into the trees. Under them, the lack of animation was stifling. I stood quietly, stalled by the hush. There are two types of stillness in nature. The first is the lull before a thunderstorm, the pause with that prickle of danger. You can smell it, a precursor to electrical violence.

I remember a moment in my childhood. It is after six, supper is done. I am standing with my father in the yard, he is speaking with the cowman. The light has an odd green tinge. A breeze blows in, stirring stone dust into spiral patterns. The stockman stops talking and looks to the east. His nose is bloated, it is like a potato. I watch the nostrils expand as he samples the air. Sensing the storm, the cowman speaks as if he is under a spell. It has a plaintive air. But this man doesn't do poetry; he has dealt in life and death since he started work at fourteen. 'She's coming,' he declares, his eyes fixed on the horizon, and I swallow, excited and frightened in equal measure.

Then there is another stillness, which is the augury of nothing. It is the stillness born from pain, from something which has passed. Certain places in nature carry this, just as some buildings do. I felt this now. The ground beneath the trees smoked with it and all that grew from it. Ferns dragged themselves from the earth, while the sweet chestnuts seemed uniquely contorted. It was this atmosphere, I was sure, which had got into Pig.

Stepping out of the trees and onto the ride, I felt relief. And there, in the track's sunlit border was a small pink flower which looked like Weasel's snout. Compared with the local plant community it seemed to quiver with joy, uninhibited by the general mood. I stood there, touched by its stubborn refusal to be cowed by Gribble.

Then out of the corner of my eye, a figure. Perhaps two hundred metres down the ride, a stranger in a black hoodie, looking towards my camp. I could make out slight movements of the head, as if he was reconnoitring the place, his neck kinking like a hunting snake. As I turned and walked down the ride towards him, he lifted an arm in greeting.

I prepared myself for confrontation. As I got closer the visitor pulled down his hood to reveal a small, bald head. He was short, perhaps five foot seven, with a rash of tattoos covering both forearms. A bright blue vintage pick-up truck monopolised one patch of skin, burlesque girls with improbably large breasts, the other. I judged him to be in his late fifties. Motioning over to a small copse across the field from Gribble, he began: 'Seen your smoke. Thought I'd come over, say 'ello. I own that wood there. Name's Leon.'

'Had it long?' I enquired.

'Bought it off the council a year back. Wanted to ask if you'd be interested in some copsin' – paid of course.' I let it hang.

'Maybe. Got a fair bit to do here first.'

There was a pause. I took him in some more. He had a sharp mouth, undercut with a strip of greying fuzz which travelled south down his chin. Nothing like a woodsman's beard, more town, was my immediate impression. As he spoke he looked shifty, his eyes unable to settle.

'So you're a charcoal burner?'

I nodded.

'Yes. I'm burning the hazel left from the thinnings last year.'

His eyes flickered across the coupe.

'Left a bloody mess didn't they – shame to see good wood wasted.'

I nodded. Another pause.

'Not many of you lot left, burnin' and livin' in the woods...'

So he knew a bit.

'Braver man than I. Wouldn't kip in this place if you paid me.'

Now I was listening.

'What do you mean?' He took his hands out of his hoodie pockets and started to roll a fag.

'The old man's family were 'orse drawn, spent most of their time round 'ere as well as on the Levels. Camped mostly down Crooked Lane. Would never stop in Gribble though, Nan wouldn't 'ave it.'

He put a filter in place, wet the paper and rolled it between finger and thumb.

'The men might go stickin' round the edges, fetchin' firewood, but Nan refused to go inside. She were a tough old bird, but you wouldn't 'ave got 'er to put a toe in Gribble. Even mention the name and she'd 'ave to cross 'erself. Said the Mulleri Mush lived here...' Leon took a Zippo from his pocket, flipped the top and set a flame to the rollie. He took a deep drag. I wanted to know more.

'Mulleri Mush?'

The stranger looked guarded and for the first time fixed me with his eyes. His voice took on a more serious tone.

'The Dead Man. Gypsies' version of the Grim Reaper.'

I felt like laughing. It was something that commonly happened when I was nervous. At that moment a green woodpecker dropped from a piece of standing deadwood, fracturing the silence with its crackpot laugh. Leon jumped.

'Bleedin' bird!'

I watched the woodpecker dissolve into the trees while Leon took another draw on his fag, as if a remedy against his angst.

'Maybe Nan was onto somethin'. Her was what they call a mirror, had a feelin' for things. Cut a long story short, I did some nosin' after I bought me wood, looked into the 'istory. Found some papers from way back which had details of all the folk 'round 'ere. Three hundred year back they 'ad a mush down in the records as livin' in Gribble – name of Edward Vowles. Law were after 'im, but they never found 'im. Well, on the census you know what they put down for 'is occupation?' I shook my head. Leon let the word fall slowly: 'Murderer.'

Leon sniffed.

'Just pleased there's a field between my wood and this place.' I nodded, but wasn't taking much else in. Leon scanned the deeper wood, his eyes had narrowed. 'Anyway, better trot on, light's goin' – old Vowles might be around.'

Leon turned down the ride, shuffling off with the tick of someone leaving a crime scene, not wanting to be noticed. Left alone, his words hung in the air. Suddenly, the wood seemed more spooky than ever, the ground in front of me practically begging for an apparition.

I turned back towards camp, twilight was now bending in. And then, as I rounded a curve in the ride, a crashing of twigs. I froze, my heart in my mouth. But it was only a badger. He pushed along a tunnel bored through a thicket, not five metres from where I stood, his salt and pepper coat as tough as a gamekeeper's thorn-proof jacket. 'Got to get on, got to get on' he seemed to be repeating to himself as he trundled past, the animal less like the over-large weasel his taxonomy dictates and more like England's only native bear.

That night, I woke with a start. In the darkness, what sounded like footsteps. I lay paralysed in the back of the truck, my eyes fixed on the mesh panel beyond my feet. My breathing became shallower, my ears super-sensors. It was probably an old male badger – a boar – perhaps the same individual I'd bumped into from before.

I waited. Again, the press of dry leaves, the steady crunch on the woodland floor. My ears made minute calibrations. The cadence was more measured, less bright than a rambling boar. It sounded bipedal. It sounded human.

Pig, the scoundrel, did nothing. Part Bull terrier, I expected at least his braver half to spring into action. Suddenly the dog kicked a leg against my side and began to whimper: I guessed he was dreaming of rabbits. I fumbled for my billhook and lay there, primed. The footsteps had stopped. All I could hear was the pumping of blood in my ears. I gripped the weapon's ash handle but felt too scared to ease myself from the sleeping bag and go outside. Minutes passed, the silence deepened – had I imagined it? Slowly, the hot flush in my chest guttered. My limbs relaxed. Sleep had me.

I awoke with the daylight. Looking out on the wood, the trees stood silent, disinclined to share their secrets. I wriggled free of the bed and in doing so exposed a hairy white trotter. The toes arched as I brushed them. My traitorous companion was still dead to the world. Only the sound of breakfast would rouse him.

Standing beside the pick-up, my eyes searched vainly for clues, but the woodland floor showed no signs of passing. Pig snapped me out of my detective work, appearing on the edge of the truck bed, looking well-rested and chipper. A sharp bark let me know he was ready for his breakfast.

'You don't deserve it.' I countered. He barked again, I stood my ground. 'You should be on half-rations for dereliction of duty.'

The dog stared into me. I returned the hard gaze, trying to match him, but it was no good, I was putty in his paws.

Pig sprang from the truck and fretted at my feet while I fixed his breakfast. Putting his bowl down he was straight into it. I left him to his gluttony and walked out onto the ride. As I stared down the green corridor, there was not a breath of wind. All animation had scarpered.

That afternoon a tall, dark figure approached from the direction of the road. The elegance with which he ducked under a low-hanging hawthorn gave him instantly away. It was Bill Cope, the land agent.

'Hello,' he projected, filling Gribble with some well-needed heart. We shook hands. Bill looked across at the area of ground I'd been clearing, the brash piles already visibly reduced.

'Made a good dent in it then.'

'Well, it's a start,' I replied, not wanting to appear too pleased with myself. Bill smiled. He had a kind, handsome face. Scanning the wood beyond the area of hazel I had cleared, he asked: 'How do you like the wood?' I didn't want to say it gave me the willies, so sugared the pill, replying it was good, and that I was happy to be there. Bill's gaze remained fixed on the deeper wood. A small furrow appeared on his forehead, but the steady smile did not wane. It was difficult to read him, perhaps he too had a feeling for Gribble's darker notes.

'Fancy a cuppa?'

Bill looked back at me suddenly, as if refocusing out of a dream.

'Yes... Good idea. Have you any coffee?'

Bill watched as I opened an old ammo box and liberated a silver brick of ground Italian coffee.

'Ah, super!'

I invited him to take a seat and put the espresso pot over the fire. Bill took off his glasses and removed a handkerchief from his jacket's inside pocket. Without them he suddenly looked older. He began cleaning the lenses.

'I was thinking of that old charcoal burner last night, the one that used to work here. Couldn't for the life of me remember his name. Then, would you believe, I woke up last night with his name ringing in my head – Obadiah Smith – if you could ever forget it.' I said nothing, letting Bill talk, but aware of the symmetry, of both of us waking in the small hours.

'He was originally from Kent – a man of the Weald – almost certainly had some Gypsy in him. It must have been about '73...'

Bill put his glasses back on, and instantly regained some of his vigour.

'... I had a conversation with him before he left. Would have been about this time of year. I was fresh out of school and rather green, but he'd always take off his hat, call me Mr. Cope. I can remember his words even now.'

At this point Bill leant forward on the bench and utterly transformed. No longer a well-to-do land agent, but an old Wealden countryman.

'"There be things which go on in woods, not all woods, but I been in many all across this South Country and some 'ave good feelings and others bad. And somethin' ain't right in this one Mr. Cope, tis a busy place."'

Bill suddenly looked younger. Perhaps it was the animation in mimicking the old Gypsy. He certainly had a flair for it, he could have been on the stage. He continued,

'I'd no idea what the old chap was talking about and told him so. I remember he had this grim laugh. He took the pipe out of his mouth and pointed the stem towards me, as if to make his point. He said quite slowly, "There be places where we're closer to the others, Mr. Cope. Places where the veil is thinner, if you follow me."'

Bill paused, to check I was still with him.

'Well I was none the wiser – had no understanding of these things back then. I asked him to explain some more. But he wouldn't be drawn, only said: "There be things you shouldn't talk on. Not wise nor respectful. I'll say no more."'

The land agent paused, looking into space. He was suddenly modern again, all head.

'Obadiah left later that year. Must be dead now, at least twenty years. A hard life like that wears a man out.'

Bill's recollections left me torn. On one hand I was spooked. Obadiah Smith was one of the old line, a man who could see beyond what the scrambled modern mind perceives. It was as if he had taken my own vague feelings about the wood and whittled them into sharper points. He had spoken with such vividness on Gribble's shadow and his observations, through Bill, had the quality of a dark poem. Yet I also felt enthused by so rich a connection. To tread in such a man's footsteps and work the same wood as him seemed significant. Suddenly I had a sense that the work I was doing was truly important. Not just making a living, but picking up where Obadiah had left off, keeping the old flame alive. Up until then, it had been a solitary path, even with the names of the old burners smouldering in my mind. Now, with such a direct link I felt less alone. Obadiah Smith had worked here, burned in this very wood, slept beneath the trees Pig and I now walked under. His spirit marked this place as real as the small pieces of riddled charcoal you'd find beneath the leaf litter if you knew where to look. Forty years in one sense is a long time, but in the grand scheme it is a blink, and I felt Obadiah and I were as close as if the old man had passed me a bucket of hot embers in his calloused hands, nodded towards the kiln and said: 'There you go, boy – now get makin'.'

The charcoal orders dried up through September and I began to turn my attention to winter work. Bill had been back in touch, calling me to ask if I'd be interested in coppicing part of the lower wood. The work would be unpaid, but I could keep the timber. I weighed it up. Cutting over-stood coppice is labour intensive and doesn't pay if you're doing it for the wood alone, but I'd need more hazel for charcoal-making late next year and had no other source of material. The small allowance to take out some larger trees for firewood also presented a bit of a lure. Logs made reasonable money and there were plenty of people wanting them. I told Bill I'd do it.

Ralph had also been in contact, leaving me an uncharacteristically chirpy message. He wanted to know if I'd be available for more hedge laying that autumn. Despite the clear danger of working with a lunatic, it would be regular, paid work – something I couldn't turn down.

What was less secure was my domestic situation. I wouldn't be staying in Gribble over the winter, that was for sure. Pig and I had roughed it in some pretty bleak places over the years, but overwintering in the back of a pick-up, in a haunted wood, really was taking the biscuit.

Yet as one soon discovers when one opens oneself up to fate, something generally pops up. It was a Saturday. Coming back from a trip to the coast I stopped at a village shop as our rations of teabags and milk were running low. An elderly lady beamed across at me as I placed the sundries and several packets of Ginger Nuts on the counter. Totting up the total, she asked where I was from. I replied I was a charcoal burner and living in the back of my van in a wood five miles away. The woman asked whether such an arrangement wasn't a bit much at this time of year. I confirmed it was, but explained local digs were hard to find.

As I handed over the cash the lady confided she knew of a place in the next village which was derelict and had a caravan in its grounds. She was friendly with the owner and would sound her out. I must have been a little sketchy from lack of food, because she looked directly at me and asked if I was alright. And here I let myself down. Desperate for winter lodgings and sensing a Good Samaritan, I played the Poor Me card. Casting my eyes over the nutritional car crash littering the counter, I replied I'd be OK once I'd had my dinner. The pensioner looked winded.

'What? This is your *dinner*?'

I paused for a second, asking myself if I could go through with such an act, then gravely nodded.

The Good Samaritan called me the next morning. She'd been in touch with the owner of the derelict property and the long and short of it was yes, I could stay in the caravan. She explained the lady lived up country and visited only once a year. The place had been her father's. There had been a house fire there in the Seventies, but the old man had continued living in one downstairs room until going into sheltered accommodation some years back. The coal yard and garden had not been touched for as long as she could remember. The deal was that I could stay in the caravan over winter and in lieu of rent tidy up the yard and garden. I thanked the old woman for going out of her way to help me. She said it was no bother and that I'd find the key to the place hidden behind one of the yard's stone entrance piers.

That afternoon I drove over to the village for a look. I parked the pick-up opposite the yard gates and went to get the key. Bending down, I found it, and beside the key, a warm pyrex dish covered over with tin foil. I peeled back the crinkly silver to reveal a homemade shepherd's pie. It smelled delicious. I shook my head at the wonder of it. And beside the offering, an envelope with a twenty-pound note tucked inside. I felt instantly terrible — donated money by a pensioner who, I was sure, was hardly flush herself. My low act now seemed even lower. Rarely have I disliked myself more.

There had been rain in the woods overnight and the sky was a battleship grey. I eased myself out of bed and onto the truck's lowered tailgate, dangling my stockinged feet over the edge. I realised I'd left my boots outside during the night and they were sopping wet. Karma perhaps.

The remains of the fire were a cold, wet gruel, a few charred sticks lying in the sodden ash. Rivulets of water ran through the camp, the only animation in a world which seemed dulled. Weather like this always got me down. I felt unmoved to light a fire despite the fact I knew it would add cheer. I thought of Joby Cutler. Even in the most horrible weather, when the woods appeared one enormous wet room, he'd exude a sense of belonging, a constant delight in the trees.

I could not kid myself that was me. At times like this I actually felt anti-wood. With no relief from the dripping canopy, I pined for a way out, an escape from the damp. In contrast, the Joby Cutlers of this world are true woodland animals. They rejoice in the stench of photosynthesis and the clinging smell of damp hummus, that particularly drear world inside a wood's borders after rain. It is my hunch that they are, in fact, ill at ease outside the wood, uncomfortable in spaces not pressed in by trees.

It was the right time to leave the wood. I looked over the pitstead, emptier now, just piles of riddled charcoal pieces glistening like wet slate. The kiln, too, felt remote. How different from the hot, sentient creature of Midsummer. My mind flipped back to the burns of late June, those magical hours when the kiln had trumpeted smoke, rejoicing in its own industry. Now that life force had drained away, sunk into the dark places, like the tail of a black snake disappearing into a drystone wall.

I spent the morning clearing the camp and packing up our stuff. We didn't have much. The four months since we'd moved to Gribble had gone so quickly. But we'd be back that winter for coppicing. Yet as I got into the truck I could feel the melancholy of being separated, of an affection for the place, despite its present gloom and ghosts. And as I drove through the gate and away I still felt no clear break, as if part of me remained fixed to Gribble and all that called it home.

14

The caravan stood at the back of the coal yard on a hard standing of old concrete.

It had seen better days. Stepping inside the interior had been vandalised, the sort of damage that is the hallmark of bored village kids. Plates and crockery were smashed, drawers rifled. A long mirror on the inside of the toilet door had also been destroyed, but thankfully the chemical loo remained intact.

The damage was hard on the eyes, but not irreversible. What offended me more was the colour of the curtains. I could not once, not for a second, see any merit in them. A tired, synthetic orange, they filtered the daylight, bathing the caravan in a tawdry, tangerine glow. At the far end of the space, another obstruction to my sanity – a built-in sofa upholstered in a brown and cream tartan. The thing set my eyes on edge.

I spent the day clearing out the trailer. Taking down the curtains and putting a throw over the sofa delivered instant relief, like taking an eye bath in strong prescription Optrex. Towards the end of the afternoon I was feeling much better about our new home when Pig snuck inside, before swiftly retreating and sitting at a distance from the doorway, sulking.

I understood what this was about. Being a Traveller's dog, he knew it wasn't a topnotch caravan. This was no luxury Roma or gleaming Buccaneer. I went outside and had words with him. As I scolded him for such ungratefulness, his dull brown eyes levelled on me, like a child disappointed at Christmas. I told him if he didn't like it he could sleep outside.

After a couple of days' work, I'd made some repairs. The water pump had been faulty but was now functioning.

I'd also bought a pair of gas cylinders – one for the hob and another for a small, mobile heater which I'd found in a shed. While there was no electricity, we had heat and water and were set fair. My only concern was the lack of light. Memories of that dark winter in Joby's wood still lingered. I had a couple of small paraffin lamps I'd brought from Gribble and hoped they would be enough to ease the cabin fever that might leach in over the dark months.

In lieu of paying rent, I started the clean-up job on the coal yard. My strategy was to go at it hard and fast, in a kind of horticultural blitzkrieg. Staring up at a tsunami of brambles, I gave the chainsaw throttle a blip. The German two-stroke screamed as if desperate to get among the thorny surge.

As I waded in, brambles tore at me like schoolgirls in a cat fight and after twenty minutes' scrapping, I reached a spreading willow, a toadish character growing from the foot of a perimeter wall. The wall itself was high and old, the lower part perfect squares of knapped flint. Above them ran courses of slim brickwork, hand-worked filets of local clay. It was fine work, probably eighteenth century and beside such sophistication, the willow appeared even more of a runt. Not only was it a bloated glutton who had slaked itself on water, but its roots were a structural risk to the wall. I restarted the saw and drove it into the trunk. The willow groaned like a fat man as I pulled the chainsaw out. A quick downward cut would sever the hinge that kept him standing.

The rest of the morning was a prolonged skirmish with more brambles, the village only getting respite from the yawling saw when I needed to refuel. I was also halted on two occasions by long-abandoned birds' nests deep in the thicket, deftly spun domes of moss and scraps of wool, the homes of warblers or wrens. Their shape and symmetry seemed proof that mechanical instinct was not the only driver in making them. Love glittered in the weave.

After lunch I reached five apple trees, what remained of an old orchard. All of them were choked with ivy and barely alive. Four collapsed as I yanked the climbers away, the inside of the trunks nothing more than friable soil. One tree, however, seemed to be hanging on. I hoped by giving it more light and air it may perk up and fruit again. Beyond the sickly Malus, more brambles and a deeper shade. Hacking into it with my slasher, I saw something take shape and slowly appear. It was an old Anderson shelter, something from the war years repurposed as a shed. The iron corrugation was generous and thick, decay had hardly touched it. I dropped the slasher and squeezed forwards. Inside, the floor was dry dirt, the air stained with fox. As my vision adjusted, I could make out the entrance to his den among bits of gardening junk, including a rusting Allen scythe, its cutting bar set like the teeth of a sawfish. And then my eyes fell on the broad curve of something older. It was the headboard of a wooden tipping cart, a tumbrel. I stepped towards it, excitement rising in my gut. Chinks of light fell on the cart's decorative scoops and hollows, beautiful embellishments made by the wagon maker's drawknife, primarily there to reduce weight. On the headboard itself, a faint impression of lettering. I rubbed the surface to shoo away the dust and a ghost appeared:

JOHN SMALL - MAKER
CLAPTON MILL 1927

A modest name for a conjurer of such beauty. Mr. Small would be dead, but the tumbrel still stood and gave him his immortality. It was anybody's guess how long she'd been retired, her function of tipping muck onto the fields superseded by mechanical spreader decades ago. Crawling underneath, I tested a cross ledge with the point of my knife. It was solid. I tried the axle – sound too. The axle-bed was a single block of heavily chamfered timber, held in place by strapping ironwork, while on each stub end perched a five-stud artillery wheel, the sort used on gun carriages during the First World War. I was spellbound.

The Autumn Equinox passed and the afternoons hurried toward darkness. I was back at Gribble cutting the hazel which lay beyond the middle ride. On overcast days the semi-darkness did not lift from the woods and night's shutter came down hard. But the work was all-consuming and most of the time I laboured in a kind of chainsaw trance. Towards the end of the day, I would raise my head and look around. Then the wood would be transformed: veteran trees dissolved, animal tracks vanished, gaps between the hazel gone. The coming night had reshaped the wood. Darkness has fast hands.

More often than not I was caught off-guard and forced to stumble back to the pick-up, blind. Tripping over tree roots, snagging tools, the silence of the wood polluted with a 'bollocks' here and a 'shit' there and always the heavy breathing of a woodsman struggling under a panoply of gear.

Getting back to the coal yard, I could dump my tools but the lack of light remained an issue. Inside the caravan, the illumination from the oil lamps cast a cosy glow, but their fetch was weak. Reading for extended periods was impossible and while the radio offered some company, the days when I would not speak to another person far outweighed those when I did. Thinking of my old therapist, this collision of circumstances would be, in his eyes, a perfect storm; isolation and darkness a ticking time bomb for anybody with mental health problems.

Yet, for the most part, I felt okay. I still had my moments, but the searing torture of the old days had largely gone. I felt content in my small world, my aluminium burrow. I took pleasure in the rituals living in a small space demands, the happy limitations it imposes on how much you can own. In that dark coal yard I was actually in a place with more light. Working in London, even with its three million sodium lamps, had often felt like the darkest place on the planet. The grim push of modern life; the rampant competitiveness; the clawing of several million applicants all after the same prize. I could not live in that world anymore, it had left me a hollow wreck.

Removing myself from that place had given me a golden pause. But I still had work to do. I had practised some meditation in London, but had never properly persevered. I resumed it now, more seriously. And then there was the same tired body from physical work which always seemed to tranquillize the mind.

Pure O. The name sounds so wholesome. But over the years I had learned its true nature. Pure O is like living in a house that is on fire. It is the logic box overheating, bringing only warped perspectives and blinding pain. Our deeper intelligence – mindful awareness – is its counter weight. To enter what feels like a vast room when we become truly still is the only way out of those burning corridors of over-thinking. Living in the woods and working my body had led me towards that beautiful space, that fire exit.

'Fuckin' tree. No good fuckin' tree.'

Ralph had been in a foul mood since ten that morning when he'd unrolled his canvas grip to find his baccy missing. Losing a decent pleacher – a nice, long, straight one at that – wasn't going to improve matters. The old hedger stood glowering at the maple which had split off at the hinge as he'd tried to lay it. Without a fag to ease the hard ball of anger calcifying inside him, he seemed lost, his mouth working ugly shapes.

We were laying a hedge which straddled a footpath and a country lane. The adjacent field belonged to a nearby abbey, the remains of a monastery which had been built in the twelfth century. It was an awkward job, the hedge bank steep and clotted with hazel. Ralph's normal pace was also hampered by a caravan of dog walkers using the footpath. It forced him to rein in his natural instincts and show caution when felling. He didn't like it.

Despite these inconveniences, we got on well that morning and the loss of the early pleacher was soon a memory. While this went some way to put Ralph in a better mood, I was beginning to feel nauseous. The hedger's old saw was belching fumes from its exhaust and while this was designed to expel pollutants away from him, I copped it head on. Very quickly a hazy feeling overtook my legs and a cold glistening bloomed on my forehead. I was slowly being poisoned. I was going to be sick.

I threw up down the hedge line, an ugly pool of breakfast remains. I toed the vomit under a filler of blackthorn at the base of the hedge. Ralph cut the chainsaw's engine and regarded me with a queer, lop-sided grin. 'Bedder?' he queried. I nodded, not wanting to engage. Knowing I was not in the right condition for eating, Ralph quickly suggested an early lunch. Other people's misfortune was always a tonic for his soul.

That afternoon fate equalled the score. We'd reached a thick stand of field maple which had thrown up dozens of shoots, eighteen feet in the air. To compound the problem, a guard of blackthorn grew bristling around them, a tough lot that would fight dirty. By the time we'd levelled the gang, light was draining in the west. But true to form, Ralph liked to joust with the dusk, to grab a few more minutes as if to get one up on the day.

The old chancer restarted his saw and ripped into the next section of hedge, a dense thicket of hazel and thorn. He'd only been going half a minute when I heard the engine stall and die. Seconds later, Ralph staggered out of the hedge as if blinded. I thought the old fool had lanced an eyeball. Ralph gurgled something incomprehensible and grasped at me for support. I was instantly hit by a diabolical stench and pulled away. As Ralph turned square on I could see he was pebble-dashed with excrement. Behind him, a glut of small black bags hung from the bushes – dog mess. The old git had cut through several, spraying their contents across his arms and chest. One piece had lodged in his hair.

Suddenly, Ralph began to tear at his clothes. I stepped back in an eruption of silent giggles. Throwing his shirt on the ground, the old hedger let rip at his persecutors, the faceless protagonists low enough to commit such an act. 'I'll murder 'em!' he declared, half-naked to the coming night. I watched with fascination as he gave vent to his feelings, bellowing to the moon like a deranged saint. As I gathered our kit, he continued to rail against the persons responsible, elaborating on the ways he was going to seek revenge, versions of torture that would shame a Baghdad jailer. But trudging back to the pick-up Ralph fell silent. It had turned cold and the low temperature seemed to have smothered his fury. Pulling away, he turned on the heater full blast and for the next half hour we were forced to endure the complex aroma of warmed-up dog shit.

When we arrived at the hedge the following day, a clearer picture emerged. For at least twenty yards the hedge was festooned with a crop of dangling black bags. We were only fifty metres from the entrance to the abbey car park and, while it seemed the local dog walkers considered it only right to clear up after their pets on a public footpath, taking it home was another matter. Even more perverse was the fact they'd figured it reasonable to throw the bags in a hedge. Decked out with foul black baubles, the bushes now appeared a collection of satanic Christmas trees.

Having walked the hedge line and exhausted the expletives available to him in the English language, Ralph prepared to get to work. While I sharpened the saws and mixed the two-stroke fuel, he went back to the pick-up and returned wearing a full-face motorcycle helmet. Locking down the tinted visor with a heavy click, it was clear the man was taking no chances.

Throughout the morning, the usual parade of dog walkers ambled by, oblivious to the enmity radiating from the hedge. Ralph stood in the bushes facing them, a kind of black-helmeted Jack-in-the-Green, mumbling blasphemies and aggressively revving his chainsaw. By lunchtime, his anger had begun to dim. Sitting at the foot of the bank in winter sunshine, Ralph poured some tea from his flask, then rearranged himself, lying out like a basking adder.

Needing a sugar hit, I rifled in my bag for some biscuits. Ralph heard the crinkle of the wrapper and looked over, with a pathetic, wheedling grin.

'I find my tea a bit wet without a biscuit.'

I threw the packet across to him and watched as his bony fingers extracted five digestives. Ralph began to nibble at the edge of the first one then took a loud slurp of tea.

The sound of his rehydrating was eclipsed by the screech of a car braking hard on the lane. The engine cut out and two doors opened. Voices floated over the hedge in a low, conspiratorial whisper. Instantly, Ralph uncoiled and moved up the bank. Reaching the top he poked his head over the hedge and quickly gestured for me to join him. I climbed up, crouching low, eager to see what had pricked his curiosity. Below, on the lane, a sporty hatchback stood idling, its boot open.

A middle-aged man appeared out of the lee of the hedge, puffy and red-faced. Pressed against his gut was a bundle of logs. He wobbled across the lane towards the car and dropped the wood into the boot, wiping his soft pink hands on immaculate slacks. From beneath the raised boot I could make out a woman who I assumed to be his wife, fat and urgent, bossing him in a low voice. The logs were the remains of the maple we'd felled the previous day, material Ralph had put aside for firewood. It was perhaps two cubic metres all told, worth well over a hundred and fifty pounds once split and seasoned.

I glanced across at Ralph whose face had passed into shadow. His cold eyes glittered with venom. It was obvious this was the final straw, all his bitterness had coalesced into this moment. Ralph put a finger to his lips and crept down the bank, collecting his motorcycle helmet and slasher. 'This'll put the wind up 'em,' he hissed as he returned, before coldly adding, 'Time to get even.' Something in his voice suggested this was not going to be a schoolboy prank and I instantly felt concerned. Ralph was a rare piece of work and in that moment I believed he was capable of anything, perhaps even murder.

The stillness of the back country lane was cleaved in two as Ralph dropped down the bank with the crazed possession of a man on fire, running towards water. As he skittered onto the lane, he quickly regathered himself, before raising the slasher over his head and charging at the pair, curses rattling the inside of his helmet. The fat man shat himself on the spot. The bundle of logs he was carrying slipped through his grasp and emptied on the lane beneath him. His wife, although equally plump, was more nimble and bolted for the car. As she squeezed into the hatchback, it rocked in violent disagreement. Meanwhile, her husband was tilting toward the getaway vehicle in a frantic waddle. As he folded himself in, the bright metal box catapulted forward, spewing two dozen logs across the lane. It was a pathetic, tragic spectacle, all of it. I watched as Ralph chased after them, raging and gesticulating and fighting the growing distance, until he could give no more. In that moment, he appeared to me a Lowry matchstick man, but all burnt out.

By December, real winter had arrived – I was glad. It had been a poor autumn, the West Country bearing the brunt of a succession of Atlantic lows, the hills binge-drinking on rain water. With some proper cold we had a few weeks of bright, settled weather.

Hedge laying, however, had been put on hold. Ralph was out of action, a message from his daughter saying he'd put out his back lifting a sofa. I imagined him stuck at home, stretched out on a linoleum floor: he would be a nightmare patient. With no hedge work I would have to tighten my belt, although the lack of income was happily offset by a freedom to pursue my own projects. I had managed to speak to the owner of the coal yard, a Mrs Legge. I'd wanted to thank her for letting me stay and to give her an update on the work I'd done there. I also wanted to sound her out about the cart.

The woman was softly spoken and explained the tumbrel was her father's. He had rescued it from a neighbouring farm in the eighties, where it had been destined for a bonfire. The cart had remained in the Anderson shelter ever since, the old fella had done nothing with it. But his daughter remembered how he'd often go out and look at it, quietly run his hands over the scoops and hollows, the fine chamfering which decorated the body. Sadly, he was now suffering from Alzheimer's and was settled in a care home. Mrs Legge explained she had no need for the cart and if I had a use for it, the tumbrel was mine. I offered her some money but she declined, adding her father would have been happy to see it go to somebody who loved it as much as he had.

So, while Ralph was grounded, I divided my time between coppicing and cart renovation. The tumbrel was a beauty and

I was hopelessly smitten. The cart, however, was more than a restoration project driven by a wish to preserve a piece of our agricultural heritage. On first seeing it, I'd thought there was a better future for it, and a more useful one, in Gribble Wood.

While the tumbrel wouldn't exactly be spacious, there was room for a single bed. And perhaps along one of the lade boards, a long trunk for a few possessions. With a bow top raised over it, the cart would be a place to sleep between kiln duties, or somewhere to shelter in if the weather turned wet. In short, a home.

I pulled the cart out of the iron shack and into daylight. I could now make a proper appraisal of the work involved. In the dim light of the shelter, its colour had been difficult to judge, but the winter sun now revealed it as a faded red. I imagined after a wipe down she might blush a little brighter. There was an argument to leave her as she was, to preserve her attractive but shabby gentility. A brush of varnish over the old paintwork would do the trick, and also honour Mr. Small by keeping him in the present. But I loved the idea of repainting the cart in my own livery, even to have a stab at branding. Perhaps I hadn't completely exorcised the adman.

December the twenty-first. The marches of Somerset had been transformed by a heavy fall of snow during the night, so that when I crawled into Gribble early that morning it was a different vision which greeted me. The whiteout – brought in by a Scandinavian low – had changed the wood not only in its appearance but also its mood, Gribble somehow relieved of its heaviness. It was as if old Vowles had retreated inside one of the urchin sallows, to sit out this raid of Viking weather.

Working that day I had a more vivid sense than usual of being alone. It was the weight of silence in the wood, snow being an excellent damper of sound. Around midday

I'd stopped to sharpen my saw and kneeling down, felt a presence behind me. This mental alert was something I had become used to, a growing sixth sense which working in nature had seemed to endow. As the chainsaw file dragged across a cutting tooth, the word 'deer' dropped into my head from nowhere. Instinctively, I swivelled around and twelve feet away stood a young roebuck, watching me. He had eyes the shape of dew ponds, glistening pools the colour of peat water. They did not so much look as absorb. The buck took a step back and turned side on to show himself to his full advantage. As he breathed out, soft parcels of lung-warmed air lifted. I remained crouched, stilling myself in body and mind, admiring the dark wooly flank and his sharp, bright hooves. The deer wandered around me in a perfect circle, never dropping his gaze. And then he bucked his head and barked at me, just once, before wandering away, at ease in his world.

Towards the end of the afternoon, however, I felt a gathering disquiet. Perhaps it was the light, an odd yellow discharge that leaked over the wood as if the sun was trying to shake off some infection. Glancing up, I guessed another twenty minutes of daylight left. Long blue shadows were bleeding out, open wounds across the woodland floor. It seemed the purity of the day had vanished. Gribble had reverted to type.

During that afternoon I'd been coppicing a rash of self-seeded holly which were in danger of over-running the coupe. Superstition made me reluctant to cut them, but since they were small, I'd convinced myself it was not too grave a trespass. With the light almost out, I bent down to finish off the last few when I felt a heavy push on my shoulders from behind. A bolt of fear went through me and earthed at my feet. I hit the saw's chain brake and swivelled around, but there was no one there. A message as clear as if it had been broadcast over tannoy throughout the wood commanded me:

'Leave. You are not welcome here.'

I killed my saw and left Gribble.

I have thought about this experience many times since and while intellect says impossible, feeling disagrees. Write it off if you will – the few people I have told mostly have, putting it down to a vivid imagination and overwork. But I know one man who would not have dismissed it. He would have listened, sucking grimly on his pipe. He would have taken the pipe from his mouth and turned the stem towards me, and with a look as old as his people, said reproachfully, 'Cutting down holly on the Solstice – what did you expect son?'

15

Gribble had given me a proper fright. What happened there had thrown not so much a spanner in the works, but a whole socket set. I had planned to return to the wood in early spring to start charcoal burning, but wasn't now sure if I had the nerve to go back at all.

It would have been easy to turn away. What I'd experienced there had seemed real. But Gribble still had a hold over me and while I was acquainted with its shadows, I also appreciated the space it gave me to live and work, the ongoing therapy of woodland life. The original job I'd set out to do was also unfinished. It had been a deal I'd made with the wood, a spit on my palm and a green handshake. I had to see it through.

We left the coal yard on the one calendar day set aside for fools. I decided to take the quietest route back to Gribble, avoiding main roads and sticking to the lanes. The tumbrel was running well. Over the previous few months I'd patched her up as best I could, even if the work was more country carpenter than craftsman. Out of expediency, I'd decided against steam bending the bow top's hoops and paid a local blacksmith to hammer some out of mild steel. The carapace itself was a collection of canvas tarps overlaid and roped down hard. It looked cobbled together and homespun, for which I liked it better. Finally, the paintwork. I had come to the conclusion that the dull rouge did not inspire, it deserved something new. Red would work for the chassis, but there was only one colour for the body: forest green.

Rising above Clapton Mill, the cart's birthplace, we hit some high country. The lanes there reminded me of west

Cornwall, high-banked and fretted with spring flowers. We passed a Celtic cross at a remote lane junction which deepened the flavour, a patch of the far west in the Dorset lanes. Over the next few miles, our route fell away further into backwater. We crossed a drain herding a slough of brown, slow-moving liquid south. The dyke was the first sign we were entering the zone of bigger skies. Only ten miles north, the land would concede to the horizontal entirely and the Somerset Levels would roll out.

As we rounded a bend, the road began to rise. A quarter of a mile ahead stood a red brick house, surrounded by dark trees. Rattling towards it, the building held my gaze. There was an ill savour to the place, a spook house watching the countryside. I felt uneasy as we passed it, a pick-up hauling a bow top, clocked for sure. A little further on, I caught my first glimpse of Gribble's southern fringe, a dark phalanx of trees. I felt a stab of anxiety – how would we be greeted? Drawing nearer, the firs seemed to close ranks, their lower branches sticking out like broken arrows.

Turning down Crooked Lane, I noticed a small, black heap in the middle of the road – a dead rook. I braked and got out and stared down at the bird. It was barely recognisable as a creature of the air. Black intestines wormed across the road and the beak was violently twisted, sticking up like a caudal lure. Joby had once told me that a dead corvid on the road was a bad sign – that to most Gypsies it imparted a single message: turn back. Black birds, he explained, were an ill-omen linked with misfortune and death and were not to be ignored. I remained fixed on the dead rook. The iridescent feathers had lost none of their lustre. But I was no Traveller and could read into it what I liked. I took a shovel from the truck and scooped the corpse off the road, laying it in the hedge.

By six o'clock that evening, we had pitched camp. While Pig had dozed, I'd levelled the wagon, gathered some firewood and prepared a fire. If anyone was watching, we'd made our intentions clear. Before supper, I thought it a good idea to take a walk through the wood, to reacquaint ourselves with its particular energy. Calling the dog, I watched as he slunk under the wagon, pretending not to hear. This was disappointing. We may have been camping in a jinxed wood, but he was a slab of canine fighting muscle and needed to step up. I pulled him out from under the cart and had words. As dusk slid in, we picked our way through Gribble. Above, the oak canopy was in early leaf, the acid green filtering what was left of the light. Several nuthatches scurried up and down the trees like blue-backed mice while the bracken fronds remained tightly closed, their sleeping heads like chameleon's eyes. In the glades, a sweep of early bluebells gushed violet. Yet, despite spring's mellowing effects, I wasn't fooled. Gribble's black heart was still there, beating darkly.

On the final straight back home, we hopped over a boundary fence and skirted the edge of the wood, glad to be out in the open. Cutting through a farm meadow, we were technically trespassing, but this seemed a lesser crime than confining ourselves to the trees, not wringing out the last drops of light from the day. The air had that unmistakable quality of spring, procreant and hopeful. Ever since I can remember, it is a smell that has made me happy. I think it is the same for every creature. I closed my eyes and took a lungful, letting every cell sing. But the moment was hijacked by a commotion behind me. Turning around, I watched as a dim russet flare shot from the wood bank, aimed straight for the dog. Pig squealed and set off in alarm, his low pink gut barreling through the grass. I laughed; my little pork scratching, never built for speed, was being seen off by a territorial fox.

Pig traced an arc in the field, the vixen glued to his back. While the terrier tucked in his tail in panic, the pursuer seemed to elongate in flight, a red bullet. The animals performed a perfect figure of eight, before the portly ace banked hard and made a direct line for me. I could see he was spooked. Skidding in behind my legs, the hair on his back was frosted with fright. I remained motionless and watched as the fox kept her line. At twenty metres she kept on coming – when would she stop? At a little over six, she put a brake on her approach and in two more halted, my dark form posing a sudden question: not a tree. Not a man. Smells like a man. Her rib cage was heaving, her red mouth open, the hot tongue hanging limp. It was whale flesh, blubber, sea-meat. But the teeth were all fox, hard, white stones which glowed in the dimsey. The vixen raised her head and faced the black tower of man.

For ten seconds or more her eyes regarded me. Not the quick, bright eyes of nature, but sad, heavy eyes. The vixen wavered another moment then turned and trotted away, until she was gone, a small red flame snuffed out by the coming night. Pig and I were stunned in our different ways. I no longer felt so alone in Gribble, so hemmed in by menace. There was good living with us in the wood, the uncomplicated virtue of a vixen protecting her young. The universe seemed in better order.

Over that first week we slowly reacclimatised to woodland living. Organising the camp seemed to bring out the domestic angel in me and as always during good weather, outdoor living seemed the life. Perhaps it was my imagination, but the bow top seemed to give the camp more heart and my enterprise a little more compass. I'd established a fire pit, and made sure the kettle was always on. I'd also knocked up a fireside bench, a simple piece of forest furniture that seemed a step up from the rounds of cordwood I'd used for sitting on the previous year.

Looking around, the whole set up reminded me of the black and white photographs I'd seen in Joby's book. Charcoal burners and woodland camps are synonymous and the pride I had in our leafy patch mirrored that of the burners featured in the old pamphlet.

Two photographs from the book stick in my memory. The first depicts a Wyre Forest charcoal burner of the 1930s standing in front of his shelter, stirring a cup of tea. His hair is combed back with what seems uncommon care. There is a modest solidity about his home, a kind of woodland wig-wam constructed from poles cut from the forest and neatly dressed with large hessian sacks. Several bottles and a flagon are positioned around the hut's doorframe. Whether the man liked a drink we will never know, but if he was a drunk, he seems a house-proud one.

The other picture shows a man, woman and boy posing stiffly outside their forest tipi. They are regarding the visiting photographer with a certain remoteness as if the stranger brings with him something distasteful, or potentially contagious. Behind them, the entrance to their sod-covered home is hung with a brushwood door. The matriarch is wearing a spotless apron tied around a dark housecoat and is holding a silver tea-pot, as if to say, 'Yes, we're respectable – now stop gawpin'!'

For my part, visitors were rare in Gribble, but my brother did appear with his kids from time to time. While they played, we would wander down the ride or sit by the fire. His life was very different from mine and with three young children to support he had weightier responsibilities. Both he and his wife worked hard at their block-printing business, but he too was a country boy and felt as I did about the woods and fields. It was always good to see him and he clearly enjoyed escaping the smell of printing ink and getting a waft of wood-land air. When he left I always felt a tinge of sadness. We were now grown-up men with quite separate lives, but for a few moments in the wood we had been our old selves once again, two twin boys poking around in nature, eternally joined.

Burn

Between the business of charcoal burning, I turned to other jobs. The pick-up needed attention, the chassis was looking woeful. I'd neglected to seal the underside the previous winter, and rust had got a foothold. A brush over with old engine oil would keep it good for another year. It wasn't exactly deep ecology performing a truck service in a wood, but apart from going out on the road, I had no choice. Driving the pick-up onto some blocks, I placed a tarpaulin underneath to ease my conscience.

Lying under the truck my world shrunk. I gazed up at the underbelly of the machine, slopping sump oil on with a three-inch brush. It had degraded from its original state, the work of lubricating an engine over ten thousand miles reducing it to a thin, carcinogenic gruel which trickled down the brush's handle and over my hands. Lying there, the present caved in, slipped like an old face. I let the oil run and lay motionless, black drip after black drip after black drip.

I had been underground for years. Ten years working the same seam, mining for light, hope, some glittering release. The weight of darkness at times had been unbearable and in that moment I felt it again. I shifted uncomfortably, the woodland floor now cold rock. Poison gas – anxiety – began to leak in. I stayed with the discomfort, tried to weather the fear. The moment was as raw and lonely as it had ever been.

Suddenly, something moving at the edge of the ride pulled me out of the darkness. It looked like a tail feather, some kind of fowl. A second later a white cockerel fell out of the grass and onto the track, like a drunk lurching out of a bar. I watched him in disbelief: a cockerel in a wood – why? I eased myself out from under the truck and walked towards him. It was immediately obvious he was in a bad way. The cockerel sat hunched, his neck limp and dangling. He made no play to escape, he had nothing left. I placed my hands on him, tried to comfort him with gentle words. His beak opened and closed, but he made no sound.

157

He was sitting like this because he could not raise his head, his neck muscles were shot. Around the nape, pin pricks of blood like a dark necklace. I figured he'd been nabbed by a fox and carried into the wood, but somehow got away. The whole thing seemed perverse. Cockerels are the archetypal strutters, proud, vigorous dandies, but this bird was none of these things. I'd never seen a more desolate creature.

I expected him to die and thought it best to leave him. But as I turned, I was snagged by guilt, a feeling I couldn't just walk away. Easing my hands under his warm body, I carried him back to the camp. Climbing the wagon steps I was worried how Pig might react to a lodger, he had become quite possessive of me. As I shouldered back the tarp and the dim light of the wood fell on the wagon bed, the dog looked up, one ear raised.

'Quiet now Pig. This fella needs some rest.'

The terrier's nose worked the air, but he made no fuss. I began to make up a hospital bed, padding out a cardboard box with my jacket, surprised by the easy acceptance the dog was showing the bird. As I placed the cockerel in the box, Pig sniffed at him gently, almost tenderly, his ears pressed back against his head. I wanted to get the bird to drink, so dabbed my finger in a bowl of water and rested it against his beak. He tried some, but alarmingly couldn't swallow. I was sure he would be dead in a few hours. Left out in the wood, he'd be dead sooner. With night sliding in, Gribble's professional killers were preparing to go to work. I wondered if I'd made a mistake, perhaps a quick death was preferable – left outside, a stoat or fox would make sure of that. But I couldn't give up on him, not yet. So I sat holding the box and watched night's ingress, the dark dye seep into the wood. The wind had died and a stillness fixed itself to every tree. Beneath me, in the bottom of the box, I could still make out the white bird, but he seemed unreachable; neither alive, nor dead, but somewhere in between.

I cooked supper over the fire. Dishing it out, I wondered why I'd bothered, the day had fleeced me of my appetite. Pushing the food around the plate I eventually gave up and went to the trunk in search of comfort. Pouring a tot of whisky into a tin cup, I stared into the fire. It appeared a molten ball caught in the black glove of the wood. A breeze danced through the camp and I shivered. I was tired. I necked my medicine and went to bed.

After two days he was still with us. It was as if he was stuck, his spirit waiting for the body to give it permission to go, while some internal mechanism dragged its feet. In hindsight, the best thing would have been to take him outside and end it quickly. I had done this several times with diseased rabbits, and although I never enjoyed killing it was the kindest thing to do. But in my confusion I took him to a vet. We were well acquainted with the surgery, an antiseptic modern block on the outskirts of Bridport. Pig had been patched up there on several occasions, a catalogue of self-inflicted woodland accidents which made his veterinary record read as one elongated mishap.

Gordon, the vet, was old school. Always dressed in a checked shirt and tie, he reeked of disinfectant. And while his manner was headmasterly, I always sensed he was rather soft on the little dog. As I entered the room with the bird in my arms, Gordon looked at me with an expression that said, 'You must be joking.' I did not react and placed the cockerel on the examination table. His neck lowered like a broken toy crane. I took in the feathers, soft as dandelion clocks. They shamed the loveless room. Gordon placed a hand underneath the bird, shifting him slightly and pressing a stethoscope to his chest. Quickly but gently, he began to feel the throat and neck, the bird pliant in his hands. The vet stood up and stepped back, the mouth a thin, dry seam.

'Well, he's not going to get better, his neck's had it.' There was a pause. 'Best thing we can do is put him down.' I felt a small stab of grief. Dying was OK, but in this place? Better all along to have gone in the spring trap of a fox's jaw, than knocked off on a sterile worktop. Gordon scooped the cockerel in his arms and turned towards a door. 'It should only take a few minutes.' As they left I caught the limp head of the bird, took in his eyes. I wanted to tell him I was sorry, but embarrassment forbade it. Five minutes later Gordon returned. 'It's done. His heart's stopped.' Another smear of sadness. I'd only known the bird for a short time but in that moment, it felt like loss. I looked up at the vet, standing across from me. 'Do you want us to deal with the body?' I shook my head, I couldn't agree to that. I wanted him buried back in the wood, away from that awful place.

'No, I'll sort it thanks.' The vet nodded, his face framed with concern. 'You're not going to eat him are you?' The question was at once obscene and utterly ridiculous, but I understood its root. Gordon caught the look on my face and softened: 'He's poisonous now, given the injection.'

'Don't worry,' I replied. 'I'll bury him.'

The vet consented with a nod.

'Just make sure it's deep.'

Driving back to the wood, I considered where I should site the grave. I knew a place under a handsome oak, a little way off one of the central rides. It was a peaceful spot that got the sun most of the day. Nearing the wood, I started having misgivings about the burial. I remembered my vixen and her cubs – I couldn't risk them being poisoned by bad meat. Then there was Pig, the inveterate digger. I couldn't watch him twenty-four seven. We turned off the main road and onto the lane which took us to Gribble. On the crest of the hill stood the spook house. As we came up opposite the gates, I slowed, took in the morbid brickwork and, to one side, a pair of colour-coded bins. I pulled over and sat for a second, the engine idling.

And then, in what felt like betrayal, I jumped out of the cab and marched around the back of the truck. Taking the cockerel in his shroud, I hopped over the gate and hurried across the pea shingle. The black council bin was for landfill. It was empty and there was a quarter of a second's silence before I heard the dull thud. I turned back to the truck as the plastic lid clattered shut, every part of me burning with shame.

Spring passed to summer in the wood and with the birds silent, Gribble felt abandoned. These were old Vowles' salad days, where the stillness and pin-drop quiet gave him fuller voice. I felt my alarm system primed: the lethargy in the wood was oppressive and could drag a mind down. Having suffered for years, I perfectly understood the mechanics of anxiety, the particularly insidious way it can claim territory inside a person. While that knowledge was a powerful ally in remaining well, it was not foolproof. The balance needed to stay healthy and has to be tuned acutely.

In response to the wood's mood I worked harder than ever. I was constantly black, my clothes stained with wood tar and thick with woodsmoke. I'd lost weight, my old belt needing a new hole, two inches from the previous setting. By my rough calculations, I was getting through five tonnes of wood a week, all of it moved by hand.

I still needed to rest. Often, after lunch, I'd take a siesta, pulling what felt like an old body up the wagon steps. The bowtop's interior always felt like a safe haven; beyond its canvas curtain old Vowles could not pass. With its simple bed and long trunk it reminded me of the abandoned shepherd's hut of my youth, a beautiful association which only gave the space more armour. Pig would follow me inside and lie down. With the even sound of his snoring and the zirr of insect life outside, this was perfect peace – better than zero sound, this was silence with a drugged edge.

In these moments I fell into a meditative half-sleep. I breathed into the wood and the wood breathed into me. Fleeting moments of grace visited, like a white moth landing on my skin. I saw my true essence. I was the whine of a hornet passing by; I was the breeze lifting the door curtain; I was the play of light on the woodland floor.

Coming to an hour later, I felt no need to rush. I had no crushing deadlines to meet, I was free. Taking one's time in an oak wood, raking over the embers of a fire, the secret of life seemed so clear. We need far less than we think. We move around too much. Plain, everyday tasks – call them rituals – are what give our lives ballast and meaning. And we are all born with an innate creativity. Pursuing that in some form will make us happy.

The renovation of the cart had been a case in point. I'm no craftsman, but the love I had poured into that process had made up for my shortcomings. While I sat beside the fire nursing a cup of tea, my eyes would linger on the cart's lines, its headboard, the curved, patchwork roof. Looking at the top rails I'd cut and shaped with a drawknife, I had surprised myself; their chamfered ends not vastly dissimilar to those originals crafted by Mr. Small, the master wagon maker. It had been a joyful process, all of it. Even the anxious moments – fitting the new rails onto the iron uprights which ran vertically through the cart – had eventually been shaded out by satisfaction. I still remember the relief of it done and the little jig in the coal yard, Pig barking in circles around my feet.

The storm broke with no warning shot. The afternoon had been unusually still, so much so I'd written in my burning notes: Aug 11. No breeze. Wood becalmed.

Burn

But sometime after midnight, I was woken by a sickening crack. The storm had relieved a nearby oak of a limb. Pig was ruined with nerves, shaking at the bottom of the bed. I tried to calm him, but my mind was elsewhere. No more than fifteen feet above the bow top roof were several tonnes of shifting oak. If that lot came down on us, it was curtains.

As the storm surge hit, the cart became a boat far out at sea. I had been caught once in a Force 8 sixty miles off Ireland – that had been no picnic. I relived it that night: the crack of the bow hitting a trough, before the sucker punch of the next wave, the whip and smack of straining canvas. The cart did all of this, or so it seemed, the hooped roof shaken this way and that. I sat bolt upright in bed, helpless, while all about the storm vented and cursed, as if settling some blood feud against the trees.

Such vulnerability is a feeling we rarely encounter in our lives. It is the sudden and terrifying realisation that you are in the wrong place at the wrong time. We see the horror of this in other people's lives, but it is always at a safe distance through the lens of the news. I thought about our neighbours in the wood. The vixen and her cubs would be safely underground, the badger too, locked down in his sett. But what of the young buck, was he out there, alone, braced in the jaws of the gale? And what of Gribble's birds? I hoped they'd sensed it coming and flown, although any late fledgers in the tree-tops would be smashed to pieces.

The storm had blown itself out by morning. Peering out of our lifeboat, I saw the wood had undergone a sea-change. The trivet had collapsed into the fire and charred sticks were scattered far and wide. Our camp kettle had relocated fifty metres down the track while a groundsheet had eloped and was nowhere to be seen. These were all small personal inconveniences, what grieved me more was the devastation

163

wrought upon the trees. Countless sweet chestnuts thrown at varying degrees, and not thirty feet from the wagon, the amputee oak, its shorn limb lying motionless.

Putting aside my feelings for the ravaged trees, what we now had on our hands was a glut of firewood. I spent the morning cutting up the fallen boughs and hauling them back to camp. It wouldn't be seasoned enough for burning yet, but if I split them now, the drying process would be quicker.

By mid-afternoon I had split and stacked two full cords, just shy of eight cubic metres. I had built them in a semi-circle around the kiln. The timber would act as a windbreak but also benefit from the kiln's ambient heat. Pondering the beauty of the woodstack, I was interrupted by the sight of Bill Cope walking towards us.

'Hello Bill, how's tricks?' The land agent stood at a short distance, surveying the camp, his lean face chiselled with concern.

'Tell me you weren't here last night.' I nodded.

'Fraid so.'

Bill frowned and looked over his spectacles like a school-master observing a very dull boy.

'But it was nigh-on a hurricane. Didn't you see yesterday's weather? It was forecast.' I shrugged, trying to play it down.

'Got no TV here Bill – and before you ask, the radio's knackered.' The land agent shook his head, looking at the wood's wreckage.

'Good God.'

'Anyway, we're all in one piece, fancy a brew?' Bill nodded and sallied forward. As he sat down on the fire-side bench, Pig fussed about him.

'How did the little chap take it?'

'It scared the bejesus out of him. Only getting back to nor-mal now.' I handed Bill a full mug. He blew over the enamel lip and surveyed the old cart.

'The wagon stood up then?'

'Yes,' I answered. 'She's pretty tough.' Bill fixed me with a serious look.

'But she wouldn't have survived a direct hit, would she?' I didn't answer. Pig had by this point climbed up onto the old man's lap and was settling down to doze.

'I've come to say goodbye. They've offered me redundancy. It's time to wrap my hand in.' I let the words sink in. I liked Bill immensely, he emanated decency. He had such a wonderful presence and even when he'd gone his energy seemed to linger in the wood.

'I don't know what to say Bill... I'll – we'll – both miss you.' The old man's form shook in the heat of the fire.

'That's kind of you, but it's time. Annie is struggling at home these days and I'm needed there.' I nodded, there was nothing to say. Bill looked across at me with an extra degree of gravity.

'You need to know that they'll be selling the wood too. Not this year, but probably next. With all the recent cuts the council are trying to liquidate some of their assets. It's short-term gain in my book, but I'm a dinosaur as far as the younger ones in the office are concerned.' He paused. 'Put it like this, it would be wise of you to start looking for a new wood.' I wasn't surprised. I'd seen one of the council farms at Barley Hill fall under the hammer and sensed a change.

'Well thanks for the nudge, Bill.'

Bill stood up and Pig slid off his lap. So this was it. He drained his mug and reached out his hand. It was a good, firm shake, no less than what I would have expected from him. Bill smiled.

'Well, good luck. Look after yourself.' As he turned to go I felt a tightening in my throat. I watched him walk down the ride for the last time. After a few steps he turned around. 'You know there are other woods Ben, happier woods. Go find yourself one.'

16

Since Bill had walked out of Gribble, I'd filled my time burning the last of the hazel, completing the task I'd set myself nearly two years earlier. It was late afternoon and standing in the camp, a mixture of exhaustion and melancholy settled over me. September was a beautiful month, but also summer's last stand. I remembered the same feelings as a boy, looking over the stubble fields which surrounded our farm. Where once they'd rippled and danced, in September they returned a harder stare.

I walked up to the pub that evening needing beer and company. The googly-eyed dragon remained there, simpering above the door. The bar was not busy, only a few regulars huddled on stools. An old man surveyed me from one corner, hunkered over his pint. I nodded at him, but his eyes beat down instantly. I guessed there would be no conversation there.

By nine o'clock, the pub was empty and reading the barmaid's face, it was clear she wanted to go home. Turning out of the pub, I had that sense of wellbeing that good beer delivers a person. It was a clear night and the moon was three-quarters full. Overhead the country lane was an arched roof of hazel, wattle work twinkling with stars. As I walked downhill, a large field stretched away in the moonlight. At random intervals up its centre stood six mature oaks. Their line and stillness stopped me. They were obviously the survivors from an ancient hedgerow which had been grubbed out, probably decades before.

Suddenly, my phone rang. I fumbled in my coat pocket and pulled it out.

'Hello?'

A man's voice was returned.

'Hello, is that Ben?'

'Speaking,' I answered.

'My name's Christopher Wardley, I got your number from my aunt, Elizabeth Cole.' The name did not register. 'She, um, knew you when you lived at the gamekeeper's lodge. I think you were friendly with her husband John.' It came back to me. John and Elizabeth, my old landlords. I used to meet them sometimes when walking the lanes.

'Oh yes, how are they?'

'Good, good...' There was a pause. 'I, er, have some woods over towards Belstone Hill, and hear you do charcoal burning.' My ears pricked up. I tried my best to sound sober.

'Yes, the burning's my summer work. I'm just finishing up for the year over in Somerset.'

'Ah, good, well, I wondered if you'd be interested in coming over our way – having a look at the woods here. The hazel's terribly over-stood and there's plenty of it.' The voice continued. 'What are you doing next week?' I paused. The beer had slowed the cogs in my head.

'Well, I've got a load of firewood to get through, but could come over on Thursday.' There was a pause.

'Thursday's good. Shall we say after lunch? I'll meet you at Greys Yard – I can text you the directions.' I dumbly agreed and mouthed my thanks. The man said goodbye twice, then hung up. I looked around the lane – just hazel and stars.

I sat in the pick-up listening to rain fettling the cab roof. As the weather dug in, the drill on the metal intensified. I had arrived at the yard early, not wanting to keep Christopher waiting. He had warned me the place was a little off the beaten track and wasn't wrong. It seemed the road had lost all ambition of going anywhere significant miles back, but as I drove towards what felt like the edge of something, I sensed a light joy rising. Even under the grey sky, there was something effervescent about the land, something gleaming just below the surface.

The rain persevered, pummelling the windscreen. It had a hard edge to it. In a field opposite, two horses pressed into each other for comfort. The windscreen began to fog, shrinking the view, but I felt a strong sense of calm. The country had echoes of downland and my heart had responded.

My daydream was broken by the arrival of a green Land Rover rattling into the yard. It braked hard and slid to a stop in the hedge. I could make out a figure through the truck's rear window, wrestling with a coat. Eventually, he unfolded from the cab, making sartorial adjustments to a wax jacket that had seen better days. The man was tall with frizzy grey hair. He looked over at me and smiled, raising a hand. I got out of the truck to introduce myself but was beaten to the draw.

'Hello, Ben, isn't it?'

'Yes,' I smiled. We shook.

'Christopher Wardley. Nice to meet you.' There was a pause as he eyed the rain front. 'Rotten weather for a tour.' He quickly motioned over to the green Land Rover. 'Shall we take mine?'

The old truck was an authentic back-country model, full to the gunnels with forestry gear. I climbed in. Christopher got in beside me, plump drops of rainwater beading his brow.

'I want to show you Badgers', he explained, as he reversed the Land Rover out of the yard. This came as a surprise. I hadn't expected a tour of the estate's fauna, I thought we were focusing on trees. I asked if they were being culled in the area, part of an initiative to control bovine TB. For half a second Christopher looked lost. Then it dawned.

'No, Badgers' is the name of the copse. But there's a sett there if you're interested.'

As we pushed through the lanes, the rain and mist had started to clear. Christopher slowed and turned onto a steep, rough track. The Land Rover shook over the stone.

'The old railway line,' Christopher explained, 'closed in '75. Used to run all the way to the coast.'

Rattling forward, I could make out the shape of a Victorian railway bridge not far ahead, an arch of blue-black brick. We passed beneath it and clearing the other side, my eyes fell on a deep railway siding. Beyond that, green fields and further still, the profile of a chalk hill which rose higher than anything else in the vicinity.

'What hill is that?' I asked. Christopher flashed an eye at the ridge.

'Belstone, an old hill fort. Stronghold of the Iron Age Durotriges – well, until the Romans took it. There's locals who won't go over it after dark. Old superstitions about ghost armies.'

I remained held by the hill. A row of limestone blocks jutted out on the seaward flank like molars on a jaw bone, while a long, elegant curve towards the western tip was a beautiful topographical flourish. But there was something deeper there than mere form. Belstone resonated age. It was old old. It felt sentient.

My view of the hill was suddenly occluded by a tall hedge so I looked the other way. In the field opposite, close to the line, a small life form. It was a man fiddling with an electric fence battery. He raised a hand and Christopher beeped.

'Francis Wilde, a tenant farmer on the estate. Those are his sheep.' Spreading across the green carpet was a flock of Dorset Horn. Finally the vehicle stopped.

'We're here.' I opened the door and got out. The land on both sides fell away steeply from the old line, so much so that for fifty yards the track resembled a causeway. As my guide picked his way down the bank, I followed. Sycamore and ash hugged the slopes, both groups of trees a considerable age.

The sycamore trunks were plated and cracked like old porcelain, a pink primer showing through the green-grey bark. Beneath the standards, old mocks of hazel, specimens so overgrown each pole was thicker than my thigh. At the bottom of the bank, a wetland area supported a sullen gang of alder.

'Good wood for charcoal,' Christopher offered, eyeing the swampy trees. I smiled and nodded, although looking at the wet ground, I didn't fancy burning there.

We turned to the hazel. Christopher asked if I'd be interested in cutting it for charcoal. Although I felt the pressure to say yes, I wasn't convinced. Working derelict coppice for the wood alone is a slippery game. If the hazel is straight and the land flat, you might just earn a penny. But this stuff was twisted and tangled and hadn't felt the bite of an axe for perhaps fifty years. To compound matters, Badgers' was wet and steep, factors that would kill any notion of a profit. I put this all to Christopher as diplomatically as I could. He looked a little wounded, but quickly rebounded.

'Not to worry – I've another job down the road if you're interested?'

I nodded, and we turned back up the slope, towards the truck. Returning down the line, I glanced again at the railway siding, now just a bare patch of ground where once it would have been a depot for engines and branch line trains. Leaving the railway line, we crested a short hill which opened out onto a wide plateau of arable land. In the distance, a plume of gulls followed a plough and, further to the south, a ridge back-lit by a luminous glimmer – the sea.

The lane dived down into a combe and we entered a village. A huddle of houses made of yellow limestone faced each other on three sides. Christopher informed me this was the Square. I immediately got a sense this place was different, at least from other Dorset villages I'd passed through. The cars parked outside the cottages were tattier; the verges more unkempt. Faint markings on the lane happy evidence of kids being creative with coloured chalk. The place felt backward in the best possible sense, a throw-back to the villages of my childhood. A time when rural second homes were the exception rather than the rule.

We passed down a narrow lane which dived around a steep bluff. At the bottom, beside a stream, stood a derelict farm. Christopher pulled up in front of a disintegrating five-bar gate. Beyond stood a fold yard running with water, several cattle hock-deep in the clay-brown flood. Behind the herd, on higher ground, a collection of outhouses raised from field rubble. We got out of the Land Rover. Christopher opened the gate and forded the flood by hopping over some river stone. An old man appeared from one of the sheds.

'Afternoon Francis, grim old day.'

The farmer was wiping his hands on a rag and by the look of the grime collecting on it, he'd been tinkering with an engine. Christopher introduced me, although I remembered him from the field of sheep. The countryman nodded, but did not smile. I tipped my hat towards him, conscious he might see the bandless, battered trilby as a sign. The two began to talk, a fencing job that needed doing. My eyes returned to the standing cattle, the flooded yard and its backdrop of dark trees. Constable could have painted this, I thought, a grimmer version of *The Hay Wain*.

My attention veered back to the two men. They were finishing off. We said our goodbyes and once again, I could feel the farmer's eyes on me – was it the Traveller's hat? Christopher and I recrossed the flood and took a hard right, up a rising footpath. My guide explained that at the top there were several Bronze Age burial mounds, hence the hump's name, Barrow Top.

'Need to show you a bank which needs thinning,' Christopher muttered, through the effort of what was becoming a steep climb. The stony path was narrow and grown-in, but you could see it had once been a farm track. Christopher seemed telepathically to confirm my thinking when he suddenly stopped and bent down, his finger tracing a long groove in one of the stones. 'A wheel rut,' he proclaimed, a sign of repeated passing when the track had been used by wagons and carts, their wooden wheels shod with iron rims.

We climbed a stile and stepped into a tunnel of hazel. The ground was muddy and puddled by hooves, I guessed from the cattle now overwintering in Francis's yard. Christopher had got his second wind and set off up the track, ducking and weaving through the overhang.

Ahead, coming down the slope, was a more diminutive figure with what appeared a grotesque hunchback. Shuffling closer I realised it was no deformity, but a faggot of sticks which the person had slung across his back. In the gloom, the whole vision felt out of kilter, as if the hazel tunnel was a wormhole in time and space. What I saw was an English peasant exercising his rights of estover, the ancient law allowing cottagers to collect firewood on a landlord's ground. At twenty metres, another shift in perspective – he was actually a she. I could see the faggot was bound with baling twine, and as she approached the dead sticks were brushing the hazel overhang, causing an eddy of movement. Christopher piped up.

'Hello Mary.'

The woman was indeed tiny, with a thick wedge of grey hair, the shape of a mixing bowl.

'Afternoon Christopher.' The landlord motioned to the bundle of firewood on her back.

'Out sticking I see.' Mary nodded, her eyes raised for a moment. She had a pleasant face, her large brown eyes the colour of the flood water running in the yard. A green bomber jacket hung loosely off her. Despite the padding it was clear she was remarkably slight. Mary motioned uphill.

'Been up on the top checkin' the cattle.' Christopher smiled.

'I see, I see.' There was an awkward pause. 'I've, er, been down the yard talking with Francis. We're going to sort that fence out next week.' Mary did not look up, only giving a slight nod of the head in acknowledgment of the news. I sensed the man was about to introduce me, but the woman cut in.

'Better git on Christopher. Gettin' dimsey. Gotta move them cattle.'

'Yes, of course.' Mary gave the hint of a smile and continued down the track.

We watched her go. There was something kindly and modest in her bearing, a good heart beyond the barriers, I thought. Christopher looked at me. 'Francis's wife – loves her cows.' The comment hovered between profound mundanity and a curious poignance.

We pushed on and in five more minutes summited the top. A sea mist had moved inland and settled on the hill and around us shapes of much larger beasts moved in the murk. I took these to be the remainder of the Wilde herd. I could hear the sucking of the mud beneath their hooves, the sound of their warm, moist breathing. It was all a little unsettling.

'Not much to see today. Usually the views are glorious.' There was a few seconds' pause. Christopher continued, 'Not far now, but keep close, don't want to lose you.' We stumbled over some rough ground. I could make out disc-shaped earthworks, barrows after which the hill was named. Christopher stopped by a hedge, a rough stretch of juvenile sycamore and thorn. Beyond it, perhaps a hundred feet below, one could just make out the grey twist of a country lane. This wasn't a bank, it was a cliff. Christopher pointed to a dozen or more trees which grew out of the scar at varying altitudes.

'All these need to go. Get much bigger and they'll rupture the bank, end up on the lane.' I felt uneasy. I'd done a fair bit of felling, but that had been at Gribble. The Somerset wood was flat, whereas this job looked like it would require ropes and carabiners and far more skill than I could claim to have. Christopher looked at me.

'You're happy to do it?' The idiot in me nodded.

'When can you start?'

'Monday,' the idiot replied.

Walking back to the Land Rover I broached the subject of moving my bow top to the estate. I was done with Gribble and it would be daft commuting if there was a possibility of living there. I understood the question was a little premature as I was still a stranger and felt some awkwardness in asking it, but Christopher seemed unruffled.

'Fine by me – where exactly were you thinking?' I already had one place in mind.

'The siding on the old railway line, just after the bridge.' I watched for his reaction and could see him framing a picture of it in his mind.

'Good idea – when will you be moving?'

'This weekend if that's okay.'

Christopher nodded. I felt relief. Being in the railway cutting we'd be afforded some shelter and if the weather got really bad, we could move in under the bridge. Back at the Land Rover I declined a lift, I felt a walk would give me more time to mull things over. I thanked Christopher for his time, we shook hands and in the dying light, parted.

I tramped back through the village revolving ideas in my mind, slightly dizzy with the speed of events. Little owls called up and down the lane, soft reverberations rippling the dark. In ten minutes I found myself back at my pick-up. As I opened the door, Pig looked up, woozy from sleep. I gave his head a rub.

'Hello boy, time to get busy.'

The dog shook himself and wagged his tail. I started the engine and pulled out onto the lane.

17

Arriving at the cliff bottom the following Monday, I felt vaguely sick. If the scarp had appeared steep from above the previous week, sitting in a deep-cut lane looking up, it now seemed even more precipitous.

There was no point stalling. I got out of the truck and locked up. Looking through the driver's window, I apologised to Pig for leaving him there – I couldn't risk him being squashed by falling trees. Turning towards the back of the pick-up to collect my chainsaw and kit, I heard a toot. It was a tractor approaching, a silage bale skewered on its front prong, fetishistic in black plastic wrap. As the Ford came alongside, the diesel engine rattled to a stop. The cab door swung open. It was Francis Wilde.

'Shady spot you in 'ere – what stops you?'

'Starting work for Christopher up on that bank. Sycamore needs thinning.'

The farmer pulled a face as if he'd found lead shot in his dinner.

'What? Could've asked me first – I rent that land!'

I instantly reddened. Upsetting the locals was the last thing I wanted, especially a man like Francis. I reckoned if you got on the wrong side of him, it would be a hard road back. While I fumbled for words the farmer held me in his eyes. It was as if I was being scanned for authenticity, like a geiger counter sweeping a body for radiation. Suddenly the old man released his silent grip.

'Never mind boy, you git on. I'll 'ave words with Mr. Wardley.' I smiled, relieved but still stung by the hectoring. Then Francis nodded towards Barrow Top...

'Just keep a look out for metal detectorists – not permitted on the Top, 'tis an ancient monument. One lanky prat always there. Gave 'im an earful t'other day. Told 'im if it's old metal he's after, I'd rattle some fillings out 'is mouth next time I catches 'im loiterin'.' I stifled a laugh. That was some dark verse. The old farmer swung the cab door shut, sealing himself in. As he pulled away, I gathered the rest of my gear and headed up the track to the base of the limestone cliff.

I allowed myself a cup of tea, a settler. Looking up at the scar, I figured if I went slowly, I'd be able to make my way across it, felling in stages. What was patently clear, however, was that pressed into the bank there was no escape route if a tree fell backwards, onto me. Deep down I knew this was dangerous work and I was not really qualified.

First, I had to rid the dropping zone of scrub. I ripped into it, processing and clearing as I went, cutting the slender trees into eight-foot lengths. The brash I dragged aside, a natural hillock of waste which I would burn up later. A few sprightly maples were just too pretty to fell, so I pollarded them. Several hawthorns I also spared. Spirited little trees, they were never going to grow to any vast size and shade out the clearing.

By mid-morning I'd coppiced at least fifty metres along the bank and the brash fire was crackling with vigour. I was enjoying the work but in the back of my mind I knew there were stiffer challenges ahead.

I started up the bank along an animal track which traversed the righthand side of the bluff. The ground lacked purchase, my heavy boots slipping on the clay surface. At about twenty-five feet, a line of sycamore dressed the cliff edge. I looked down over the ground I'd worked, took in the piles of cordwood and the brash fire glowing in the bottom. Good work I thought. But behind the satisfaction crept a shadow. Felling sycamore is dangerous. It is a brittle hardwood and prone to split off prematurely at the hinge. Get it wrong and the tree can land anywhere.

I put my saw on the ground and yanked the starter. From now on it got serious. Leaning around the righthand side of the tree I put in the gob cut, the initial incision which determines the direction of fall. That done, I peeled off the tree and stood back. The lean was definitely away from me, towards the void. If there was any risk at all, it was that the trunk could split up the middle if I stalled with the felling cut and the back half of it fly up towards my head. Woodsman call this phenomenon a 'barber's chair'. If it catches you, you are very probably dead. I breathed out, flipped down my visor. Taking my line a couple of inches above the gob cut, I set the saw into the tree, spraying out pale sawdust. I kept my eye on the top of the sycamore for any movement, a shift in the tree's balance. With the saw revving hard I was deaf to the inner workings of the tree, the nascent grumbling which lets you know it is about to fall. I leant in to pinch a couple more inches from the hinge. Then no mistake: the dry wrenching of wood fibres escalating to a searing crack. The sycamore was on its way.

I stepped back as the tree pitched forward, diving into space in what seemed like slow motion. One beat of silence, then two, before the shudder of its deadweight hit the cliff bottom. I stood on the edge, looking down. Below, a cord of hazel had been scattered like cast seed. The shocking absence of sound pressed in, slowly giving birth to clarity. It is a clarity which holds every woodcutter. For a second you feel the power, the frisson of being able to impose your will over much larger, living things. Then there is shame. A proud tree levelled, forty years of growth undone in minutes. My eyes settled on the trunk, the limber boughs, the delicacy of branch and twig. And silence.

I had another cup of tea, gave myself five minutes. Hiking back up the bluff, I considered my next move. Part of me wanted to level the sycamores in one fell swoop; to get the job done before bad luck pitched up. But I knew that would be rash, the dropping zone would be a senseless tangle of wood, difficult and dangerous to work. The right way would be to fell and cross-cut each individual tree before moving onto the next.

It took me the bulk of the afternoon to get through them. While sycamore is soft, processing any broadleaf tree is time-consuming. There's the tension and compression in heavy limbs to navigate, the manhandling and stacking of the material too. But eventually it was done, bar one straggler high up on the eastern end of the scar, a leering, semi-juvenile, full of sap and attitude. I had deliberately left him to last. I refuelled my saw and went to him.

Setting myself at the tree's base, I checked the escape routes – non-existent. I pulled the starter cord and gave myself up to fate. Chewing through the front of the tree to make the gob cut, the chainsaw rattled and spat. Repositioning myself, I began with the felling cut. As the saw came through, the sycamore began to mither. I prepared to step away. But suddenly and violently, the tree split at the hinge and lurched forward. I fell back, rolling my ankle, as a side-root exploded from the bank, lifting the ground around me. Lying on my back, in some pain, I could hear the scream of my saw somewhere below, its throttle pinched on high revs. I stared at the carnage all around. The tattered root, a full hand span in diameter, hung inches from my shin; it was only luck that had kept my leg in one piece. The relief I should have felt was clotted with shock. The power of natural forces had been like a mine detonating. I tried my ankle – tender but not broken – pulled myself up and limped down to safer ground.

After ten days I'd thinned the remainder of the bank. Christopher had blown in to check on progress and seemed delighted with the transformation. The old ground had been liberated from its shadow and rung out more brightly. I stood among the corded piles of sycamore, my reconfigured trees. A deep peace settled over me. Dozens of birds became animate, drawn out of their hiding by the hush. Pig was quiet too, dozing in a sunlit patch of sawdust. For a long while I gazed on the gentle rise and fall of his ribcage, and was made aware of my own steady breath, too.

My mind started to pick over figures. Four cords of firewood, plus the charcoaling wood were my payment. The firewood, sold as logs, would bring in at least a thousand pounds, the charcoal, perhaps half that again. After costs, maybe twelve hundred quid. Not much for two week's danger work. But what did that matter? The whole exercise hadn't been about money, but winning Christopher's trust.

By late October the heat had gone out of the sun. I'd finished the day hauling the last of the felled sycamore back from the cliff bottom and stacked it in the railway siding. It had been a good day, the air crisp and dry, but now the light was slipping away. Sitting beside the fire, my surroundings had a comforting echo. I had vivid memories of spending time in a similar place as a boy. As six-year-olds my brother and I had been free to wander in the woods and fields around our home. We'd spend hours exploring, only coming home when we lost the light. The railway cutting was our secret place, a world beyond the furthest field. Down its steep banks, the modern world was excluded; down there, the air was different. Relieved of its iron and shuffling branch line trains, it was now a green way of silence, a place with palpable ghosts. Where the sway of a foxglove indicated a passing supernatural presence rather than plain breeze. The cutting was a haunt, too, of vivid creatures: the first place I'd seen an adder and on regular occasions a green woodpecker, which rose and dipped down the line.

Through middle-aged eyes I was now looking on an updated version. The Dorset cutting had the same steep banks, the same sense of removal from the world, but also featured a flickering campfire and a green bow top. I wondered what my young eyes would have made of it? A vision of perfection perhaps.

My daydreaming was disturbed by Pig. His bark had a skull-splitting quality. I looked behind me and saw a pick-up approaching further down the line. I got out of my chair and walked towards it. The truck slowed and halted. An electric window buzzed down and Francis Wilde's face mooned out. His eyes fell on the cords of wood, then the wagon: 'Pert little dray you got there – ol' muck-cart in't it?'

At first I didn't hear the question, his tone had so surprised me. Francis seemed engaged, even friendly.

'Sorry, didn't catch you.'

'That cart. 'Aven't seen one of them in years. Used to lug the shit out on the fields when I was a boy.'

'Yes, I think that's what it was used for – well, that and other glamorous chores.' The visitor remained fixed on the tumbrel.

'See you put a roof on 'e. So that's yer 'abitation is it?'

'Yes, at least for the time being.' The old man looked at me harder.

'Gonna git cold 'ere – frost pocket. You'd do bedder in bricks.'

'We're working on that,' I lied. Again the forensic stare and a weighted pause.

'How did yer get on at Barrow Top? All done?

'Yep, finished last week.' I nodded over to the cordwood stacked in the railway siding. 'Twenty six trees cross-cut and drying.'

Burn

The farmer scanned the woodpile. I noticed his eyes, the irises flecked a light green-brown, the pupils almost oblong. Fringed by thick grey curls, he resembled an old ram.

'Probably more work for you round 'ere – Christopher always tinkerin' with 'is trees.' I smiled. Francis looked across to his flock in the adjacent field.

'Right then, bedder get on, feed these sheep.' I nodded and stepped back as the large head retreated inside the cab. He raised a hand and the pick-up crawled away.

Francis Wilde wasn't the only person to pass that week. A couple of days later a light tipper lorry went by, carrying a cargo of willow cuttings. The man driving didn't stop, but the camp was enough of a novelty to make him touch the brakes and ogle. As he disappeared down the line, it struck me there was often some reticence on the part of people to reach across to us. While the bow top was a draw, it also aroused suspicion. If only they'd known I was nothing more threatening than an ex-adman trying to get through his life, more might have come forward.

That Friday, Christopher appeared at the camp. He hadn't visited before and seemed quite taken with the set up. I offered him a coffee and pulled up my best bentwood chair, but declined the seat, preferring a round of sycamore at the edge of the fire. Watching him park himself on the low stump of wood was comical, akin to observing a giraffe sit down on a toddler's potty. I took him in some more. Christopher was a handsome man, lean and definitively aristocratic. A pair of long sideburns ran inward, razored points contouring his cheeks. It struck me they were the only thing which seemed manicured in him and a kind of facial anachronism. While my landlord may have been the height of a Zulu warrior, his sideburns were that of a nineteenth-century British redcoat, the military overlord they had tried to kill.

Ben Short

While we waited for the coffee we talked forestry. Christopher was a fan of larch and Douglas fir, both of which were grown on the estate. He planned to plant more sweet chestnut and pined for Japanese red cedar. I learnt he'd studied engineering at university and had spent time in Africa, working on building projects. In Christopher, the tree lover and engineer naturally coalesced. He not only loved trees for their own sake, but also for their utility.

The coffee pot sounded, liberating a genie of steam into the air. I poured and passed a mug across to my guest. We got down to business. Christopher had come to see if I was interested in laying a few hedges. He explained the estate had some stewardship funding from Natural England and that they were obliged to spend it before the end of the year. I told him I would be happy to have a look. Smiling, he drained his mug and we agreed to meet at the end of the day.

It was no hedge. Sheep could have waltzed through it, cattle sashayed. The problem was that it had been left unmanaged for years. I walked the eastern perimeter with Christopher, lodging notes in my mind. There was evidence of former laying, but many of the old pleachers were dead or dying; dry, purpling husks of wood. Several ash mocks had grown to immense proportions, bloated and unrecognisable. In between it all, a mangy infill of dog rose, elder and hazel; and along the northern rim, a stream. My heart sank. Laying a hedge so badly let go is hard enough without getting wet feet.

Christopher asked me how long the work would take. I tried to sound positive. If I wasn't hindered by weather and went at it hard, it could be finished by the end of November. Christopher solemnly nodded, although I sensed he hadn't heard. Casually, he pointed at one of the field maples growing in the hedge.

'Leave the maiden maples if you don't mind, they're rather lovely.'

Burn

Not the worst crime to be distracted by a tree. And certainly, *Acer campestre* is lovely, one could even say poetic. Bare and leafless it is a scrappy half-pint, but in the autumn it comes into its own, the leaves a dream coat of tattered gold.

I returned to the hedge just before eight the following morning. It was a perfect winter's day, the sky white-blue and the mud in the field entrance glinting with points of silver. Such mornings are the dream of all hedgers: dry, cold and energising.

I got out of the truck and re-walked the hedge line. Blackthorn had encroached into the field, stealing metres. Cutting that would give Christopher an extra acre at least. A handsome cock pheasant strutted about on the far side of the field. I found myself wishing the old bird some luck. With the shooting season underway, it would be a precarious time for him.

That first morning went well. By eleven o'clock I'd laid five metres. I had pinned the hazel pleachers down hard with crooks cut from the hedge. Where they brushed the ground, the bottoms would root giving the plant more vigour. While I worked, Pig gambolled about in the field, immersed in his own game of sticks. I occasionally looked up to watch him. He'd come a long way from the skinny, loveless stray and I found myself smiling.

Getting back to work, I came across a single spindle in the hedge, a small, humble tree, more like a woody shrub. It was not uncommon, but certainly not abundant in the local hedges. Making the pleach down its stem, I talked to it gently. I realised as I laid it down that I loved it, I cared about it, a single quite smelly plant among the countless different species growing in the landscape. Was I going a bit daft? Perhaps there is such a thing as getting too much fresh air.

As the day drew out, I noticed the hedge becoming poorer. The hazel which had provided such good material to lay in

183

the field corner had thinned to virtually nothing. Over three to four metres I did what I could, trying to make something out of such a barren stretch. Packing up my tools at the end of the day, I wasn't satisfied. The laid hedge lacked heart. I asked myself if it was the fault of the hedger, some skill set I'd been lacking. But no, the problem had been the pressure of so many hedgerow trees. They had shaded out the bank and compromised plant growth. I'd been like a drystone waller with a paucity of stone.

The next day, things didn't go much better. A large mock of ash cut into my morning, stalling progress. Sometimes with coppice trees it is a brain teaser. The multiple poles criss-cross, jostle, play tricks and you are forced to work out a cutting order to get through the mayhem above you. The ash did all this and more. Slowly my day devolved from a sincere attempt at hedge husbandry to a bitter tug-of-war between man and tree. A hedger swears a lot. I realised I was beginning to sound like Ralph.

At just gone four and on the cusp of calling it a day, I caught the slow creep of a figure along the field's southern edge. I kept my head down, pretending I hadn't noticed. A minute later, I stole another glance. The visitor had left the cover of the hedge and was now walking towards me. His sheer length seemed uncomfortable in the expanse of the field and I realised it was Christopher. At forty yards, my watcher stopped and crouched down low. I made out a camera. He pointed it towards me and I instantly felt my shame on the lens. The hedge was not something I wanted documented, it was not my best work. A moment later he was upon me.

'Afternoon Christopher.' The man returned a wide, awkward smile, as if his teeth were clogged with glue.

'You don't mind? A few snaps for the parish magazine.'

'No problem. You carry on.' I felt the burn of self-consciousness as the shooter clicked away. I pulled a whetstone from my bag and gave the billhook's edge a few strokes but the action felt overdone. I turned back to the hedge and started to pull over another hazel stick, but a knot of ivy in the top held it firm.

'Let me help you.' Christopher climbed over the hedge to add his weight. A brief scuffle and the hazel broke free. We lay it down. As I flexed a hazel binder across my knee, my co-worker threw in a tangent.

'Would you like to ring? I'm trying to get some new blood involved.' I paused from my work and looked at him, square on.

'What? Church bells?'

'Yes, it's a while since we had a group of village ringers. I'm trying to get some younger people together and thought of you. We've got the heaviest bells in Dorset – could do with some muscle.' I took it as a compliment that he should ask me. It was a measure of trust and, I suppose, a sign he thought I was alright. I weighed it up. As much as I loved Pig, his conversation was limited and my life had, for some time, been more solitary than was perhaps healthy.

'Yes, I don't see why not.' Christopher's normal reticence evaporated and a smile broke across his face.

'We ring on Thursday evenings. Meet at the church at seven-thirty. Some of the ringers go to the pub afterwards.'

'You're on.'

Christopher made his excuses to go and turned away. I watched as his stooping figure receded, slowly melding with the high hedge on the far side of the field. A thoroughly nice man, I thought, but remote. Perhaps it was a bearing he had been forced to cultivate due to his position; to keep some distance from the villagers who were either tenants or employees or both. I could see it was a necessary tactic, but also a kind of curse. I considered my own loneliness, spending long evenings in a railway cutting with just a dog for company. While

Christopher lived in a beautiful Queen Anne house with his family, his was a different kind of isolation and not necessarily less lonely.

Last light had skipped camp as I got back to the wagon. My world had become reduced to an ellipse of dim white light thrown from a failing head torch. Scuffing through the dark, my feet found the edges of the camp fire. It was almost out. I raked the ash with a stick and kicked some charred ends back into the centre. Sitting on the wagon steps I took off my wellies. My socks were damp and wrinkled, as if expressing their contempt at being incarcerated in a rubber cell all day. It hadn't been wet but the exertion of the day meant one would always unpeel, rather than undress. I removed my work clothes, towelled off, shivered. I quickly pulled on a dry vest and long johns. As I pushed my head through a sweater, I saw that the kindling had caught, rousing a flicker of cheer. I crawled up into the wagon and lit a paraffin lamp. Two lines of baling twine stretched across the interior. I hung the damp clothes over them. It was the usual routine. All the while Pig fussed about, impatient for his dinner.

My first priority however was firewood. I collected a bundle of dry sticks from under the wagon and placed them on the fire. The tinder crackled, sending fireflies into the night. I sat down beside the fire to chop more batons. Pig continued to fret. He knew it was his time and brewed a bark. I cut him short.

'Quiet! Wait.' Pig retaliated, jabbing me with his nose. I glowered at him, half-serious. The animal was an irrepressible clown. 'OK Pig, bugger the fire. Have it your way.' I rose and rifled through the long trunk for his victuals. As I prepared the meal, he danced under my feet. I turned towards him with the silver bowl. He was into it before it touched the ground. Like all Bull terriers, he loved his scran.

Burn

I turned on the radio for company. *Just A Minute*'s cool metropolitan banter joined the sharp percussion of ash sticks on the fire and the clanking sound of Pig nosing his bowl around somewhere in the darkness. He reappeared a minute later and stood looking at me, sated. He licked his black lips and belched. I took that as his goodnight. Sure enough, Pig turned and climbed the old wooden hill – the wagon steps – up to his bed.

I stared into the fire. Its glow spread over the near ground, embracing me in its halo.

Tiredness clawed at me. But it was a pleasant fatigue won from the working day, the natural after-glow of manual work. Behind the wagon curtain, the dog had begun to snore. I set an iron pan on the trivet, poured a small pool of oil in its centre and watched it thin as the metal took the heat into itself. The onions fell from the chopping board and danced in the pan. Omelette tonight.

Life wasn't bad. I had money in my pocket and a purpose to my days. But I knew the current situation was unsustainable. I remembered Francis' comment that we'd be better off in bricks and couldn't disagree. Living in a makeshift bow top over winter was just not practicable. I knew if I tried, reality would come crashing down around my feet and with all the positive momentum I'd made in regards to my mental health, that was a risk not worth taking. Some people could do it – I was not one of them. Real Travelling folk are born into it. They have modern caravans, family around them and a tangible community. They are not cooped up alone, in a railway siding, waiting for the morning. I was in truth no Gypsy. And besides, the onions were burning.

18

A cold day in the fields at the back end of the year. Bogged down in a stretch of bramble and suckering willow, the hedge had started to drag. I'd taken five minutes to sharpen a dull chain when I spied Christopher coming across the field, his loping gait accentuated by a pair of orange chainsaw wellies. As he raised a hand, the dog catapulted out of the hedge to meet him.

'Hello Pig.'

The white terrier sniffed at him, his tail a lazy tick-tock. I unscrewed the top of my flask and poured some tea, offering the man a cup.

'No thank you, just had one at the farm.' I nodded and took a sip, having momentarily lost the knack of small talk. A buzzard wheeled above us, calling plaintively for its mate.

'So, all good?' Christopher began.

'Yes, all good thanks.'

'Still in the wagon?'

'Yep. Just about holding out.' A small frown appeared on Christopher's forehead. I felt his eyes settle on me.

'I know of a place going in the village if you're interested – Claypit Cottage – been empty a while.'

I suddenly felt lighter.

'Really? Whereabouts?'

'A short way down from the pub. Next to the old orchard.' I knew of the place, a small stone cottage I'd passed on my way to Barrow Top. 'I'll text you the number of the owner. Do call her.'

'I will. Thanks.' The man's mouth peeled into a wide grin.

'Glad to help.'

Burn

The buzzard had slid west. Christopher turned to go, then stalled. 'Oh, and the bell ringing this evening – you will come?' I held his gaze and nodded.

'Sure, seven thirty.'

With only a sliver of new moon, the path to the church was in black out. In darkness I spent two minutes simply working out how to open the gate, then followed a wide flagstone path to the church door. Pushing it open, I was immediately met with the stock-in-trade smell of every country church, that lean fragrance of ancient timbers, stone dust and heavy vestibule curtains. Since I was little, it always held such a precise odour and in that moment I put my finger on it: *it smelt of time.* Walking over the threshold, I looked up.

Across the entire facing wall, a block-printed motif of holly and ivy, pagan symbols rehashed by the Christian church. I thought of the ivy I tangled with in the hedges, the peculiar tenacity with which it remained fixed, however violently you shook the tree. The religious motifs had the same bloody-minded quality and, over millennia, had clung on.

Out of sight, lowered voices. I rounded the corner and came upon at least ten pairs of eyes which swivelled towards me. At the back of the group stood Christopher.

'Ah, glad you could make it.' I nodded a little self-consciously, never comfortable in the limelight.

'Evening.'

A murmur was returned across the space. I picked on several faces, but they seemed unwilling to meet my eye. Bar Christopher, I recognised only one other, the man I'd seen driving past our camp with his cargo of willow. He raised his hand with a polite, if contained smile. It struck me he was bigger than he'd appeared behind the wheel, a bit of a unit. He had a floppy grey fringe which fell down over a pair of round spectacles and could have been William Butler Yeats's heftier half-brother. Christopher piped up.

'I'm afraid it's a washout tonight. Had a death in the parish. Ringing's cancelled.' This was something I later learned was always observed. Yet this deference to parish sensitivities did not mean the whole evening was shelved. While ringing was deemed disrespectful, drinking was sacrosanct. A voice emerged from the group; it came from a short, brusque young man who was already putting on his coat.

'Right, who's wantin' a drink?'

As we left the church, collars were pulled up against the cold, a couple of cigarettes lit. I felt a lightening in the group. Subdued church voices became more animated, a mix of broad Dorset and English public school. The most voluble of the group seemed to be the young man who'd first got the group moving and despite his age, appeared to carry an odd seniority. It was too dark to see much but I noticed he moved awkwardly, as if stricken with sciatica. It was the classic sideways crab of an old farmer.

I slipped in behind to eavesdrop. The young man was regaling two other ringers with details of the deceased, an octogenarian who'd fallen off a stepladder while pruning her roses. There was a journalistic brio to his report, and I imagined him a well of village gossip. His commentary was punctuated by frequent pauses as he pulled heavily on a fag.

We reached the pub. The Farriers Arms was an unpretentious Victorian building built of brick and limestone block. Under the glare thrown from several exterior wall lights, it had all the warmth of a maiden aunt. We pushed through the front door and I hung my coat on a low brass hook, Christopher tapped me on the shoulder.

'What are you drinking?'

'Lager please.'

Burn

The bar was a long sweep of varnished wood which ran down one side of the room, enough space, I estimated, for two dozen drinkers. My immediate impression of the pub's interior was a bit like its outside – inoffensive, workaday, but a bit short on charm. The walls were clad in vintage tongue and groove which had been stripped and heavily stained, making the wood appear a tacky burnt orange. The only distinguishing feature was a narrow band of thatch running the entire length of the bar, an agricultural reworking of the beach bar aesthetic. The original colour of the straw had been transformed by decades of tobacco smoke to a used, teabag brown. I noticed several places where the material had been scorched. I later found out this was the doing of an eccentric local, an ex-naval officer who necked pink gin and found it amusing to set fire to the thatch so he could watch the barmaids get on a wiggle.

I looked back at the bell-ringers. It seemed a split had developed, several of the group had moved further down the bar. Two sat on bar stools – one of them the willow man – while the rest remained standing. Their voices and laughter had an easy confidence about them. To a man they looked like artisanal types, the sort who shun a salary and a weekday suit. Closer to me the second group were getting stuck into their pints. Their talisman seemed to be the young farmer, who was leaning against the bar, pressed in closely to a mate. The vowels rising from this group were far broader, hints of old Dorset dialect rung out. I studied the leader. He had a soft, pink face fringed with blonde hair. Looking at him, I couldn't help thinking of a choirboy. But the boyishness was offset by a hard, contrary mouth and a well-developed beer gut which left the shiny chorister stained, as if harried by work and drink and years.

His mate was a short, breezy character with a seamy brow and dark, cropped hair – I put him at about fifty. He had an old-time face; the sort of physiognomy reminiscent of a First World War Tommy. There was a guileless honesty in it, that rare look one hardly encounters these days – worldliness and vanity has bred it out of us. While the ruined choirboy ordered drinks, his right-hand man doled out the pints.

Behind the pair stood a tall, wiry creature with red hair and a patchy beard, his long face verging on malnourished. As the short man passed him a half of lager and he mouthed his thanks, I detected a slight foreign accent, German, perhaps. Pressed into the corner of the bar was the only female in the group, a big-boned woman in her thirties. She had a clear, honest face, the sort that blushes easily. A pair of thick bottle lenses sat on her nose, the whole arrangement framed by a short bob haircut. South of her neck was a gargantuan bosom and further still, strong thighs housed in pale denim. I noticed her gaze levelled at the choirboy leader and behind the glasses, her eyes had gone soft. He was in the middle of a joke, and catching bits of it, the sort that wouldn't go down well in liberal circles. As he delivered the punchline, the group fell about, but rising above it all was the woman's shrill titter. It had the cut-through of a hen-night bride tanked up on cider and black. Christopher appeared beside me with a pint. He motioned towards the pub jester.

'Roly Grist. Always good for a laugh.' Christopher passed me the lager.

'Cheers Christopher.' The man leant in.

'Call me Christo – everyone else here does.'

I nodded and watched as he veered back to the first group which had decamped further down the bar. They appeared a monoculture of age, race and possibly political bent. I later learned they all rented workshops off the estate and had lived and worked under Belstone for years. Why they had all gravitated here I did not know, but I guessed it was something to do with Christopher's reputation as a benevolent landlord;

one who had a soft spot for all those that made a living with their hands.

I was drawn from my thoughts by a rising clamour. The young woman had just let slip it was her birthday and Roly had not hesitated in ordering a round of whisky chasers to celebrate. The woman, whose name was Helen, was clearly uncomfortable in the spotlight and had shrunk into the corner, squirming. Roly began teasing her, guessing her age. He started low, throwing twenty-six into the ring. She burned up. He chucked twenty-eight at her. She reddened some more.

'Come on Helen you can't be more than thirty!' insisted Roly, the rest of the group getting behind him. Helen shook her head, grinning self-consciously. Roly spat thirty-two.

The girl's shoulders rounded and her knees crept inwards.

'Stop teasin' me you girt clown. You know I'm older – look at my lines!' Helen pulled off her glasses, pointing at faint seams of age around her eyes. At that moment the short, dark fellow cut in.

'Don't worry my love. Just take off that bra and you'll soon straighten out those wrinkles.' The whole group ruptured, Helen's face, purpling.

'Stop it! I'll wet meself!'

The short, dark man turned towards me. He looked down at my half empty glass.

'We're 'ere to drink, not shake 'ands with it! You wan' another one?' I felt suitably reprimanded.

'Er, yes, thanks... Didn't get your name.' The question stilled him. He fixed me with his brown face-marbles: 'Brian Marwood.'

It was the best sort of evening, a kind of pub ambush. By the end of it we were all reeling, bar Roly who seemed impervious to alcohol. Brian, too, seemed to possess an impressive capacity, but a hairline fracture in his eyes suggested the whisky had made a dent. I looked over at the other ringers.

The red-bearded half-pinter had vanished, while down the bar, William Butler Yeats's half-brother was still hunkered over his beer, slurring some point of sheep husbandry with another man. Christopher stood behind them all, swaying. I noticed Brian was watching him. The small, dark man caught my gaze and leaned in.

'Look at Christo, poor bugger. Don't know if he's on foot or horseback.'

The hedge was finished by the first week in December. Christopher seemed pleased. I sensed he knew the job had been a bit of a hospital pass and was just happy it was done. I'd also made progress on the domestic front and had contacted the owner of Claypit Cottage. She had seemed pleasant enough and explained I could pick up the key from The Farriers as she was currently away up country. It was the sort of arrangement I liked, simple and trusting.

The cottage sat on a quiet bend in the lane, on the eastern edge of the village, just a short walk down from the pub. The back entrance was a plain plank door, and set in the bottom, I noticed a plastic cat flap. I put the key in the lock, turned it and the door swung open. Across the threshold stood a modest kitchen, its floor a beige linoleum and screwed to the ceiling, a single strip light.

Ducking through the doorway and into the next room my eyes fell on an even more spartan space. No carpet, no rug, no floorboards, just a twelve-foot square of concrete. Any potential warmth in the place was suggested by an ancient inglenook fireplace, its heavy oak lintel warped and cracked. I noticed Pig had picked up a scent along one of the skirting boards and was pressing his nose against the old gloss. Perhaps he could smell the cat? I just hoped it wasn't rats.

I ducked down and turned up a short, narrow run of stairs which led to a tiny landing. Off it, two small bedrooms and a bathroom. The bath, sink and toilet were a tart 1970's lemon – funky in an odd kind of way. There were night storage heaters on the bedroom walls which were less pleasing – I wasn't keen on being mugged. I figured my best bet would be to live downstairs, put some rugs down and try and keep the fire going around the clock. It wasn't as if we were short of logs.

I went downstairs and stood in the centre of the concrete patch. On one of the deep sills sat a telephone. It had a line. I called the woman back, asking what she wanted for rent. Four hundred pounds a month was her answer. A pleasant surprise – I'd expected more. I paused, intending to haggle, but thinking I'd be lucky if she'd accept less. The line crackled and the woman's voice returned down the phone.

'OK, three fifty.'

I smiled. The power of silent barter. The owner confirmed she'd send a tenancy agreement in the post, but didn't mention a deposit. It all seemed so breezy. I asked when I could move in. The woman replied whenever was convenient. I paused, gritted my teeth, and suggested now. 'Don't see why not,' came her simple reply. I stood grinning in that cold room. All I could do was thank her. She told me it was Christopher I should thank – he'd given me a favourable reference.

We moved into Claypits the next day. I didn't have much stuff to furnish the place, most of the furniture from my London years long gone. But my brother had looked after a few of my old possessions and I called on them now to make the cottage more homely.

A primitive wooden armchair found its place next to the fire. I had bought it years before in a junk shop off the Essex Road. It had a thick green seat and a wonky, rounded back inset with fine spindles. I also hung a couple of rugs on the walls and rolled out some carpet underlay on the concrete floor to warm the place up. The underlay I'd salvaged out of a skip. It was made of furrowed black rubber and, spread out across the floor, reminded me of the fields of tilled black earth I'd seen in Fenland.

The kitchen doubled as a workshop, chainsaw parts and tools scattered around. I hung my pots and pans off brass hooks screwed in the ceiling beams. Their blackened sides and bottoms, charred by the flames of wood fires, whispered the truth that although we were now in bricks, we were essentially still camping.

One final survivor from my London life had made it this far: an oil painting of Somerset, done in 1957. The thing was like an old friend and never failed to give me comfort. It depicts a squally late afternoon in March, a dyke animated by the liquid fleck of a passing shower. The palate is subtle – grey-blues, clay reds, dull greens – and thickly applied with a knife. In the foreground, concentric rings from falling raindrops echo out on the water's surface, giving the painting a powerful geometry, while in the far distance, a ridge is rendered blue-grey under the advancing storm front. The painting resounds with a powerful melancholy, but that is not the conquering emotion. Hope sings in it from a thin seam of white light picked out along the horizon. Looking at it, as I did every day, it was on that glow that my eyes always settled. Love resided there. Some call it God.

With our domestic situation better served, I turned my attention to wood. I had, for some time, suffered a nagging feeling my stockpile of charcoaling material for the summer wasn't enough. I had mentioned this to Christopher who'd kindly suggested another patch of woodland on the estate which could provide me with the shortfall. It went by the name of Rag Copse.

I visited the wood on a bright, cold weekday. It was only a short drive from my camp on the railway line, accessed by a narrow farm track which ran steeply uphill, directly off the cutting. At some point further on, the track reached a solitary cottage. I never got that far, but it was by all accounts a lonely spot, one that would be all the more desolate now since the tenant, the estate's gamekeeper, had recently died.

Wending my way up through the trees, I reached the top. Rag Copse was a narrow splinter of woodland connecting a higher lump of ground to the east with a shallow escarpment of pasture, running west. Inside the copse, pale columns of ash dominated, while a tangle of hazel claimed the under storey. Clematis vines hung in the coppice trees and cob nuts littered the ground. Picking one up I noticed the contents had been burgled. A smooth circular incision in the shell told me there were dormice about.

The area I was planning to cut was at least two acres in size. It had never been proper hazel coppice – nothing like the dreamy coppice plots found further east – and much of the hazel was in poor condition, the underwood suffering from a lack of light. It was the right thing to coppice it, but part of me also knew that without proper deer fencing, the regrowth from the stumps would be decimated. I could lay brash over the mocks to make it harder for the fallow to claim their free meal, but that would only go a small way in protecting the coupe. I had the pressure of making a living and was aware it wasn't a perfect solution.

My head ran through a list of works. At least two-thirds of the large trees would have to be felled to allow enough light for the hazel to regenerate. The ash grew to perhaps sixty feet and would provide me with first-class firewood which I could sell the following winter. Again, I wobbled between conscience and my yearning for more wood. I knew that the right thing to do – the correct, long-term approach – would be to fell, coppice and fence it. Wading in with my chainsaw and ignoring that final step would be an abdication of responsibility. I wavered, knowing I couldn't afford the cost of deer fencing, and that the right course was to walk away. I am not proud to say I fell on the side of money.

Beyond the practical observations, I undertook a deeper survey. Rag was not one wood, there was a step change in feeling between east and west. Towards the western end was a certain lightness, the copse washed through with sea breezes off the bay. In the other direction, a heavier atmosphere. Locals called this part of the wood 'High Rag' and walking towards it, the airiness of the lower copse drained away.

At its eastern extremity, the slopes of the prow were colonised by enormous mocks of hazel, the biggest I'd ever seen. These monsters had outgrown their identity as hazel; *Corylus avellana* no longer, but vast hulks which had burst the seams of their Latin clothes. I gazed on their physicality, the fluted, silver limbs hanging with emerald moss. The air in the coppice was cold and wired. The hazel, earthed deep in the hill, were transmitting to something far off, something unnameable.

I began cutting at Rag Copse the following day. As always, the first job was to get a fire going. I rooted around for some dry sticks and spent a few moments nursing a flame. Once the fire was established, I put my coffee pot over the heat and got busy erecting a tarpaulin shelter a short distance away. Five minutes passed and the stove top gurgled. Steam rolled from the spout and into the copse. A fire and coffee. Ritual.

Fortified by two mugs, I ripped into the hazel, hungry for wood. At these times it is never one's impulse to consider the amount of work one is committing to, the mind is too full of wood-lust. One's body chemistry soon makes the adjustment, however. When all adrenalin is spent, a clearer picture is revealed and the eternal truth booms loud and clear: cutting over-stood hazel is a beast of a job.

Throughout the day I would take short breaks to refuel myself and the saw. I would also tend the fire – it was important that it never died. To look up and see woodsmoke was to give one heart. It was evidence of life, of a kindred spirit that would stay the course, something affirming and good among the cold, damp carnage of sticks.

Cutting each mock, the poles fell away, pointing out from the centre like star bursts of wood. As I dragged the brash and piled it in long rows, the catkins released drifts of pollen as a soundless green mist. I worked through the copse, dismantling the over-stood hazel and building neat stacks of charcoaling wood, so that the underwood came to resemble an archipelago of timber islands rising from the woodland floor. I was never bored. In a wood you are always watching. A robin monitored my progress and gave me reason to smile. I was visited more than once by a curious hare, a quivering inspector who came loping along the ride. His arrival always commanded me to stop. It was the upright pose and the ears – those long, soft, sensing apparatus. Looking at him, I couldn't help notice the eyes, set so high in his head. They stood remarkably proud of the skull, the dark iris like a black planet hanging in amber space. He legged it when I got too close, burning out of the wood at warp speed, the sort of encounter that makes your day.

Deer were also about. In the early morning I would come upon them as I clattered into the wood. With the noise they would melt away, but come dusk they'd reappear, a dim caravan of shapes moving through the trees. Walking through Rag I would sometimes come across the places they'd lie up, personal, private quarters which I felt I wasn't meant to see. The impressions in the ground were so deer-like, so vivid. They reminded me of a photograph in a book from my childhood which showed the imprint of a man on a patch of ground, daisies and meadow grass pressed in the shape of a head, torso and splayed limbs. Below it ran the haunting caption: 'Impression left by an airman fallen from a zeppelin.' Unlike the dead airman, the animal shapes did not make me linger in morbid fascination. But they did offer a glimpse of the deer's private world and I lingered long on the privilege.

The copse work took me six weeks. Over thirty days of cutting and stacking and only one accident. The morning had been a grisly affair: freezing mizzle and the wood a dull monochrome, while Belstone sulked in cloud. The weather put me in a poor mood and I felt none of the natural joy one gets from working steadily and productively in a dry wood. There are days when you just want to go home.

I'd reached the far end of the copse. The hazel here was thicker and the ground beyond a Hindenburg line of briar and bramble. I waded in and the mocks shook bright tears as I cut them. At some point I pinched my saw and was unable to dislodge it. I quickly reached for my billhook. I'd hack into the hazel to release the tension and liberate the saw. But the billhook handle was wet and slippery and as I cut down the hook bounced off the hazel and lodged squarely in my hand. I looked down to see the curved bill sunk just below my thumb knuckle, the wound curling in a rictus grin. There was no immediate pain, my hand anaesthetised by cold. The cut was clean, exposing flesh-fat, the dull white of a squid ring. Was it bad enough to merit a visit to A & E? I figured it would need a few stitches, but that would mean I'd lose part of the afternoon. I stood for a few minutes undecided what to do.

I had not completely developed the brazenness of Ralph Watts, but in that moment his spirit worked in me and I closed my mind to the idea of quitting. Leaving the saw in the tree I traipsed back to my gear which lay disgorged under the tarp. I had some gauze bandage and antiseptic in a small field kit. Cleaning the wound, I saw for the first time how deep the old hook had penetrated.

If stitches were out I was darned if I knew how to fix my hand. Then I remembered I had some superglue in my tool box. I rummaged through it and found a small white tube among the fluff and chainsaw files. I ran a thin line along the edge of the wound, then pinched it shut. After five minutes, human skin had bonded. I wrapped it in a bandage and tied the ends. Working my hand in and out of a fist, there was no hint of red, no seepage. I shook my head at my own absurdity and thought of Ralph. He might have smiled.

19

Bell ringing had not been going well. There had been complaints in the village. Brian Marwood had bumped into Francis Wilde the previous week while shopping in Lidl and been told our efforts sounded like six blokes straightening out a plough share with sledgehammers. You could rely on the old farmer not to spare feelings.

The man's hawkishness aside, he had a point. We were a rabble and over the past few months my experience on a bell rope had cemented only one thing – that it was awfully hard. If you'd asked me my thoughts on bell ringing before I'd started, I would have most likely expressed the common prejudice that it was a sport for old fogies, or people of a churchy bent. How wrong can one be? The reality was that to be a ringer of any note, one needed a ton of skill and a heavy dollop of nerve.

I'd been assigned the number five bell, the second heaviest in the belfry. The real mother – number six – was entrusted to Helen. Not only was she physically strong, but she also had experience, having rung at a neighbouring belfry for years. She was always a patient and nurturing presence and during those early days, it was comforting to have her near. For, just like tree felling, when bell ringing goes wrong, it does so with terrible rapidity.

We had close shaves every month. One Thursday evening, the hefty willow man – a certain Jack Windle – was liberated of his specs when a bell rope whipped around his neck, nearly garrotting him. A couple of weeks later, Roly lost control of his bell and was lifted violently off the floor, his ascent only thwarted by Christopher who dived in around his legs, hanging on like a purple-faced tree-hugger. I had courted disaster on several occasions, twice breaking the 'stay', the piece of wood designed to stop the bell doing a full revolution on its wheel, from over-zealous pulling. There are few things more alarming than a bell rope going fully slack above you. Several hundred-weight of rogue metal doing its own thing is no laughing matter.

It was clear we needed some coaching and Helen suggested a man who could help. By all accounts he was well regarded in the bell ringing game, a bit of a fixer. Virgil Judd was a barrel of a man, short and bald with what looked like rosacea, a skin condition which made his face permanently flushed – I was reminded of a gammon joint. Out of the meat feast peered pale, watery eyes. Passing him in the street one might take him for a mild man, but that would be an error. There was nothing meek about Mr. Judd.

One only had to spend a few minutes in his presence to realise he was a man who burned with a passion. Bell-ringing was his life. We forgave him the self-aggrandising tales he could stray into during a coaching session – stories of three-hour peals and world record attempts in which he always emerged the hero. His involvement came from the right place, heart, and that was something you had to respect him for. But beyond this, I found I actually liked him, even if he did pick on me more than most. I was never sure why I was so often the target of his critical eye; I didn't think I was the worst ringer, but then again I certainly wasn't the best. That accolade went to Brian Marwood who appeared so relaxed with several hundredweight of iron on the end of his rope that he might as well have been pulling the light cord on and off in his bathroom. The wiry redhead also seemed a natural. I'd learned his name was Erwin Krause and that he was originally from Hamburg. He had been floating around the West Country for two decades and worked as gardener in a big house down the road.

Thursday evening was bell ringing night. With Virgil in tow, what had always felt more like a social gathering and an excuse to have a drink suddenly turned into something more sober. Our teacher started by taking us back to basics and watched us like a hawk. We covered the nuances of raising and lowering the bells, the fine motor skills involved in the 'handstroke' and 'backstroke'. Like so many things, the art in ringing came from feel. One can intellectually understand the mechanics of what one is aiming at, but it is the magic of muscle memory which takes somebody from a novice ringer to one who does not have to think. Developing such skill cannot be done by short cut and is only achieved by hours on a bell rope.

One evening Virgil had halted ringing to pick us up on a technical point. This had quickly unravelled into another saga of his own bell-ringing prowess, a three-hour peal in Coventry Cathedral ringing two bells simultaneously, after a fellow ringer had fallen ill. We all let it go, giving the man his moment, when the German broke rank.

'This is not relevant.'

For a moment, Virgil looked like he'd been hit over the head with a blackthorn cudgel.

'What d'yer say, boy?' Erwin held his gaze.

'We are here to ring. You talk too much.'

Technically, he was right. But the manner of his delivery was just too direct. We Brits are mostly spineless when it comes to saying it how it is and, while there may be a strength in such straight talking, it didn't sit well on English ears. Virgil blinked and looked at the floor. From the corners of his mouth, I noticed a kind of electrical, pulsing twitch.

I scanned the group. Christopher, always the paragon of good manners, stood paralysed, a man caught between intense discomfort and the natural desire to smooth things over; Brian and Roly were staring at their shoes; Helen, shuttered behind thick bifocals, glowed red.

Jack Windle cut in with forced levity, piping up that it was time to lower the bells and get to the pub – our curfew of 9pm had passed. As we lowered them, Virgil reached a short arm up and gathered his thick, black coat. Remaining fixed on Erwin, he pulled it on violently and turning up the collar strode through the middle of the ringing circle and out towards the door.

To say we were unqualified to ring at our first wedding would be an understatement. Christopher had tried to patch things up with Virgil and left several phone messages but none had been returned. We were on our own.

It was halfway through April and the big day arrived. As the guests filed into the church I began to feel nervous. I'd been assigned the No.4 bell which was notoriously skittish. My usual bell, No.5, had been handed to Jack.

Brian, ringing at No.1, soberly gave the command and we began. Magically, we all remained in time and our usual din evolved into something almost musical. After several minutes, and the church full, Brian gave the order to 'stand', something which always gave me anxiety. To stand a bell is to stop it ringing by finding the sweet spot on its arc, the place where the momentum is just enough for it to dock gently into an inverted position. Achieving this means exerting exactly the right amount of pull on the rope. The command to 'stand' also required every ringer to do this simultaneously, six bells falling silent together. Brian counted down.

'In three, two, one…'

All the bells obeyed and were silent. For half a second I felt rather pleased with myself, a small personal victory ringing out in a perfect hush. But then, disaster. The bell rope started to travel back through my hands, swiftly and horribly fast.

As the bell swung back through its arc, the clapper struck the sound bow; alone, it had a funereal quality. The other ringers froze, their eyes willing me to stand it. I felt myself redden, but tried to remain calm. But just as I thought I'd done it, the bell would refuse the invitation and fall away again. As the clapper struck over and over, my imagination unravelled. Ding! I saw roses in hats and lapels curling from sheer embarrassment. Ding! Images of the Apostles in the stained glass animating – Luke staring at his sandals; Paul covering his face; John the Baptist, waist deep in water, shaking his head and submerging entirely. Ding! The whole ancient fabric of the church cowering in one giant, ecclesiastical cringe. Brian was looking into me now, rather than at me, trying to project all his haptic skill across the six feet of space between us. People in the congregation had started to cough, shift. From the chancel, I could feel the vicar's death stare, see his fat neck pinking above his dog collar. He would be set on his own dark spells.

Salvation came from my left via a strong arm which reached across and grabbed the bell rope. On the end of it, smiling sweetly, was Helen. She stood the bell on the second stroke and the church was silent. Tension released like the popping of a blood blister. I looked over at her, had the strongest urge to kiss her, to plant my lips all over her big, beautiful face. A wedding march wheezed from the church organ and a shy, pretty bride walked through the church door and down the aisle towards her husband-to-be. I hoped they would have more luck.

Early May in the copse. I'd been burning for six weeks and Rag was looking handsome, neat piles of wood dotted between the trees waiting to be converted into char. Pig and I had popped into town that morning to get more sand to bank up the kiln when, arriving back, I noticed Jack Windle's tipper parked at the edge of the ride. Getting out of the truck,

I spied him across the far side of the coppice. He had his head down. As we approached, he looked up.

'Herb Paris, rare.' The man was botanising. At his feet sticking up through the leaf litter was a splayed, four-leaved plant with what looked like a single blueberry protruding from a flimsy central stalk. Jack fingered the specimen. 'Don't come across these too often, a sure sign of old woodland.' I asked Jack why. He explained plants like herb paris, bluebells and dog's mercury were, in the lexicon of ecology, 'ancient woodland indicators'. The reason for this is that they colonise ground very slowly and require long-term, stable woodland cover to survive. I remained fixed on the moist green thing, not knowing what to say. It looked very poisonous. While I could just about call myself a woodsman, as a plantsman I was still a dud.

I changed tack and asked Jack what had brought him to the wood. He said he'd been sitting at his breakfast table putting off going to the workshop, when he'd seen smoke rising from the copse and guessed it was us. He rented the gardener's cottage down by the Manor and from the kitchen window could survey the whole of Rag, as well as a long curving section of the old railway line. Jack said he hadn't seen a burn for a good few years and felt nostalgic for a peek.

For someone who seemed so inveterate a countryman, I was surprised he'd not had a rural start. Jack explained his early years had been spent in suburban Essex but in those days the woods and fields weren't that far away. He described mudlarking on the Thames and perch fishing in old chalk pits, long days out on his bicycle with the dreamy smell of fennel and Alexanders filling the lanes. His great-grandmother had been a Traveller and had hailed from the orchard country around Evesham. There was some Irish in there, too.

Later, as a student, Jack had moved to Kent. He'd poked about in the county's sweet chestnut coppices, rubbed up

with some of the old Wealden woodsmen. He had dim memories of Fordson Major tractors powering belt-driven saw
benches although he couldn't remember seeing any horses.
He described the men, tough characters who smoked Cap-
stan Full Strength and swore like sailors. Talking about the
old days, Jack did confess memory was not always reliable,
but felt in the early eighties there had still been a connection
to something deeper, something more real. While the woodsmen had appeared old-fashioned to him back then, they had
not seemed entirely out of context – somehow the world still
had room for them. I listened, remembering some of the old
Hampshire characters from my childhood and understood
what he meant. Jack mumbled something about modern
society's distorted value system and our dismissal of manual
work. Said the problem with too many people these days was
that they were 'allergic to wood'. I didn't understand what he
meant. Smiling, he nodded to the rake and shovel propped
against the kiln, and murmured: 'Anything with a handle.'

We got to work, shovelling the aggregate off the truck.
Jack seemed to enjoy the exercise and, in ten minutes, we
were done. I'd loaded the kiln the previous day and standing beside it, Jack asked why I hadn't left an open shoot in
the centre, a cavity down which to drop hot embers – after
all, that's how they'd done it in Kent. I explained I'd never
bothered with a central shoot, didn't see the benefit. A cavity
in the stack meant less wood in the kiln which would mean
less charcoal. Instead I'd light a fuel-soaked rag and push it
through one of the air inlets with a stick. Jack said nothing. I
think he preferred the Kentish way.

We let the free burn take hold. Gentle beginnings. Twenty
minutes later a corkscrew of thick smoke lifted into the air.
While I started to bank up the kiln sides with sand, Jack
fetched the kiln's lid, rolling it from its resting post against
a tree. We heaved the lid up, sliding its steel edge across the

kiln's rim, before dropping it down. I set the kiln's chimneys and waited to check the flues were drawing evenly.

Meanwhile, the campfire required nursing, so Jack busied himself fetching some sticks from under the trees. He reminded me of an overgrown boy scout. A neat pile of twigs was deposited on top of the embers and slowly started to smoke – even damp wood burns eventually. Sitting beside the fire, neither of us felt the need to talk. After a while Jack trod the trivet low into the embers and put on the kettle. Pig had grown weary of his game of sticks and had returned, lying down to sleep at my feet. We wet the tea and talked some more. By the third cup, Jack said he couldn't put the workshop off any longer and left me to my burning. It would be seven hours before I needed to change the chimneys so I woke the dog. We could do with a walk.

We headed down the landward side of Rag, through hangars of ash and oak. Pig gambolled ahead, occasionally stopping to check I was following. The slope was covered in bluebells and the white stars of flowering ramsons, the air giddy with the smell of garlic. In the softness of May the old wood had an enchanted feeling. I imagined Pan kicking back in the crook of a tree, a hairy leg swinging lazily in the air. Across the slope, I could make out animal by-ways, paths of badger and deer. A crab apple flashed its knickerbocker blossom, all Moulin Rouge. We passed from wood to field and hugged the hedge line up towards the lane. Drifts of downy white seed from hedgerow willows carried on the wind, as if piloted drunk. Halfway up, a blackbird fired out of the hedge through my bow wave of air. I watched as he flew on an arc before turning back and repeating the sortie. Was this a game or a warning? A few yards further on, a chaffinch shot from cover and flew about my face like a catatonic hummingbird. It was nesting season and the parents were edgy.

Turning up the lane towards Belstone we passed Brian Marwood running the first cut of silage back to the clamp at the dairy. He waved from the tractor's bowl-like cab, and dressed in an orange tractor suit, I thought of a goldfish. His dog, a tatty Patterdale, was pressed in beside him and went berserk on seeing the stocky white terrier at my feet. But over the sound of the engine, the dog's vitriol was silenced, just an angry black mutt in a vacuum. Territorial birds, territorial dogs.

We cut up an old chalk track which climbed onto Belstone. I looked up at Belstone's southern face to clumps of gorse in flower. The bushes crackled from the ground. They resembled petrified explosions of ordnance, as if Belstone was being shelled by distant artillery. Among these odd vegetable eruptions, the flowers glittered gold, precious mineral nuggets thrown up by the shelling. We reached a wooden gate on the path, a portal onto Belstone's higher slopes.

Pushing through we walked higher. Cuckoo flowers danced on the verges. I took a deep breath. Chalk grassland, my soul country. The feelings welled up, the land was just too beautiful. I was immediately back in the summer of 1976, a five-year-old idling on the top of Old Winchester Hill. The sound of skylarks and day trippers blissed out on the view, a table of yellowing wheat which rolled out beneath them. I remembered skinny young men in denim flares, arm-in-arm with pretty girls. In the car park, a pink ice-cream van and a blue Beetle.

I'd been daydreaming and lost Pig. I turned around and saw his four feet in the air, just visible over a hillock. The dirty tyke was rolling in something. I called him but he ignored me and continued twisting in the grass. I called again and he momentarily stopped, glancing sideways, before giving it some more. I walked up to him.

'You filthy animal!' Pig rolled upright and shook himself, not caring a jot. Dark streaks smeared his back making the thick ridge hair stick up as if styled with some foul-smelling gel.

'Get on!' I ordered, and the dog trotted off a short way, before shoving his nose in the wind. I looked down at the dark fecal mounds in the grass, tarry black swabs like oil paint, the end of each turd pinched, as if severed by a cigar cutter. Badgers have strong jaws. It seemed their arses were equally formidable.

We reached the top, standing on a raised bank, the last of a concentric ring of earthworks encircling the hill. They had been dug by people using antler pick and wooden spade, thousands of tonnes of soil shifted to create the defensive ditches and ramparts that would protect the hill-fort from hostile attack. To realise such a thing with so primitive a technology was awe-inspiring – you could almost say they had moved mountains.

Inside the earthworks lay an expanse of flat ground, perhaps twenty acres. This was the old Iron Age camp, now only gorse, wild flowers and a few scratchy thorn trees inhabiting the space. The hill was all earth but its ruling element was air. The thorns were full of it, the orchids danced in it. I stood and looked out into a dramatic gulf of nothingness that found landfall eight hundred feet below. Beyond, a land of tumps and bumps which was ended in the west by a stagger of blue sea cliffs and a silver sea.

To the south, Rag Copse. The recent thinning had let more light bleed in from the seaward side, so it now appeared covered in a crackle-glaze of gold. Through the trees a white mist rose – the smoke from my kiln. I stood on top of the hill a while longer, absorbing the landscape and its thousand parts. Here the land was loaded with visible history: valleys and green funnels scored into the earth from glacial movements before time was even a word; tumuli-littered ridges, the Bronze Age burial mounds of great men and women which had been built in the high places for all of their kind to see; and wide steps in the hills, the medieval plough lanes of peasant farmers who had cultivated these slopes in an attempt to ward off famine. We talk of places being loaded with history, as if history is a deadweight, but I found no heaviness there. Like the smoke which lifted through the trees, the past simply rose off the land, joyful and weightless. I stood on the edge looking out and felt my own density lift. A joy rose in me – intense feelings of love and connection – which I could hardly contain. I burst like a seed head, sowings of memory and gratitude scattered. It had always been about the land, ever since I was a boy. I could never feel alone here.

The weather held for the first part of the summer and we spent all our time out of doors. I'd occasionally pop back to Claypits for a bath but my heart remained in the wagon. With the sustained good weather and people in the mood to barbecue, there was pressure to keep burning. I'd also started doing a stall at Bridport market every Saturday. Selling direct to the public and losing the middle-man meant a better return, and while this was the main reason for doing it, there was also the sociability and buzz of a market town on a Saturday, a pleasant change from the wood.

Naturally, I was there to sell charcoal, but also felt there was an opportunity to educate the public on why they should buy British. Beyond the direct consumer benefits – the wonderful heat performance, the absence of chemicals – there was also the positive ripples that choosing native charcoal brings to our woods. A charcoal burner cutting over stood hazel will not only be returning a derelict patch of woodland into the coppice cycle, but his or her intervention will also create new habitats for a host of woodland species, including dormice and rare fritillary butterflies which will thrive there.

Despite these glaring positives, I knew cold lecturing rarely works – target imagination first, then the public might listen. I started with branding. My brother had created a new logo for me, a beautiful block print of an adder in a box. His inspiration for the design had been the charcoal burners in Arthur Ransome's *Swallows & Amazons* series, a half-feral father-and-son team called Young and Old Billy, who tend their burns in the silence of the fells. The two men keep a viper in a wooden box lined with sphagnum moss and when they are asked why they have the snake, Young Billy replies 'For luck.' Old Billy adds that his own father had always kept an adder and 'he was burning on these fells a hundred years ago.'

Printed on the simple brown sack, the new logo looked perfect and with the talisman serpent gracing my bags, I felt confident my enterprise would be a success. Turning the screw some more, I towed my bow top into town. The wagon was a statement, a challenge to anyone with feeling not to have their romance pricked and be drawn to the stall.

Plenty took the bait. They would gaze on the bow top and the brown sacks and ask how the charcoal was made. I impressed on them the multiple strands involved in its production, the particularly beautiful way in which the process enfolds the whole year. Barbecues might be a summer thing, but the material garnered for my kiln came out of hedges and woods, cut during the cold, dark months when the sap was down.

I felt I was getting through, but the charcoal message always seemed trumped by the simple presence of the bow top. On more than one occasion I had people queuing to go inside. They'd pull back the canvas curtain and peer in, shaking their heads as if gazing on something infinitely beautiful. A good number said they would live like that too, if it wasn't for the mortgage or kids. I explained the great rewards I'd felt from simplifying my life and living closer to nature. They hung on every word. A few poor souls actually looked wounded, as if I was offering them a vision of something they desperately wanted, yet knew they could never have.

Yet the novelty of such a ready audience began to pale. I started to feel uncomfortable and realised I was spouting too much sugar. I had a responsibility to give them the bad as well as the good, so tried to provide some counter-narrative, a more balanced picture of the challenges one faces when living this way. I talked of the physical realities of the work too – scalds from the kiln and the numerous septic cuts from laying blackthorn hedges, and they would nod, and murmur a yes, but I could see a glaze had fallen over their eyes, and their grins harden. They did not want the truth, they wanted the fairytale, and like so many others in town on a Saturday they were shopping for a quick hit, something cheap and easy to fill the void. The whole truth was not in their budget.

20

I packed up the kiln, another charcoal season done. Rag Copse had been transformed. Eight months earlier it had been a derelict patch of forgotten woodland. Now silver-grey pillars of ash lifted from a woodland floor relieved of its tangle; proud and spruce, it seemed the copse had graduated into something more noble. Even the winding drifts of brash and the scorched black circles which marked my old burning places had an aesthetic rigour about them.

I'd agreed to buy the standing wood from Christopher and we'd spent a morning measuring and marking the trees to be felled. Nearly ninety were designated for the chop. Christopher tagged the doomed ash with a blaze of red from a forester's aerosol, soberly and deliberately, like a Brahmin marking a Hindu brow.

The following week I set about felling them. I did not rush. The ash is an explosive tree and among woodsman is referred to as a 'widow maker'. The reason for this can be found in the extraordinary elasticity of its wood fibres. Ash's ability to flex and its tolerance to vibration accounts for the reason it was always the favoured timber for tool handles. But what are useful qualities in a billhook grip, are less attractive in a tree you're squaring to fell.

With this in mind, I went very soberly from tree to tree. I also had a clear picture where I wanted them to drop – the brushy tops away from the woodland ride, so the trunks could be more easily extracted. But being exposed on a hill, most of the ash had been influenced by the prevailing south westerlies and grown at an angle counter to the direction in which I wanted them to fall. Such is the wood cutter's lot.

Copse work is rarely easy, there are always snags. Happily, most woodsmen cultivate a sanguine acceptance to the niggles which dog their day. It is best that way. Getting frustrated and rushing will often only end badly.

Over several weeks, the trees generally fell where they were supposed to, bar half a dozen refusers. Looking down at their stumps I noticed I had a tendency to overshoot things and leave only the ghost of a hinge which wouldn't pass muster with a forestry examiner: 'could do better' rung in my head. Still, the trees were safely down and I now had close to a hundred cubic metres of firewood lying on the deck. The next challenge was moving it. I had considered asking Brian if he'd like some cash-in-hand work; he had his own forestry tractor that would easily do the job. But there was also a man in the village who did horse-logging. Christopher had mentioned him before in passing and while I knew Brian and trusted his abilities, I was curious about the man and horse.

A Friday night in The Farriers. The crush of early evening drinkers had thinned and by nine o'clock there was only a smattering of regulars. Ordering a pint, I settled on a stool, happy to take the weight off my feet after what had been a heavy day. A little further down the bar sat two men. They'd both scrubbed up for the pub in the way most working countrymen do; clean collars rising to red faces, raw from weather or sun. Looking down, I was somewhat less spruce. I'd often go straight to the pub in my work clothes, a jumper misted with sawdust, trousers stained by chainsaw grease. This, I knew, was a kind of affectation. Coming into the pub literally covered in the residue of my work, was – at least in my mind – a statement of authenticity. But the uniform was not necessary and pointed to what was still, in some ways, a fragile ego. Despite the distance I'd travelled from my old life, and the time I'd spent in the woods and fields, there still remained a part of me which felt I had something to prove, evidence I was for real.

I took a sip of lager and swivelled my eyes down the bar. The man nearest to me was swarthy and lean with tight, black curls on the turn to grey. The other fellow was younger, although he was already losing his hair. He was a big lump with eyes that possessed a striking vacancy. I watched as he tipped back on his stool. He started to slur.

'Last night I killed a shrew with a chair leg.'

The older man pulled back from his pint.

'*Why?*'

His mate looked dully forward.

'They're venomous.' The wiry man's brow crinkled.

'Venomous!? Maybe to an earthworm, but not a great lummox like you! You can't be murderin' shrews, they're protected by the 1981 Wildlife and Countryside Act.' The callow, grey eyes showed no emotion.

'The missus thought it was a rat.'

The older man sneered.

'A shrew looks nothin' like a rat. And why a chair leg? Bit heavy-handed i'n't it?' The killer pulled an empty grin and shaped to get up.

'Looks like I been told.' I watched as he drained his pint, and with a 'Night all' left the bar. Keeping my head down I took a long pull on my lager. Suddenly the other man spoke. I realised he was talking to me.

'You're that charcoal burner.' I looked over and nodded, word had obviously got round. 'Seen your smoke from the village. Do it pay good?'

'When the sun's shining.' I replied.

'Never tried it meself. Done plenty of forestry work, mind. Felled all that conifer on Poorstock Common a few year back. Took it out with the 'orse.' My mind cracked a smile — so this was the horse-logger. The man continued: 'Were a poor job, ended up well out of pocket. They'd wanted a price before I started. Impossible to judge. Ended up workin' seven-day weeks and the 'orse was knackered.'

I expressed my sympathy. It's easy to get shafted on woodland work, I'd realised that in my own short experience. Most of the time jobs took longer than expected; there were the perennial snags. Best to load the scales a shade in one's favour when pricing a job, that way you'd hopefully come out of it in the black. We carried on talking, emptied another pint. Gently, I broached the subject of him skidding out the ash at Rag. He paused, rolling the possibility around his head, then said he'd pop up over the next few days and take a look.

Sean Hooley pitched up early the following Tuesday. A twenty-minute scout around the wood and he agreed to do it. He explained that he wouldn't be able to start immediately, he had a couple of pressing jobs to finish first. I asked what he was up to. He replied he was in the middle of a big fencing contract on a posh estate up country and also had a dozen donkeys that needed their feet trimming near Weymouth. Sean, in his own words, was a 'professional dabbler'.

During his working life he'd been a dairy hand, a forestry worker, a fruit picker, a mole catcher, a farrier and a chimney sweep. The farrier work had been the mainstay of his income over the last decade but he said he was out of love with horses having been kicked and bitten so many times. I could see by the way he walked that his body was prematurely aged, not only from the abuse meted out by striking hooves, but decades of physical work. Sean told me he was one year away from fifty but needed a hip replacement. His body was wrecked.

I asked him more about his past. He told me he had grown up on a council estate in Bridgewater. Been into motorbikes and pot. At seventeen he'd left home and done a stint as a tractor driver on a large arable farm in Norfolk. He'd then moved on to work in a dairy but that had ended badly when he'd had enough of the bullying manager and, in his own words, 'lifted him up against the parlour wall by his face'. After that, he'd spent twelve years on the road in a horse drawn wagon. Talking to him, I quickly gathered he'd not chosen the life out of any romantic impulse. The bow top had been offered to him cheap when he had nowhere to live. It was only six months later that he acquired a horse and started travelling around the country, at first fruit picking, and later offering his services as a horse-logger.

But the nomadic life had not been without its challenges. Sean had been young and despite a certain maturity and talent for self-reliance he had always had problems with other Travellers. He'd learned ways of avoiding trouble, but the bow top and the horse, he explained, had always made him a target and the fact he was a non-Gypsy living that lifestyle, was, as he put it, 'the cherry on the top'. They'd pitch up and the most important thing, he explained, was never let them get out of their truck. Go straight over, talk them to death, appear *mad*. That was the only way. If they got out, you'd had it. Once mobile, they'd pick around your camp and take anything they wanted. He'd lost horse tack, chainsaws, even one of his dogs once. There was nothing you could do. Sean grizzled, 'you could be parked down the end of a quiet lane mindin' your own business, but they'd always find you, they're always around.' It was obvious Sean had had a rough time at the hands of some fairly unsavoury characters, but I wasn't entirely comfortable with his generalisations. It seemed the man had long switched off to the possibility there was any such thing as a decent Traveller.

Despite the fact that we both knew woods, we were polar opposites. Sean had the natural instinct of an engineer and tinkered with engines for fun. It was clear he possessed that enviable facility of understanding how things work – stuff I could never retain. Sean always serviced and repaired his own chainsaws, his van too. He'd also designed and made the gas forge which sat in the back of the Transit. This do-it-yourself attitude even extended to his dogs. One day, over coffee, he spent ten minutes explaining how he would always sew up his lurchers when they cut themselves while out coursing – on the road, paying a vet hadn't been an option. He even recalled how he'd once buried one of his old dogs on a roundabout outside Swindon, digging up the central flower bed in the early hours. Talking of the animal he showed little emotion, only commenting that the greyhound collie cross had been an excellent fetcher of hares. I asked him the reason for this and he gave me some poacher's wisdom.

'A pure-bred greyhound will seldom catch a hare; a good lurcher will, because he uses 'is head as well as 'is legs.'

Sean had always done things on his own terms and had tried, as much as is possible when on the road, to be self-sufficient. He had kept a box of bantams on the wagon's tail rack, for eggs. And if he stopped near a chalk stream, he would always bait a hook. He'd even knocked up a contraption for making lead ammo for his catapult and would often poach for his supper, creeping around downland copses after dark, no gun shot to give him away.

According to Sean, at one time he counted twenty-eight legs in his caravan menagerie, not counting the two he stood on. Yet he would not give you a penny for art or literature and told me he had no time for 'arty types'. The irony was that I figured his wagon life had been a creative performance in the most colourful sense.

Towards the second week in October Sean started moving the ash from Rag. His horse was the same one who'd pulled his vardo around England eighteen years earlier, a dapple-grey cob called Doctor. The beast stood at around sixteen hands with a heavy back end. I was fascinated watching them work together, although I did not get the feeling there was much love there. Sean was hard on the old horse. It was obvious that the animal was looked after – his ribs were well-covered and his coat shone – but emotionally there was little softness. Sean would often give the horse a dig, call him every name under the sun. At these moments the cob's eyes would blaze, and I'd watch him step back, the hind quarters immense.

It took the pair six days to clear the wood, moving the ash onto a ride which ran down one side of the copse towards a field gate. At the end of the job it resembled a river of wood. Sean was as hard as a coffin nail and apart from the odd fag break and swig of tea, would not stop all day. As I watched him, the name of Jim Shady ghosted through my mind, that tea-drinking solitary of the Wyre Forest. Dead now, but another who had understood the art in manual work.

While Sean and Doctor hauled out the ash trunks, I remained on the saw, cross-cutting the timber into four-foot lengths. It was heavy work. Once they were cut and loaded onto the trailer, I'd haul the wood down to the railway siding, and stack it beside my wagon. Processed into firewood logs the ash would bring in a middling profit. But looking at the work done and the work still to do, most people would have written the whole thing off as too much sweat for too little gain. But I didn't want an easy life. I wanted a beautiful one.

Getting to know Sean was part of that rich tapestry. It struck me as both wonderful and odd how we'd found ourselves working together. I thought of the old me, sitting in a meeting in Manhattan, before jumping on the red-eye back to London, business class pampering all the way. At the same time Sean would have been working sixteen-hour days in dark summer woods, felling conifers on piecework, half-blinded by the murk and the sweat. Or on the old common rolling bracken and dodging adders, working till his bones ached. Two worlds that had no right to come together but were now brewing up alongside one another on an ash log.

Sean asked me what I used to do and I told him. He didn't seem fazed. Most in his position would have written me off, cast me as a dreamer on a middle-class whim, but Sean displayed no such prejudice. He always shared his knowledge freely and we went about things as equals.

At the end of each day Sean would put his kit in an old army Bergen and sling it on his back, the orange chainsaw scabbard sticking proud of the top. Then he'd swing a leg over the saddleless cob and turn home. It appeared neither man nor horse was in a hurry. As they receded down the ride, I could see Sean had rolled a fag and was drawing on it slowly. Sitting tall on Doctor's back, to most people he would have seemed a throwback, but not to me. From where I stood, Sean was uniquely modern, perhaps even a vision from the future. I was fascinated by his story and in awe of his self-reliance and speculated the world would need more men like him, perhaps in my lifetime.

The farm track bolted away from the metalled lane and quickly became lost in a fold of hills and high hedges. It was country I'd not yet explored. Christopher had told me the hedge he wanted laying was 'a bit remote'. Knowing the man's talent for understatement that sounded ominous.

After a fifteen-minute drive, the track petered out to nothing. The ground beyond was soft and I decided not to risk pressing forward and getting stuck. Parking the truck and gathering my kit, I headed downhill past a quarry engorged with old farm scrap. While Pig sniffed around a badger sett, I poked about and found two artillery wheels, the same exact five-stud variety as the ones on our wagon. They were too gripped by rust and years to prize off their axle and it pained me to leave them.

Burn

Moving on, we approached a narrow copse. The ground inside was riven by a goyle from which came the sound of running water. As we rounded the end of the wood, I caught the white tip of a fox's brush as the animal sought cover. I stopped and put down my tools. I had always known this corner of Dorset was absurdly beautiful, but this was a different level. The land here was deep and ragged and wild. Across the vale were steep slopes covered in huge grey stones and the relentless march of bracken. To the west primeval alder swamp. Perhaps it was the remoteness of the spot and sense of almost clandestine beauty which made the effect so penetrating.

A raven passed overhead and acknowledged me with a cronk. The noise made me start. I watched as he disappeared over the hill, his wingbeat sounding like a rapid succession of exhalings. Deep silence returned and the craggy sentries of elder stared. I knew the old red dog in the hazel copse would still be watching. Man had been here before. But rarely.

I turned my attention to practical matters. There was immediate disquiet, that low-level anxiety which goes with an understanding of the task ahead. The hedge was long and dark and wide, more like a linear wood. It ran for over a third of a mile and looking on it I muttered to myself the first line in the hedger's rulebook: *Keep your head down. Take it metre by metre. One day at a time.* Sometimes it can be crushing to realise just how much hedge is ahead of you.

Through November and December the valley was scoured by a vicious east wind, a wind that did not care. These were tough days and I often struggled to work as the hazel knocked violently above me. One morning, while I hunkered for shelter, the wind blew harder and meaner than ever. I looked across the valley to the opposite hillside. The oak and ash were being churned by the gale. The canopy pulsated, drawing itself in and out like a lung. I watched, mesmerised by the movement, a beautiful choreography which desensitises us to the forces involved. It seemed the violence of the wind, however, was trumped by the physical intelligence of the trees, which used the gale's strength against itself, throwing the gusts over their backs, like judoka.

Mercifully at least, it remained dry. But through the hardship of those weeks, a beauty formed. Just as in Gribble, I felt a honing of my senses, a sharpening vision. But this time – perhaps because of the season and the character of the land – the focus felt even more pared down. I would be engrossed in my work, bending to find a fixing point for a binder or in the act of cutting a pleach, when the picture of an animal would blow into my mind from nowhere and hang somewhere in that starry space beyond thought. Immediately I'd look up and there would be the creature foretold – a deer or hawk, hare or fox – looking back. These were special moments and happened on so many occasions I could not write them off as coincidence. As the days advanced I became less surprised by these snatches of connection; they settled on me as completely natural. We all have this ability in us, but the noise and grab of modern life robs us of the gift. It is, however, never entirely lost. Given the right conditions, our sight can return.

I had one other visitor during my days working in the lost valley. He appeared every day, over three weeks. At first, I thought I was mistaken. Catching a dark shade on the edge of my vision, I put it down to the black hinge on my forestry helmet playing tricks. But over several days, the sense of something *other* persisted. The strong feeling I had was that it was a man. He would sometimes appear in the morning, but more often towards the close of day, a black scribble of male energy beside me. I had the definite feeling he chose to be there, although I had no idea why. He kept regular habits and would only ever appear when my whole attention was focused on the task in hand. When I turned towards him, the shade would vanish and my eyes would be left clutching sky, field, hedge. One day towards the end of my work there, he failed to show. As I packed up my kit, I almost hoped to see him, but my close orbit remained a blank. The following afternoon, empty too. I have never understood why he appeared for those few weeks in that remote valley beside me. And like that lost tract of land, he only lingers in memory now.

21

The letter 'P' had been sprayed in red paint on the walnut tree. A drip had run down the trunk before drying had caught up with it, leaving a raised pimple. 'P' stood for pollard and it was Christopher's wish that the trees thus marked should be cut six feet from the ground. These pollards would sprout from where they were cut and send out more poles, an elevated form of coppicing.

Partway Copse had been planted in 1989 by Christopher's father on a cold, north-facing slope. Because of the field's orientation, grass had always struggled to grow there. Planting it with trees, the thinking had been that, one day, the ground might return a profit in the shape of timber. Back then, they'd gone with a mix of beech, oak, walnut and cherry. Unfortunately, the walnut and beech had suffered badly from squirrel damage, the bark of these trees seemingly irresistible to the vandal's palate. Yet what was good eating for the squirrels was heartbreak for a forester. All the trees which had been gnawed around their circumference were dead or dying in their tops. These doomed specimens made up the mainstay of the felling crop.

Christopher was paying myself and Sean to thin Partway. The plan was that given the copse's steep ground, he would skid out the felled timber with his horse and stack it beside the lane. I had agreed to buy all the branch wood from Christopher for charcoal. There was a level ride which ran through the middle of the copse which would double as a timber depot. I'd stockpile the branch wood there, and at the start of the burning season move in my kiln and wagon. I estimated there was sufficient material for forty burns, enough to keep me occupied all summer.

The first job every morning was to light a fire. We both knew working in a winter wood without one was missing a trick. Sean, as always, had come prepared and would produce a pack of fire-lighters from his bergen – it seemed he wasn't proud. I watched as he built a hillock of sticks stuffed with spools of Old Man's Beard and a couple of the chemical-white cubes. As he set a match to them, the firelighters would quickly catch and Sean would start up his biggest saw, sticking its nose towards the flame and get trigger happy. While there was some fascination in his method, I felt uncomfortable, the protracted scream of the 70cc engine inconsistent with the settled peace of the wood. But as an alternative bellows, the chainsaw seemed effective. The flames grew stronger. The fire flexed its muscular heat.

I turned away and knelt down with my saw. Taking a few minutes to set it up properly was always time well spent. Sean was now doing the same, working a file across the crescent cutters, so they resembled miniature silver moons. We worked in silence, just the crackle of the fire and the rhythmic sound of sharpening. With the chains doctored and the saws fuelled, we kicked some larger logs onto the fire and walked up into the trees.

Despite their relative youth, the beech were thick in body and heavily branched. Felling them was not difficult, it was the snedding of their limbs which took the time. Sean wanted the main part of the tree perfectly streamlined. As 'clean as snooker cues' was how he put it. It would be these trunks he'd be skidding out with the horse, so any branch that wasn't cut perfectly flush could dig in the ground. The horse logger's other bugbear was safety. There wasn't a day when he wouldn't mention a possible hazard in the wood. I had never met someone more meticulous when it came to safe practice; Ralph Watts he was not. On more than one occasion Sean scolded me for not putting on my chainsaw gloves and absolutely refused to work beside anyone not wearing the correct PPE. Over one tea break he told me the story of a man he'd been cutting gorse with the previous winter. The site had been on a remote hillside and on the first morning his co-worker had turned up with no chainsaw trousers. To Sean, this was unthinkable; not only unprofessional, but an insult to the man you're working with.

'What 'appens if the saw kicks back and hits a femoral artery? Air ambulance wouldn't get there quick enough, tourniquet wouldn't save 'im. You'd 'ave to 'old 'im, try and remember 'is last words, then watch 'im bleed out.'

As his tirade trailed off, Sean looked haunted, his face twisted in a Lady Macbeth mask. I wondered why this acute sensitivity – had there been a tragedy somewhere in the past? Listening to him, I couldn't quite square the man who'd lived twelve years on the road with one so allergic to physical hazards. Run-ins with Travellers and having to poach for your supper is no country for cautious men.

By four o'clock we would call it a day. We'd both been on the saw for the best part of seven hours and were exhausted. Even if we had wanted to carry on, the day was starting to go and neither of us would risk felling in bad light. Packing up, we'd fall into the sort of uninspired conversation which is the sign of dwindling energy reserves. Sean would always enquire what I was having for my dinner. Every time, the question seemed odd. The man himself had no interest in food – the only things to pass his lips each day were nicotine and milky tea – yet he seemed perennially fascinated by my own culinary plans. Over time, I began to feel the persistence of the question deserved a more interesting response. In the end, desperation had me looking up recipes from an old cookery book, a 1960s paperback entitled *French Provincial Cooking* which had been left in the cottage by a previous tenant. The handbook offered the kind of recipes which had been collected to appeal to that particular kind of dated suburban snob, the Margot Leadbetter type. Most of them I had no intention of cooking, but they sounded good: *Rogons de boeuf à la charentaise* (Ox kidney stewed in wine with mushrooms); *Grondin au fromage* (Red gurnard with cheese sauce); *Roulade de porc a l à gelée* (Rolled leg of pork in jelly). Listening to me reel off a different one each day, Sean would stop what he was doing, take a long draw on his fag and look at me as if a warning klaxon was going off in his head. His sensitive stomach for risk clearly extended to cooking.

Over the weeks, I couldn't help ramping things up - the look on Sean's face was too delicious. When, one day, I told him I was planning on a truffle omelette for supper, I think he smelled a rat. 'Ow you gonna find one of them then?' he quizzed sourly. I gestured over to Pig who was snoring beside the fire. Sean's eyes narrowed on the white terrier. 'Don't look much like a truffle hound to me.' I shook my head in disagreement.

'Got a rare nose on him. Can smell one at two hundred feet.'

Sean pulled an uncertain smile and took another draw on his fag before turning away. I watched as he gathered his kit and led Doctor down through the trees. With the man and horse gone, I sat down beside the fire. The cold cottage did not call me, nor the idea of cooking.

A breeze had got up and the flames splayed flat, squashed by wind. A drift of woodsmoke blew across. I closed my eyes and let it wash over me. Opening my eyes, I noticed a partridge was skirting the near ground, a solitary red leg. I'd seen him there before. The bird had been poking around for over a week, hoovering up the corn I'd shaken out from some hessian sacks which I'd used for carrying my gear. The corn was musty and old but the tramp bird was not fussed. With a glance to check he was safe, the partridge started to peck at the corn. My eye took in the barred wing and the red flanks, the automaton stab of the pecking head. I felt cheered by his presence, happy he had found some luck in what would probably be a short life.

I turned back to the fire, an anchor point for my meditation. I had continued with my mindfulness work, and tried to set aside some time each day to the discipline of just sitting. But in the woods it felt different. In the cottage it was a more conscious action – positioning the cushion, settling in the chair, an eye on the clock before I started, so I could gauge the length of my practice. In the wood, these moments came upon me more freely and with extraordinary grace. Surrounded by nature, I was already halfway there.

I slipped into the gap where one is no longer thinking, only aware. The rewards of meditation are real, although in writing about them I am conscious it is easy to sound preachy. Allow me to say this. If you are suffering with anxiety or intrusive thoughts, meditation is the key. It will serve you better in the long run than any therapy or pill. The space it will give you inside yourself is a lifeline. Moments avail themselves to you, special moments. In these fleeting snatches you are separate from your thoughts, you break free from your mind. With practice, these moments expand, become deeper, and a vast nourishing space is revealed. Once experienced, you know it forever.

The sitting ended. The copse had grown dark. I felt strong, good. I stared into the wood. The fuzzy shapes of individual trees throbbed on my retina, black on a deep Rothko blue. Christopher's pollarding marks were gone, but in my mind I could still read them: 'P' for perfect; 'P' for peace.

22

Winter was slow to shift that year, frosts laying claim to mornings deep into April. Mercifully, the fag end of the cold season had been dry and working in Partway I was able to drag the bulk of the kiln wood down to the ride without the ground turning to mush. By the time we were done, I estimated we had thirty tonnes waiting there, ready to burn.

Meanwhile, Sean and Doctor had been skidding beech trunks down to the stacking area, beside the lane. Most of the time we were lost in our own rhythms, but occasionally the peace of the copse would be undone by cursing, choice words which would float into ear shot, depending on the horse-logger's proximity. The problem was that while Doctor was not exactly work-shy, age had diminished his enthusiasm for the job. In his softer moments, Sean admitted the cob was getting too old to lug timber and should be put out to grass, yet at times in the copse he forgot this, and harsh words would spill from his mouth and carry.

Most of the verbals were ignored by Doctor, who'd remain stubbornly immobile, his woolly ears switching back and forth. This would only antagonise Sean further and he'd revert to giving the old nag a dig in the ribs to get him moving. Such action would invariably result in the man being pulled down the slope a shade quicker than looked comfortable, as if hanging on to an out-of-control train. Part of me enjoyed witnessing these moments of equine revenge. It was clear Doctor knew what he was doing. His eyes shone with the game.

With all the charcoal wood hauled down onto the ride, the only thing left to do was collect the kiln and bow top.

I had considered leaving the wagon on the old railway line, and travelling to the woods to work, but that would mean a nocturnal commute every time we burned, to check on the kiln and switch the chimneys. Although I had done this while working at Rag, Partway Copse was that little bit further. It made sense to relocate to the woods.

We moved the kiln first, pulling it into Partway on a borrowed farm trailer. Rolling the steel round off the flat bed, I was once again hit by the happy smell of baking wood; that sweet, smokey taint captured in the tarry crud which clung to the kiln's insides. With that smell, six months of winter fell away and I was catapulted towards summer.

Next came the bow top. It was a mile and a half back to the old camp and as I drove through the lanes, life felt good. The hedgerows were bubbling with new growth and fizzing with colour, as if shaken violently by spring. Once we got back to the cutting, I loaded the pick-up with our domestic essentials – the chairs, trivets, pots and pans which were the mainstay of camp life. Finally, with the cart hitched and the tarpaulins roped down, I looked over the ground. Bar the cords of ash left to season there, it was now just a tired rectangle of dirt. Nostalgia ghosted through me. The old place already felt remote, the sense of home had eloped cruelly fast. I looked over it one last time, then turned away.

Back on the metalled lane, the cart was running well, but half a mile from Partway our luck ran out – around a bend, approaching slowly, was a herd of dairy cows. I pulled up hard against the hedge and killed the engine; we would have to wait. Bringing up the rear of the milking herd was a man holding a length of blue water pipe. From the slow, crabbing gait I recognised him instantly. It was Roly Grist.

The farmer eventually came alongside the truck, giving one of the stragglers a sharp whack on its flank with the blue plastic. The cow skittered forward and Roly stuck his head towards the open window. It was a bad move. Pig instantly flew across at him, territorially wired. I grabbed the dog's collar and yanked him back, but the animal had seen red and bit down on my hand. In anger, I twisted the mongrel's collar tight, part throttling him. Angry gurgling noises rose from his throat while Roly tittered – apparently this was entertainment.

'Bloody terriers – born assholes.'

I let go of the collar, seething, while Pig sat for a moment, curbed. Looking down at my hand, I saw that several depressions in the skin were already turning purple. Roly leant in, his eyes on the white menace.

'Used to 'ave a ferret like that – evil bugger – would jus' latch on and hang.' Pig's nose wrinkled and his gums drew back. It was not a good look. The dog was always twitchy about his truck, but this had a nasty edge. I stared him down.

'Leave it!'

Pig grumbled back. Then I caught the right-hand side of Roly's face and realised why the animal had taken so violently against him. It was horribly disfigured with bloating, some allergic reaction to a sting.

'Christ, what happened to you?'

'Big stripey bastard got me in the milkin' parlour this mornin'. Size of a light aircraft.' I cringed at the vision.

'You wanna see a doctor Roly, get something to ease the swelling.' The farmer shook his head and the engorged face juddered.

'Don't bother with they, tis nothin' a bit o' brown drinkin' water can't cure.' Roly's hand slipped into his coat pocket and pulled out a small bottle of Scotch. He unscrewed the cap, threw back his head, and poured a generous dose down his throat. Wiping his mouth with the back of his hand, he shot a look up the road. 'See that boss cow's pushin' on, bedder make tracks.' The dairyman moved out of the framing of the truck window, leaving only hedge and the taint of whisky.

We swung off the lane into Partway's entrance, a circle of open ground. Along the far edge stood a curving wall of wood, the beech trunks Doctor had dragged down that winter. As the truck idled, I briefly considered the spot as a stopping place for the wagon. It was level and open and got the sun. But my nightly excursions to the kiln would be uphill, and there was also security to think about. While the lane was a quiet one, the camp with its bow top and campfire would be a powerful magnet for the wrong sort, the kind of men who offer you a chainsaw out the back of their van, or a generator for fifty quid. I didn't want to sleep with one eye open. It would be better to camp among the trees.

We drove up the track. Pig had by now migrated onto my lap and was shaking with anticipation – entering a wood always got him excited. We pulled onto the central ride, slowed and stopped. I turned the key. Apart from the cooling tick of the engine there was complete silence. In front of us, a long ride now doubling as a wood depot. The simple order of it made me smile, the track with its neat servings of beech like a long table set for supper.

I opened the door and Pig leapt out, eager to get among the trees. I watched as he skipped over drifts of brash, and up along the old skidding trails left by Sean and Doctor. My eyes slipped off the dog and up towards a higher stand of trees. The energy there was different. As I gazed upon it, Pig returned with a flat look which said 'nothing to report'. Remaining fixed on the trees, I sensed he was wrong.

Uncoupling the bow top from the truck, I decided against sorting the camp out immediately – I wanted to do my own sweep of the wood. We picked our way up the slope and into a steep young plantation of beech and oak. Underfoot, barely any humus, just greensand and clay. Towards the top, the ground flattened out, and beyond a narrow band of veteran trees, the copse ended at a ploughed field.

We turned left and headed east around the top of the wood. In the far distance was the curving prow of Belstone. Despite being camouflaged against a backdrop of trees, its gaze seemed to follow us – the hill missed nothing. We continued our easterly curve along the rim of the wood, while below us, dropping steeply away, was a dungeon of green. Pig had pulled ahead but after a couple of minutes I noticed he'd stopped and was looking back. I knew that look. I grinned at my old friend and with a sharp whistle turned into the trees. Crashing through nettle, hazel and briar we tumbled down onto a wide terrace. The dog barked, high on the green energy. I stood transfixed. We'd landed on a ghost, the remains of a medieval plough lane. Looking down, another, then another fell away, like a giant's staircase, before ending at the new plantation fifty metres below.

The land here seemed to specialise in them – what field walkers call 'strip lynchets'. Pacing the width of the terrace I estimated it was a good ten metres across, each lynchet running for perhaps a hundred and fifty metres, east to west. I stood hushed under the trees, the air thick as green milk. What had once been cultivated ground had long returned to nature. Poignancy seemed to abound there.

On one level, these lynchets stand as memorials, evidence of a medieval peasantry's efforts to bring marginal hilly ground under plough. Those peasant farmers who had struggled to farm these hillsides had lived hard lives. Many of them had died horribly too. It is generally understood that this higher ground was cultivated out of a need for more food, brought on by a rapidly expanding population. The Black Death in the fourteenth century had put paid to that need, over a third of Britain wiped out in the most unpleasant way. In the fallow patch of human activity following the Plague, both the need for these marginal strips of food production and the workforce required to maintain them had died away. As ever, nature sees an opportunity. The trees had moved in and never left.

We wandered back towards the truck, stumbling on one more find at the far edge of the wood, a cast iron bathtub. The white enamel was dulled by age and weather, but it was far too useful a thing to leave behind. Filled with leaf rot and rainwater it weighed a tonne, and although I managed to turn it on its side and empty the stinking stew, it was still a major operation to get it back. Yet as the old adage goes, where there is a will, there is a way. Swearing a lot helps too.

A vintage roll top in a charcoal burner's camp. Perhaps a bit much, but we would manage. The bones from my charcoal burns – the partly charcoaled wood – would be perfect fuel for the fires I'd light underneath to heat the water. I could now get properly clean. They wouldn't know me in the pub.

I pitched camp in a light and airy glade. A gale had knocked out several young trees and left a large gap in the canopy. With the wagon level and an awning raised, it was time to set the kiln. I decided on a patch of ground about two hundred metres east of the glade. The first job was to cut a wide circle in the turf, creating a clean and level hearth. As I attacked the surface with a spade, I could half-hear Jim Shady telling me the ground there was clay and not good: clay was cold; clay would suck the heat out of the kiln and burn more wood to get it up to temperature, meaning less charcoal.

'It can't be helped, Jim,' I heard myself argue back. The land all around was clay, or at least a clay-greensand mix; I wasn't lucky enough to be burning on the light, acid soils of his patch. Then another voice pitched in, softer, more paternal. It was Obadiah: 'Check the ground for critter-runs boy – give it a good heel.' I knew the routine. Make sure there were no burrows or runs beneath the hearth; no subterranean airways that would stymie my efforts at regulating the amount of oxygen entering the kiln. So I gave the ground a sharp heel, even though I doubted there was anything there, for Obadiah, for old times' sake. Satisfied, I rolled the burner into place and dropped it down.

With the kiln set, I began to fill it. After an hour or so it was done, a tonne of beech piled inside. I cut a long hazel stick from the hedge and wrapping an old rag around its end, sloshed on a bit of red diesel. I set a lighter to the soaked cloth and the flame quickly bit. Satisfied, Jim and Obadiah walked away into the trees. Another burning season was underway.

Over the next few weeks Pig and I reverted to our wilder selves, bending to the natural rhythms of the charcoal burning life. We'd rise early and get stuck into the heavy stuff before the heat of the day took hold, bagging up the char and reloading the kiln. The afternoons called for wood-cutting, converting the long lengths of beech into shorter batons, more food for the kiln.

Moving wood, I would often bump into Toad. There was always that fork of fright, that deep-wired fear of snakes, instantly activated when, lifting a log, something shifted underneath. But there were no vipers. Every time, it was just plain old Toad. He'd squirm into the wood-mulch, trying to hide, his chubby back legs working like a crawling baby. I'd reach down and grab him, wanting to put him out of harm's way, but each time the intention was stalled by the translucent, metallic eyes and the wide, lipless face – such unnerving symmetry.

The kiln would be lit around four o'clock. I'd rotate the chimneys just once during the burn, after eight hours. Despite several charcoal seasons under my belt, the fascination of this never waned, the nocturnal rituals held the same magic they always had done.

Waking just before midnight, having fallen asleep in my fireside chair, I'd plunge into darkness and lurch down the ride, the beam of my head-torch reflecting the eyes of at least two dozen larger animals, higher up, among the trees. Sleepiness seemed to take the edge off the old atavistic fears, or perhaps I had simply become a true woodland animal just like the watching deer.

As I reached the kiln, the head-torch threw a beam across the smoke which rose silently from its three chimneys. It had lost that puffy, cotton-wool quality and was now a dingy swirl, the colour of flood water. I put on my gloves and began to rotate them. As each flue was placed on a new vent, there was an unearthly roar, a supernatural whooshing as flames drew up the pipe, spitting fire at the stars. The sight and sound of it was thrilling but, in that moment, there was also a spike of fear. It was as if all the sentience in the kiln was fully charged, and any darker forces in the wood drawn towards it by such a show of weaponry and wit. For a short moment the whole process felt like witchcraft and, alone in the wood, I was uneasy.

I had been cleaning my airgun beside the campfire when Christopher appeared out of the trees, carrying a telescopic pruning saw. It was good to see him and, as usual when out foresting, he seemed in good humour.

'Afternoon! Bit hot and sticky for your game.'

I shook my black head.

'Can't complain Christopher. Got fifty-seven bags out of the kiln this morning. For that we can put up with a bit of heatstroke.'

The man smiled and using every inch of his 6' 4" frame, began harvesting cherries off the nearest tree. Looking on him, I was again reminded of the sort of steely character who'd held the mission station at Rorke's Drift. It was the lean, tanned face and the old-time sideburns. Unfortunately, the cherry juice which was running down his chin also played to the idea of a man with a spear in his back. Christopher motioned towards my rifle, propped up against the wagon.

'Nice light gun you've got there – had any squirrels?'

I shook my head.

'Fraid not, only tin cans.'

The man looked disappointed. Christopher was in no way a natural killer but when he talked of squirrels something changed behind his eyes. I knew he would have liked me to cull as many as possible while I was living in the copse, they were a blight on the young trees.

'It would help if you could. They're a nuisance, a real pest.'

I let it hang. Christopher eyed me quizzically and spat out a cherry stone.

'Have you ever *tried* squirrel?'

I had. But that had been in a past life, back in my old advertising days. I vaguely remembered an evening out in a restaurant near Smithfield. Inside it was a minimalist cube, the whitewashed walls an arch counter to the visceral blood-iness splattered across the menu. I remembered I'd drunk too much and in a moment of bravado had ordered the squirrel. I looked back at Christopher. The dish was now so fresh in my mind, I could taste it.

'Yes Christo. Small, greasy and a bit like chicken.'

A couple of days later I had reason to pick up my gun. It was hot and muggy and I had been enjoying a siesta when I was woken by the sound of flapping in one of the nearby trees. Peering through a rip in the bow top's canvas, I spied a bird, the colour of a rain cloud, gorging on wild cherries. The wood pigeon was a hefty fellow and would look good on a plate.

I quietly reached for my gun and loaded a .22 pellet. Looking back through the tear in the canvas I could see the pigeon was still there. I noted the bird was in the killing zone, about forty metres away. I poked the barrel through the hole and settled my cheek against the stock. Part of me still saw the living bird, but that part had mostly been elbowed aside. I was now a colder animal – one with an empty stomach.

The airgun kicked back as I pulled the trigger and the bird dropped out of the tree. I jumped down the steps and ran towards him, but stopping at the foot of the cherry, I could see he was not dead. The poor creature tried to get away, heading across the slope while trailing a damaged wing. He was attempting to fly, beating his good wing frantically, but physics would not have it. I crashed after him, the end of my gun like the nose of an iron dog, hunting him down. I quickly re-loaded and delivered another shot inches from his back. The working wing flapped one more time and was still. I saw the bright red feet clench and unclench as life left him. I stood in silence. There are few things more sobering than a bad kill. In that moment, reality slapped me and I saw myself exactly as I was: the taker of a life, nothing more than a thick ape.

The Midsummer Solstice passed and I decided to let go of the cottage. I had lost all inclination to be there. Back in the woods, I lived in a sort of dream. Summer held its dry grip and half feral in shorts and a vest, I felt deeply connected. I would often wander barefoot along the woodland rides feeling the rise and fall of the ground, the tickle of the grasses. A sense of health and happiness drifted over me, as pungent as woodsmoke. I could lose chunks of the day just gazing at the kiln's white drift moving through the trees, the hypnotic migration of fret through the underwood. I thought back to my days at George's watching the smoke trails rise from Joby's wood, the agony of being so close, yet so removed.

I thought about the illness too, how during that summer it had returned and temporarily robbed me of all sunshine. Here in the copse and the surroundings of my own camp, that darkness seemed so far away. Sitting on the wagon steps I saw the curve of my own journey from London, to the Fens and finally down to Dorset, to this hidden patch of wood. Wherever I went, the illness would always be there, a sleeping cell inside me. There was a fear in that, but a good fear. To remain wary, to really know the horror of a mental health disorder, is to respect it. I had no illusions that I would ever be fully cured. I remembered my own feelings lying under the truck in Gribble Wood. That storm surge of fear, that weight of darkness. Once you have been there, it can return in a blink. But the country, especially the land in which I now found myself, seemed to have worked some kind of healing effect. Nature had blessed me and showed me a stillness which was the crux of staying well. It could be found in the woods and the rhythm of my work; in the exercise of my body and its sweet ache; in a personal universe with less noise, less rush; and in broadening one's centre of intelligence from the head to the gut, even into the soles of one's feet.

You could say the woods had worked for me. But in fighting poor mental health I would not prescribe a life among the trees as the only way. Each person must find their own path. What I can say is this: if you are suffering, *know that you are loved*. It is dark yes, but in that darkness there is a universe of tenderness surrounding you. All the men and women that have been there and found a way back are with you, a halo in that darkness. You are not alone. You can make it back.

I was black from head to foot with charcoal dust and had just filled the bath, when I heard the sound of Sean's bike pull up at the bottom of the copse. It was dusk and the red sun was gone behind the ridge, the copse prickling in the afterglow. Pig had hared off at the sound of the visitor, barking nonsense, while I perked up the camp fire embers with a stick. A couple of minutes later Sean appeared on the threshold of the camp, a couple of cans dangling from his fingers.

'Evenin'.'

'Alright there.'

I motioned for him to take a seat. Sean stepped inside the circle and plonked himself in a chair.

'Don't fancy a tea?'

Sean shook his head and raised up the cans.

'Been a warm day. Got a cider thirst on.'

I let the kettle sit and reached over for one that was offered. 'Cheers.'

Sean broke into his and took a long draw. As he drank I noticed his eyes scanning the camp, checking out the new canvas awning, the boxes of tools and the stainless steel pots hanging off a string line at the back of the wagon. He swallowed and said his piece.

'See you're losin' your tail.'

By that, I knew what he meant. In Sean's eyes I was getting the hang of it, I was no longer green. Delivered from his unsentimental mouth, it actually meant something.

'Thanks. We're getting there.'

Silence followed while Sean relaxed back into the chair. He seemed at ease in the camp surroundings, something about the simplicity and beauty of it stirred even his pragmatic soul. The man's eyes fell on me, the dusty black sitter.

'How's business?'

'Good. With this weather orders are flying in.' Sean nodded and looked down the ride, towards the emptied kiln.

'Should get another one, have two on the go. More productive, more time efficient.' He was probably right. Something I'd consider the following year. I looked back at my visitor. He was staring into the fire.

'Thorn smoke – blackthorn in't it?' I nodded. Sean continued: 'Reminds me of a stopping place I once 'ad on Salisbury Plain.'

He started to reminisce. It was Christmas Eve and he had been trying to get over to Tisbury to meet up with friends, but the ice on the roads had been too bad. In the end, he had pulled the wagon up an old drove road to sit it out, just him and his animals. Christmas Day he had woken to a complete white-out, the Plain under a thick blanket of snow. He had been out and fed the animals, poked about for firewood. The hedges along the track were mainly thorn, so he had gathered the dry stuff from the hedge bottoms to make up the fire.

Back inside the wagon, Sean chivvied the stove, got the place nice and cosy. Radio 3 was on for company, carols ringing out from the bow top's half-open stable door. His dinner was fried egg sandwiches and a bottle of spiced rum, liberated from the wagon's belly box. I listened to his words in the stillness of the summer night – it sounded perfect. As usual, it was information he imparted in a matter-of-fact way, which for me was part of the poetry. The way Sean talked was always with the bones of language, a style which perfectly suited his own lean existence. The only vague nod to sentimentality was the conclusion he allowed himself at the end.

'Best Christmas I ever 'ad.'

Sean finished his can, crushed it and threw it in the fire. Darkness was now on the wood. I looked across at my friend. The fire illuminated the high cheekbones, but also the deep-scored lines in his face. He'd had a hard life and it showed. Sean stared beyond the fetch of the fire into the wood and pulled on his fag. It was another of those moments where talking was not necessary, where silence was preferable. After a while he looked up.

'Well, you've found a good place 'ere.'

I smiled.

'Think I have.'

The visitor stayed forty minutes more. It was nice to have the company. Eventually, he got up, ready for his bed. I told him I'd see him another time and he nodded and walked out of the firelight. Everything seemed at peace. A couple of minutes later I heard his bike start up and sat listening as it accelerated away, the howl of the four-cylinder persisting for at least half a mile until I could hear it no more and the valley reverted to silence.

Left alone after company, I felt solitude pressing in. The moon was waxing, a couple of night's off full, and from my chair a trick of perspective had it cradled between the crossed sticks of the awning poles. Looking at it I, too, felt held. It was a poacher's night, the countryside lit up by the moon in moments, then falling into darkness behind tracing clouds, time enough to see where the burrow exits were, then darkness to cover you as you set your nets.

I got up and walked over to the bath – it was time to get clean. The fire was by now a bed of glowing embers under the tub, steam rising off the water's surface. I threw a few more sticks underneath, stripped off and eased myself in. Splashing water over my face, shoulders and chest, I felt the working day begin to run off me, particles of charcoal dust marbling the water's surface, a patina of dark swirls. In minutes I sat in a warm, black lake. A light breeze stirred and I felt the chill of it on my wet shoulders. The smell of the camp fire drifted across, scattering Sean's blackthorn memories through the trees. I looked across at Pig. He was asleep under the wagon, the place every good Traveller's dog should be. Stillness, complete stillness, water, earth, air and fire all around. My edges melted away, I was element rich. I could hear the fire beneath the tub, feel its bright clean soul working into the black water. I closed my eyes and sank beneath the surface and the wood was gone. Submerged in darkness – just as I had been for years – I held my breath, held it some more, held it until my lungs burned, then came up taking a gulp of cool night air and the clouds had shifted and moonlight was flooding the glade and everything was new, glowing.

Acknowledgements

Thank you to my agent, Ludo Cinelli of Eve White Literary Agency, who first took a punt on me, an unknown out of left field – or should that be green field? If we ever have that drink, it's on me.

I am also indebted to my editor, Juliet Brooke, who saw something in my initial submission and believed enough in the writing to commit. Your support and nudging have made *Burn* a better book.

My humble thanks to all those who have offered advice and suggestions along the way: Sarah Grasshoff, Berry D'Arcy, Cameron Short, Professor Hilton Davis, Paul Lamb, Paul Hackman and 'old hawk eyes' herself, my dear mum, most diligent of proofreaders.

Thank you to Pig for propping me up over the years and sitting on my lap while I wrote this book. The white hairs on my trousers were a minor sacrifice.

Finally, my love and gratitude to Holly who, throughout the writing, balanced the insecurities of a fledgling author with the pressing needs of our baby son.